# YEMEN

# YEMEN

## DANCING ON THE HEADS OF SNAKES

VICTORIA CLARK

YALE UNIVERSITY PRESS
NEW HAVEN AND LONDON

For information about this and other Yale University Press publications, please contact:
U.S. Office: sales.press@yale.edu     yalebooks.com
Europe Office: sales@yaleup.co.uk     www.yalebooks.co.uk

Set in Janson by IDSUK (DataConnection) Ltd.
Printed in the United States of America
Map by Martin Brown Design

Library of Congress Cataloging-in-Publication Data

Clark, Victoria.
Yemen : dancing on the heads of snakes / Victoria Clark.
p. cm.
Includes bibliographical references and index.
ISBN 978-0-300-11701-1 (cloth : alk. paper)
1. Yemen (Republic)—History. 2. Yemen (Republic)—Religious life and customs. 3. Islamic fundamentalism—Yemen (Republic) 4. Jihad. 5. War—Religious aspects—Islam. 6. Yemen (Republic)—Description and travel. 7. Clark, Victoria—Travel—Yemen (Republic) I. Title.
DS247.Y48C53 2010
953.3—dc22

2009047235

A catalogue record for this book is available from the British Library.

10 9 8 7 6 5 4 3 2 1

2014 2013 2012 2011 2010

# CONTENTS

# LIST OF ILLUSTRATIONS



## PLATE SECTION

In memory of my father, Noel Clark, who died in December 2004, while I was away in Yemen

# ACKNOWLEDGEMENTS

I have my parents to thank for the genesis of myself and this book because I was born in Britain's Crown colony of Aden in 1961, while my father was the BBC's South Arabia correspondent. A happy accident has therefore given me a ready-made reason to take an interest in a place few people know about.

My warmest thanks, of course, go to all the Yemenis I encountered, who were unfailingly generous with their time and suggestions, not to mention their hospitality. Yemenis are not hard to contact and meet, and mobile-phone technology seems to have made them uniquely approachable. Khaled al-Yemani at the embassy in London and Faris al-Sanabani in Sanaa were kind enough to set my research ball rolling with plenty of contacts.

Stephen Day and John Shipman, both of whom spent much of their youths in what is now southern Yemen in the 1960s as members of the Colonial Service, were constantly helpful with contacts, expertise and enthusiasm. Sarah Phillips and Tim Mackintosh-Smith in Sanaa and Henry Thompson and Ginny Hill in the UK were all hugely generous with their insights and suggestions. All passionately bound up with

Yemen and especially its people and fearful about its future, they reassured me that a book about an obscure and impoverished country was worth writing. Gregory D. Johnsen and Brian O'Neill in the US, via their excellent blog *Waq al-Waq*, were constantly helpful.

James Meek has been a source of constant support as well as constructive criticism. Charlie Foster-Hall, Joan Baranski and my brother Dominic, likewise born in Aden, all kindly provided material for the photo section.

I owe a large debt of gratitude to Robert Baldock at Yale for commissioning the book but still more to my editor, Phoebe Clapham, who had to exercise a vast amount of patience and forbearance while I fought to arrange my thoughts, impressions and knowledge about Yemen in an order that might be intelligible to a western readership.

*'Ruling Yemen is like dancing on the heads of snakes'*

President Ali Abdullah Salih,
interview in London's *Al-Hayat* newspaper,
28 March 2009

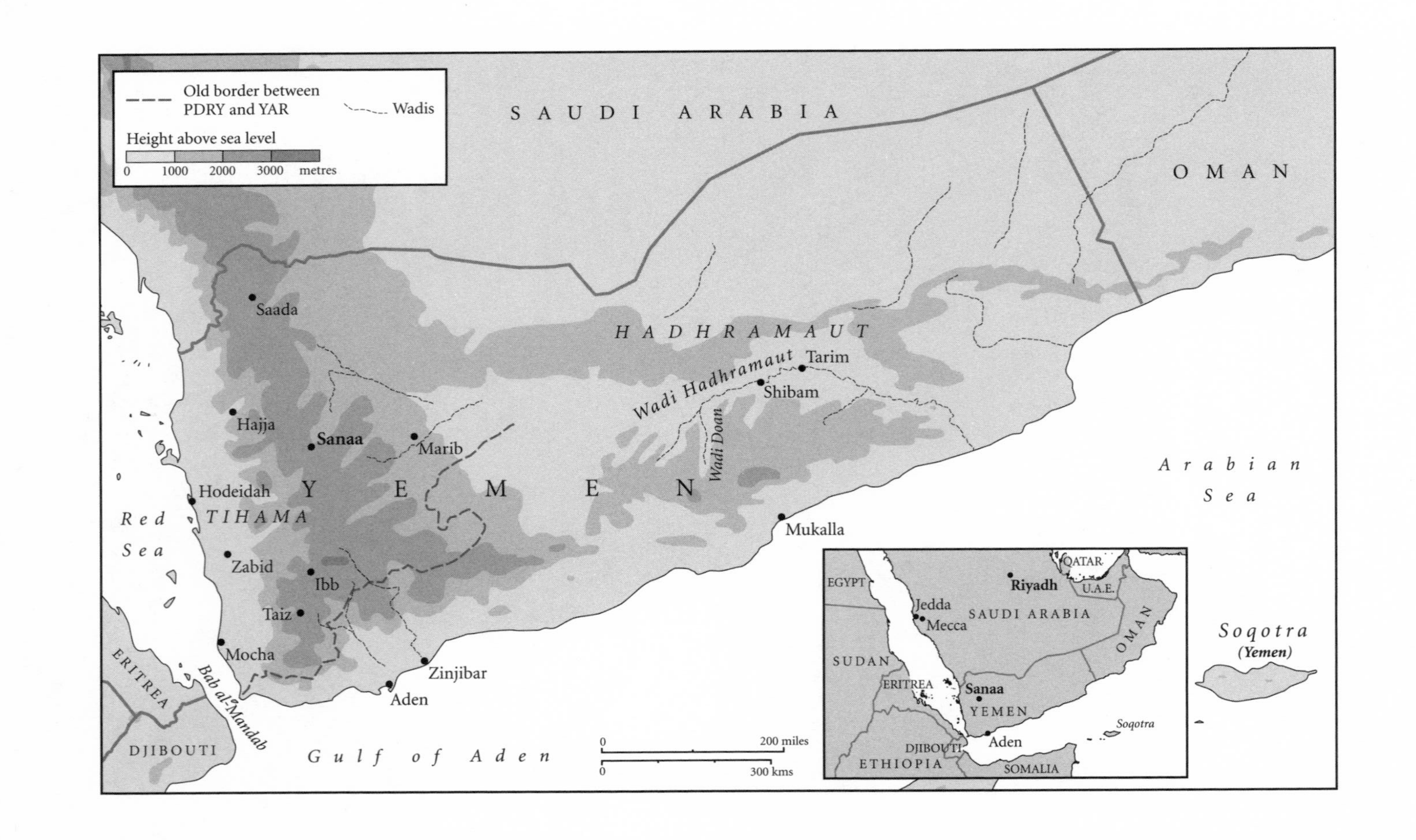
Old border between PDRY and YAR
Wadis
Height above sea level
0 1000 2000 3000 metres
SAUDI ARABIA
OMAN
HADHRAMAUT
Tarim
Wadi Hadhramaut
Shibam
Wadi Doan
Saada
Hajja
Sanaa
Marib
YEMEN
Hodeidah
TIHAMA
Red Sea
Zabid
Ibb
Taiz
Mocha
Zinjibar
Aden
Mukalla
Arabian Sea
ERITREA
DJIBOUTI
Bab al-Mandab
Gulf of Aden
0 200 miles
0 300 kms
Soqotra
(Yemen)
EGYPT
QATAR
Riyadh
U.A.E.
Jedda
Mecca
SAUDI ARABIA
OMAN
SUDAN
ERITREA
Sanaa
YEMEN
Soqotra
Aden
DJIBOUTI
ETHIOPIA
SOMALIA

# INTRODUCTION

'More tea?'

The man politely refilling my cup is Nasir al-Bahri, Osama bin Laden's former chief bodyguard, the person the world's most wanted terrorist entrusted with the delicate tasks of procuring him a Yemeni fourth wife and shooting him if he was ever in danger of being captured alive.

His manner is warm and lively, embellished with eloquent hand gestures and flashes of a dazzling smile. Charming, urbane and dressed in a freshly pressed shirt, expensive watch and soberly patterned *futa*,* al-Bahri is far removed from any western idea of a violent jihadist. I can only assume that he has seen the error of his ways and thoroughly reinvented himself.

At the Sanaa home of a mutual acquaintance, in a room lined in the comfortable Middle Eastern way with floor-level cushioned seating, we have been whiling away an afternoon in friendly conversation about his life. The fact that I am an honorary Yemeni by virtue of having been

---

* A Yemeni sarong, typically worn in southern and eastern regions of the country.

born in 1961 in Aden – now Yemen's second city but then still a British colony – has helped the flow of conversation. A southern Yemeni himself, al-Bahri has revealed that he was also born in a foreign port city, in Jeddah, where both his father and his grandfather worked as mechanics for the Bin Laden construction company. I have discovered that he left Saudi Arabia in 1990, at the age of eighteen, after hearing Osama bin Laden preach, to fight jihad against the Russians in Afghanistan. In Bosnia, where we both spent time in the early 1990s – he as a jihadist, me as a reporter – al-Bahri was involved in checking the religious motivations of jihadist recruits to the Bosnian Muslim cause.

He joined bin Laden in Kandahar in 1996 but was out of Afghanistan by October 2000, having fallen out with some of his companions when he was arrested and jailed in Sanaa following the attack on the USS *Cole* in Aden. A gold mine of information for visiting US interrogators filling in the background to the 9/11 plot, he was released after agreeing to undergo a short course of religious re-education and making a solemn promise to God that he would do nothing to damage President Ali Abdullah Salih's government. Since 2002, his activities have included the begetting of four of his five children, some taxi-driving, three friendly meetings with the president and courses in marketing, sales and the fashionable quasi-science of neuro-linguistic programming.

Now this man who once begged bin Laden's for permission to take part in a martyrdom operation has an exciting business idea to share with me. News has reached him that President Barack Obama will fail to keep his promise to close down the infamous Guantanamo Bay prison camp for suspected jihadists by January 2010. Without firm guarantees that its remaining 215 or so detainees will be incarcerated or closely supervised once back home – guarantees that Yemen, over ninety of whose citizens make up the largest national grouping in the camp, has shown itself incapable of providing – America deems the risk involved in emptying the camp too great. Obama's conundrum has got al-Bahri thinking: if America's president cannot trust President Salih to keep Yemeni detainees out of jihad trouble, why should not he commission him, Nasir al-Bahri, to establish and run a secure rehabilitation and re-education centre for them? Who better than an ex-jihadist – now equipped with his neuro-linguistic powers of persuasion – to understand and help other jihadists?

If our conversation had ended there, I might have been persuaded of the viability of such a plan. But it did not, and what al-Bahri went on to say suggested that, personable and energetic as he was, he was not a man the United States could do counter-terrorism business with.

My doubts did not surface immediately, because al-Bahri was certainly not alone in warning that Yemen was shaping up into a second Afghanistan, a vacuum which al-Qaeda would have no trouble exploiting and filling. But I began to notice the glee with which he was laying out a wider vision, of a Saudi Arabia trapped in a hostile pincer movement between an Iraq in which jihadists had filled the vacuum left by departing US troops and a recently created Islamist state of Yemen, with Somalia across the Red Sea going the same way. 'Then it'll be "you're either with us or against us", like Bush said,' he declared, his eyes bright with enthusiasm. 'You see, throughout the Islamic world al-Qaeda is the only group with a coherent programme for the future. We want the whole Muslim world to be united and on a par with the West and China and India!'

'Wait a minute, Nasir,' I interrupted, astonished. 'How can you be thinking of re-educating jihadists for the Americans? Why aren't you still with bin Laden in Waziristan, or wherever he is?'

'You are right to ask that question! I freely admit that I am weak,' he said, placing a hand over his heart to emphasise his sincerity. 'I do wish now that I had never left Afghanistan, that I was still with my sheikh.'

'So you were in favour of your sheikh's attacks on America?'

'Yes,' he replied, offering me the stock rationale, 'because it was time for western societies to taste some of the bitterness that the Muslim world is tasting. But we are against the governments, not the people.'

'What about all those innocent people dropping out of the Twin Towers?'

'Westerners are free to replace their governments when they don't like what they do,' he countered. Boosted by this reasoning, he went on to declare, 'I hope that one day I will be able to return to jihad but if I don't, I hope that my son will fight jihad.'

'Is he showing any interest yet?'

'No,' he laughed, 'he's only eleven. Right now, he wants to be a mechanic.'

Enlightening as it had been, my afternoon with al-Bahri left me baffled and uneasy. Clearly neither foolish nor naïve, he was forcing me to two conclusions: first, that being an ex-jihadist was not the same as being a reformed jihadist, and second, that enthusiastically embracing western business practices and dreaming of a contract with the US government was no natural barrier to committing divinely sanctioned atrocities against the same US government and the American people. Not for the first time in my five-year acquaintance with the country, I had been reminded of how Yemen manages to challenge and scramble the logical progressions and neat narratives that westerners prefer to deal in.

The limitations this important discrepancy imposes on an outsider's ability to understand the country and its people may in part explain why Yemen is neither as scrutinised nor as understood as neighbouring Saudi Arabia and the other Gulf States. Security concerns may be another contributing factor. Currently rated by western governments as too dangerous for anyone without essential business there to visit, the poorest and most tribal state on the Arabian Peninsula is awash with weaponry, corruptly governed and racked by two domestic insurgencies, one of them spilling over into neighbouring Saudi Arabia.

For so long briefly dismissed in agency news reports as 'Osama bin Laden's ancestral homeland', Yemen was commanding more of the world's attention by the beginning of 2010 than ever before. On Christmas Day 2009, a would-be suicide bomber tried – but failed – to bring down a flight from Amsterdam over Detroit. The plot was traced back to Yemen, where, according to the suspect, he had been trained and armed with the device he attempted to set off on board the plane. Now second only to Pakistan and Afghanistan in the business of breeding, training and sheltering terrorists, Yemen is – finally – seen as presenting a serious threat to global security, with an emergency international conference on the country hastily scheduled in London for late January 2010.

My aim in writing this book has been to provide the general western reader with an account of, but also an accounting for, the genesis and growth of contemporary jihadism in this wildest and most obscure part of its Arabian heartland. Much has been written and said about how the United States' support for Israel and reaction to 9/11 have acted as recruiting sergeants for the movement; much less about the contribution made to the spread of jihadism by conditions in its heartlands. The question of how or if such a country – or, for that matter Pakistan, Afghanistan or Somalia – can be governed as a modern nation state has a crucial bearing on its ruler's ability to combat jihadism. If, as President Ali Abdullah Salih likes to complain to foreign journalists, ruling Yemen is as delicate and dangerous as dancing on the heads of snakes, the implications for the West are serious. Yemen's usefulness as an ally of the West in the global campaign against violent jihad is bound to be very limited. But President Salih might, as many Yemenis believe, simply be trying to shift the blame for his own failings as a leader onto them.

The truth may be somewhere in between, but I have set out to present the evidence for both views. The first section of the book, a brief survey of Yemeni history from the mid-sixteenth century until 2000, lays out the case for there being, just as President Salih claims, special difficulties involved in ruling the south-western end of the peninsula. This modern history is not one Yemenis take much pride in, unlike their early story which is richly studded with kingdoms and civilisations grown so wealthy on tolls levied on passing frankincense caravans that one of them, the Sabean kingdom, built a wonder of the world, the great Marib Dam in the eighth century BC. The ancient Romans knew what is now Yemen as such a prosperous and fertile place they called it 'Arabia Felix', Lucky Arabia. Generally lucky it remained, until the mid-sixth century AD when the Marib Dam burst and the land flooded, and then dried out and emptied of its inhabitants, an event so cataclysmic that it merited a special mention in the Koran in the following century and scattered a diaspora of Yemeni tribes all over the Arab world. A hundred years later, however, the Prophet Mohammed reportedly described those Yemenis who had remained as faithful and wise, uncommonly quick and eager to espouse his Islam.

Yemenis' modern history is less lucky but at least as dramatic. Positioned at the far end of the Arabian Peninsula near the lower opening of the Red Sea, only a short distance from the Horn of Africa, their land has never escaped foreign attention for long. The story of their last half-millennium can be briefly summarised as a series of failed attempts on the part of outside powers to substitute Yemenis' hardy tribal structures and values with those of first Ottoman and British imperialism, then Nasserite Arab nationalism and Soviet-style Marxism. Although the end of the Cold War enabled Yemenis to unite their fragmented fortunes in a single state at last, the over-hasty merger agreed by Sanaa and Aden in 1990 had led to a short, sharp civil war by 1994. Six years later the odds on the Republic of Yemen prospering were being drastically lengthened again by the spread of jihadism.

By the first decade of the new millennium there were plenty of other indicators pointing to Yemen's suitability as a recruiting ground for jihadists in both the short and longer term. Its population, already judged to be the largest on the peninsula and set to double by 2035, was growing at an annual rate of 3.46 per cent, with two-thirds of it under the age of twenty-four and each woman producing an average of almost six children. Literacy rates were reported to be 33 per cent among women, 49 per cent for men and unemployment around the 40 per cent mark, with the same proportion of the population reportedly living on only two dollars a day.[1] The country's modest oil reserves accounted for 90 per cent of its exports and more than three-quarters of its revenues, but production was declining at the rate of 10 per cent a year and was scheduled to end by 2017,[2] at around the same time as Sanaa's water supply has been forecast to run out. Over a third of the country's fertile land was given over to the cultivation of qat, an evergreen shrub whose tender top leaves are chewed for hours every day by 72 per cent of Yemeni men and approximately half that number of women for their amphetamine content and mild hallucinogenic properties. It was largely thanks to the qat plant's thirst that the only country on the peninsula to rejoice in a cool enough climate to be able to feed itself was failing to do so.

The chapters comprising the second part of the book follow a rough chronology from 2000 to 2009. More thematic, they set Yemen's part in the story of radical Islam today in both a national and regional context. Meetings with Yemen's best-known jihadist, Tariq al-Fadhli, in the southern governorate of Abyan illuminate the legacy of the anti-Soviet jihad in Afghanistan on Yemen. An expedition to the oil fields east of the capital, around Marib, with a Yemeni oil worker who wishes he had fought jihad in Iraq, provides the setting for a discussion of how Yemen's largely tribal society has both facilitated and hindered jihadism. From the vantage point of eastern Yemen's magnificent Wadi Doan, the remote fertile canyon from which Osama bin Laden's father emigrated to Saudi Arabia in 1930, I examine what Yemen's powerful Saudi neighbour has contributed to the spread of radical Islam in Yemen. A brief misadventure at an Aden checkpoint while in the company of southern separatists sets the scene for a discussion of the extent to which two deep-rooted and worsening domestic secessionist movements – one in the south, one in the north-west corner of the country – are demanding more of the regime's limited resources than the West-run campaign against violent jihad. Finally, in the capital, Sanaa, I estimate the degree to which a combination of Yemen's deepening poverty and the twilight of President Salih's thirty years of rule are fuelling a popular dissatisfaction which is playing straight into the hands of a consolidated and thriving regional organisation that has made its home base in Yemen – 'Al-Qaeda in the Arabian Peninsula'.

# PART ONE

## CHAPTER ONE
# UNWANTED VISITORS (1538–1918)

### THE WORLD'S COFFEE CAPITAL

Nothing is left of what was once the busiest and richest port on the Red Sea – just sand and a few crumbling facades, the abandoned homes and 'factories' (trading posts) that used to 'display a very handsome appearance towards the sea'.[1]

No one seemed to care that these vestiges of Mocha's heyday lie half-buried under sand and strewn with plastic refuse, or that only dogs come to this wasteland between the sprawling new town and the shore. Modern Mochans' failure to derive any income from the fact that their town is the only Yemeni name still recognised all over the coffee-drinking world seemed surprising. No one had opened a café selling the authentic beverage. There were no postcards, or maps or guide books or key rings or T-shirts for sale. But the driver of a passing Toyota Land Cruiser hailed me in English across the sandy expanse, 'You are welcome! Come to my house! Meet my family!' Better one personal invitation than a thousand tourist trinkets and packets of 'authentic' Mocha coffee, I decided.

On our way, bumping softly along a sandy track, my host introduced himself as a local agent for a Malaysian shipping firm. When I enquired whether any coffee still shipped out of Mocha, he told me, 'No. Ships bring in palm oil and livestock mostly, but they usually leave empty.' As a barely face-saving afterthought he added, 'Sometimes we send sweets and biscuits to Somalia.' We were headed, he told me, towards the third Mocha. The first, whose sad relics I had just been inspecting, was ruined and buried centuries ago, and replaced by a second which was suddenly drowned by a tsunami 'about ninety years ago'. The third had a flimsy, provisional look about it; there were plenty of the rackety Japanese motorbikes doing duty as taxis, and the usual late morning hubbub around the qat shop.

A low door in a blank expanse of high white-washed wall opened off the sandy lane we had stopped in, straight onto a large, shady courtyard that was wet from a recent hosing down. In the main room of the house, sparsely furnished in the usual comfortable Arab way, with floor-level cushions and arm rests along all the walls and a television tuned to an Egyptian soap opera, I met my host's daughter. Although advantageously married to an army officer in the capital, Sanaa, she was adamant she preferred to be here at home, in this decayed and steamy backwater, among people her father described to me as peaceful and calm – 'as quiet as fish'. Implied by his simile was the usual distrust of the northern interior of the country, where Sanaa and Yemen's northern highlands are located.

In theory, Yemenis have stood a better chance of success at forging themselves into a modern nation state than either Pakistanis or Afghans, or dozens of African peoples. They are proud of the fact that they have been regarded as a single, distinct people since at least the seventh-century era of the Prophet. Noting that his missionaries were getting a particularly warm reception at the southernmost end of the Arabian Peninsula, Mohammed reportedly declared that Yemenis 'have the kindest and gentlest hearts of all. Faith is Yemeni, wisdom is Yemeni.'

These days, however, Yemenis' pronounced sense of regional identity easily trumps their consciousness of belonging to a modern nation state. Accent and dress, let alone different histories, vastly varying geography and inequalities of life opportunities, all act as powerfully polarising forces which only the ubiquity of qat and the country's swiftly growing network of roads have even begun to counteract. Few inhabitants of Tihama, where the pace and way of life closely resembles that of East Africans on the opposite side of the Red Sea, would think of wearing the traditional northern highland tribesman's curved dagger, the *jambiyah*, let alone a gun. Half East African himself, my host was relaxed in a *futa*, suitably loose attire in the sweltering climate that prevails in Tihama as well as in Aden and Hadhramaut and Mahra to the east, but is much less seen in the highlands. Instead of offering me coffee or tea, the kind shipping agent showcased his coast dweller's hospitality, his tolerance of strangers and their infidel ways, by serving me a can of black-market lager.

The impetus to unite all Yemenis into a single polity has usually been stronger in the country's tribal northern highlands than on the coast, let alone in Hadhramaut, the high, baking plateau deeply etched with fertile *wadis* (canyons) to the east, for the simple reason that the northern tribes have always lacked the wherewithal – either in the form of arable land or other natural resources – to survive in their lofty fastnesses without exploiting the coast and the verdant southern highlands. But those same rapacious northern highlanders have also acted as the sole defenders of Yemen's freedom from foreign domination through the centuries.

## THIEVING OTTOMANS AND FRANKS

Five hundred years ago, when the Ottoman Turks sailed into the Red Sea to secure the precious Muslim Holy Places of Mecca and Medina and see off the Portuguese 'Frankish' threat, the Tihamans welcomed them in much the same open-hearted manner as my kind host had welcomed me.

Unlike the Zaydi Shiite* northern highlanders who make up perhaps a quarter of Yemen's population today, Tihamans are Shafai Sunnnis. Weary of exploitation by those hungry northern tribes led by a Zaydi Shiite priestly caste of descendants of the Prophet Mohammed, rulers known as imams, it was only to be expected that Tihamans would welcome Sunni Ottoman influence. But the Ottomans – intent on uniting the entire Muslim *umma*, Sunni and Shiite, under their caliphate – were not content with going where they were wanted. Penetrating inland towards those northern highlands, they soon encountered Zaydi resistance. Imam Sharaf al-Din and his tribes may have been too weak at the time to expel the Turks from Aden and the coastal regions, but he would not surrender his southern highland stronghold of Taiz, barely an hour's drive inland from Mocha today, let alone his northern highland capital of Sanaa.

Nevertheless, during that first decade of Ottoman presence in Yemen, the 1540s, it looked as if the Turks would be able to complete their conquest. Not until 1547 was their progress halted by Imam Sharif al-Din's son Mutahhar who, having retreated to Thula – a rocky highland fastness to the north of Sanaa – managed to withstand a forty-day siege there. At last accepting there was no dislodging him, the Turks acknowledged his dominion over swathes of the northern highlands and a gentlemanly truce was agreed when Mutahhar pledged a nominal obedience to the Ottoman Sultan. He could congratulate himself on having achieved what all future imams and the Zaydi highlanders would achieve up to and even beyond the formal abolition of the imamate four centuries later: the exclusion of any foreign invader – whether Muslim or infidel – from most of their northern highlands. He was to accomplish a great deal more than that over the

* After the death of the fourth Shia Imam, Ali Zain al-Abidin, a minority in northern Iran recognised his younger son Zayd as Imam rather than his eldest son. Doctrinally, Zaydism is as close to Sunnism as possible. Yemen is the only centre of Zaydism today, but between the ninth and twelfth centuries there was another Zaydi state located south of the Caspian Sea.

next twenty years, largely thanks to the Ottomans' waning interest in their distant and irritatingly inhospitable acquisition.

Increasingly preoccupied with the conquest of central Europe and especially Vienna, the Ottomans allowed South Arabia to slip down their list of priorities. With its ferociously hostile northern tribes and equally repellent terrain – craggily mountainous and cold inland, oppressively hot on the coast – the region had nothing whatsoever to recommend it except its strategic position at the lower opening to the Red Sea and its proximity to Islam's Holy Places. The Sublime Porte would maintain a military presence there and collect as many taxes as possible rather than attempt to establish a full-scale occupation. Despite having subjugated much more than Tihama and Aden and all the southern highlands, the Ottomans were soon gladly delegating the tax farming and administration to local sheikhs. Naturally, for those sheikhs to agree to collect taxes to enrich the Sultan 'it was necessary', as a French historian puts it, 'to constantly shower them with gifts'.[2] The sheikhs commanded a higher and higher price for their loyalty, which meant there was less and less profit to be made by a succession of pashas who bemoaned their miserable lot and pined for plum postings in places where the living was easier and the pickings far richer – Cairo, Damascus or Basra. They vented their spleen and frustrated ambition in savage over-taxation of the natives. Swathes of fertile land in the southern highlands were deserted by peasants fleeing taxes too punitive to pay. In this way, portions of the population who, like the Tihamans, had at first been amenable to Ottoman rule, were needlessly alienated.

A desperately greedy Mahmud Pasha meddled with the mint, devaluing the coinage by tampering with its gold content and pocketing the spare gold himself. Soon noticing that their local currency salaries were not buying them nearly as much as those of their peers in Anatolia or Egypt, Ottoman soldiers fell to making up the shortfall by extortion from the locals. When that resource ran dry they began flogging off their personal possessions and even their weapons. Mahmud Pasha bled

Yemen as dry as he could for seven years before bribing his way into a posting to Cairo. His departure in February 1565 was a memorable enough affair to have warranted recording; his entourage comprised a personal guard of a hundred slaves and his luggage included a throne and many chests of treasure. A side effect of an Ottoman decision to divide the province of Yemen in two after his complaint that its extent and terrain made communications too slow, was that his successor's opportunities for personal gain were dramatically restricted. The fiefdom of Ridvan Pasha who took charge of the north-western half of the province – in effect the fortified towns of Sanaa and Saada – was not half as rich a prize as the peacefully prospering Tihama with its Red Sea ports, and the central southern highlands where a promising export commodity, coffee, was starting to thrive.

Dissatisfied, Ridvan Pasha lost no time in trying to improve his situation. Insisting on a renegotiation of the thirteen-year-old truce with Mutahhar al-Din, he sent a tactlessly high-handed *qadhi** to open talks, with predictably damaging results. Deciding that he was no longer bound by the truce, Mutahhar began to foment fresh trouble for the Turks and Ridvan Pasha's determination to extend taxation to Mutahhar's northern highlands gave him the perfect *casus belli.* He fired the first shot, at a Turkish tax collector. What followed was the steady reconquest of the country by and for Mutahhar's Zaydi highlander tribesmen, beginning with the capture of the fortress at Saada, the only stronghold north of Sanaa that the Ottomans controlled. By January 1567 all the northern highlands except for Sanaa and Amran were under his control, with Ridvan Pasha suing for peace before being recalled to Constantinople to be punished for his incompetence with three years in jail. While besieging Sanaa, Mutahhar ensured that the southern and western routes to the capital were closed to prevent any Turkish reinforcements under the pasha of the south, Murad the One-Eyed, coming to Sanaa's aid.

---

* Muslim judge.

When Murad the One-Eyed did belatedly stir himself to relieve Sanaa, Mutahhar was ready for him. In June, in a narrow defile, Muttahar's Zaydi fighters managed to ambush a hundred Ottoman horsemen and slaughter every one of them. Playing on mounting popular hatred of the Turks, Mutahhar then called for a general uprising against Ottoman domination, whipping up righteous outrage at the Turks' lax standards of Muslim observance: 'So where is the fury? Where has the passion gone? While these men [the Turks] degrade women of high status, taking them off to evil haunts where they can take their pleasure . . . you eat, drink, dance and play music.'[3]

Soon even the Sunni southern highlands and coastal regions were heeding the Zaydi call to rise and throw off the Ottoman yoke. After guaranteeing its Turkish garrison's safe passage back to Taiz, the southern highland town of Jiblah took a gleeful revenge by slaughtering every Ottoman soldier as soon as they left their fortress. Abandoning Sanaa to its fate, desperate to return to the southern highland town of Taiz where the Ottoman treasury was kept, Murad the One-Eyed risked relying on a local tribesman to guide him back south. Immediately, he was double-crossed. In a narrow mountain pass, his cavalcade was bombarded by boulders hurled by tribesmen infesting the mountains. In a valley transformed into a mud bath after tribesmen had flooded it by diverting a stream, his soldiers blundered about helplessly, sitting ducks for the enemy above them.

Sanaa fell to Mutahhar in the summer of 1567 and the new pasha who arrived to take up his post in the south was appalled to discover how little land there was left for him to squeeze for taxes. Encircled by hostile tribes, Taiz and its treasury was perilously isolated and nearby Zabid overrun with Turks who had fled there from every other part of the province. No wiser than any of his predecessors, the newcomer delegated the job of raising more taxes to an unscrupulous *qadhi* from Mocha. By October 1567 he had lost Taiz and his treasury. To the south in Aden a tiny 200-strong Turkish garrison surrendered without a fight, its Ottoman governor fleeing by sea.

Only then did alarm bells start clanging at the Porte. In the words of one contemporary Turkish writer, it was only the loss of one of the world's finest natural harbours that finally awakened a terror in the Ottomans. They feared 'the cursed Franks' would seize Aden. They knew that the Europeans' superior 'knowledge of artillery and cannon fire and their care for ports and castles'[4] would make it hard to recapture again and they trembled at the prospect of losing their Holy Places. Only a massive task force, mustered in Egypt, could save the situation, they believed, but, despite an Ottoman chronicler's proud boast that every Egyptian, 'save the useless, such as a very old sheikh, or child, or the like'[5] rushed to sign up for the Yemen campaign, inefficiency and power struggles delayed its departure for nine months. Not until December 1558 did a fresh pasha cross the Red Sea with an army of 3,000 to start the reconquest, and it was not until spring the following year that the Ottomans turned the tide in their favour with the overland arrival of the then Ottoman ruler of Egypt, Sinan Pasha, at the head of a main force that rejoiced in 4,000 horses, 10,000 camels, 'great pavilions, pedigree horses dressed in gold with bridles of gold and silver, weapons, armour and helmets', to say nothing of the heavy guns and supplies sent by sea.

Naturally biased in favour of the Ottomans, the main Turkish chronicler of the reconquest refers to Imam Mutahhar's forces as heretic Zaydis and takes cheap shots at the lame Imam himself by referring to him as a 'cripple' and emphasising his pathetic inability to ride anything but a donkey. But there is much that rings thrillingly true and vivid in his description of the miseries the Turks faced in recapturing Yemen. The appalling harshness of so much of the highlands struck the chronicler again and again: 'there was nothing human or friendly there: the land was lost only to gazelle and camels the colour of the desert: behind every rock lurked a pack of monkeys or a pride of lions . . . nothing but the howling of jackals, the hooting of owls and the sound of crows.'[6] Oxen could pull their heavy gun carriages on flat land, but only manpower could heave them over mountain passes too steep and narrow for wheeled transport. The author complains of a *wadi* that 'curves like a snake and anyone who takes it would risk being poisoned by the string of vipers coiled in its dangerous crannies', where 'horses would wade up to the belly and stirrup'. He describes a place whose mountains 'pierce the clouds, a place where there was only pain'.[7] He also details an engagement in which Zaydi tribesmen 'of extreme coarseness'[8] were occupying a mountain top, 'spreading out behind the rocks like cockroaches and beetles' and rolling giant boulders down onto the Turks, who responded with great blasts from their cannons, 'throwing up sparks like castles'.[9]

The Zaydi tribes were no match for the Ottomans' determined assault with their new-fangled artillery. Imam Mutahhar, who had fled to Kawkaban, another rocky mountain-top fastness not far from Sanaa, was forced to descend to parley with Sinan Pasha, an occasion apparently ominously marred by his donkey transport breaking wind on departure. Sinan Pasha graciously granted Mutahhar the governorship of the area around Saada, but the Ottomans were back in charge by 1571, reunited in a single *vilayet* under his firm rule. Imam Mutahhar's death the following year spelt the end of his dynasty. Rival families disputed the succession until, in the closing years of the sixteenth century, a new dynasty of imams emerged, the al-Qasim, to trouble the Turks again. Yet another 8,000-strong force of Egyptians was mustered, but only with great difficulty. Many soldiers had to be forced on board ship at Cairo and the army was soon decimated by casualties, desertion and disease.

This third and final effort to secure Yemen for the Ottoman caliphate lacked conviction. The Porte was losing interest in holding Yemen. With the golden prize of Vienna still untaken, the *vilayet* of Yemen was judged just too costly in manpower and materiel to be bothering with any longer. With Portuguese power in the Arabian Sea and Indian Ocean waning, the Turks' terror of Franks capturing the Muslim holy places was also fading, especially as they were on better terms with the latest Frankish powers to take an interest in the region – the British and the Dutch – than they had ever been with the Portuguese. Mocha, their last toehold, was growing rich by its coffee trade and already home to both the British and Dutch East India companies' trading posts by 1636, when the last Ottoman governor of the port acknowledged the obvious, gathered up his tiny remaining garrison, and boarded a ship for Egypt.

Yemenis were slow to realise it, but the British and Dutch vessels crowding into Mocha to buy coffee in the early seventeenth century represented a far greater long-term threat to their prosperity and independence than any Ottoman army intent on subjugating their precious highlands. English East India Company merchants had first put in to Ottoman Mocha in January 1609, twenty-three years before the Turks abandoned Yemen. In spite of finding it 'unreasonable hot', a merchant named John Jourdain had judged the port 'a very plesaunt place to bide in, were it not for the Turkes' tyrannie'.[10] He had soon been disappointed to discover that he would need special permission from the Sultan in Constantinople if he wanted to set up a 'factory' (trading post) there and begin buying a commodity he called 'cohoo'.* Coffee's special stimulating effects were a secret known only to the Muslim world at the time, so the plant intrigued Jourdain. On his trek inland into the mountains to Sanaa to parley with the pasha, he had noticed how jealously the Yemenis guarded their lucrative export, wrapping it in mystery and wonder – 'it is reported this seede will growe at noe other place but neere this mountaine',[11] he wrote.

Ever interested in turning a profit from their troublesome southernmost province, the Ottomans had been encouraging coffee production and, with it, Mocha's prominence. The southern highlands behind the Red Sea coastal plain, through which Jourdain must have passed en route for Sanaa, had experienced the equivalent of a Gold Rush. Its mountainsides had been transformed by an intricate lacework of terraces designed to take maximum advantage of the flash flood monsoon rains. A French visitor noted admiringly that 'the greatest

* The Arabic for coffee is *qahwa*.

piece of husbandry that belongs to them [Yemenis], consists in turning the course of Rivulets and Springs, that descend from the Mountains into their Nurseries, conveying the Water by little Canals to the Foot of the Trees'.[12] Those patterned mountainsides where a little coffee but more qat is grown these days remain one of the most beautiful and impressively workmanlike features of western Yemen, a startling testament to the people's ingenuity and fortitude.

Back in the early seventeenth century, detachments of Ottoman soldiers guarded the precious coffee plantations and anyone apprehended in the act of trying to smuggle coffee seedlings out of the country was heavily fined. It was a disincentive that failed to deter the first Dutch visitor to Mocha, a merchant named Pieter van der Broeck, from removing a few to the Dutch Republic in 1616 and planting them in a greenhouse. That theft enabled a group of Amsterdam grandees to present the king of France with a single coffee sapling, a curiosity for his own Paris greenhouse. Yemenis were about to learn that if the Muslim Turks had come to their country to fight and steal, the Christian Franks who had come to trade and steal were not so different.

In 1618, the Porte had granted permission to both the English and Dutch to establish their 'factories' in Mocha. By the middle of the century, with the Turks gone, the port's coffee trade with Europe was expanding fast and Yemen thriving. By the century's end Mocha was reportedly exporting some ten million kilos of coffee a year.[13] However, the effect of that first Dutch theft was about to be sorely felt. Yemenis were soon to lose their world coffee monopoly. In European colonies in south-east Asia, and South America and Africa, the precious plant could now be grown more cheaply thanks to colonised slave labour. The growing failure to compete would lead not only to the decay of Mocha and the southern highlands, but also to the impoverishment of the northern highlands that had so richly benefited from the trade since the Turks' departure.

But Mocha has furnished Yemenis with some small consolation for their loss in the form of another plant – qat (*catha edulis*). A Koranically permitted stimulant derived from chewing the evergreen qat shrub's tenderest top leaves for up to six hours a day, qat has long been as emblematic of Yemeni culture as the wearing of the *jambiyah* or the *futa*. Yemenis believe the life-enhancing properties of both coffee and qat were discovered at precisely the same time by a fourteenth-century Sufi named Ali Ibn Umar al-Shadhili who, while residing as a hermit in the vicinity of Mocha for twenty years, nourished himself and his meditations on both substances. There was a time, probably as far back as the sixteenth century, when coffee and qat vied for pole position in Yemenis' hearts, a state of affairs reflected in this imagined debate between the two substances:

> Qat says: they take off your husk and crush you. They force you in the fire and pound you. I seek refuge in God from people created by fire.
>
> Coffee says: A prize can be hidden in ritual. The diamond comes clear after the fire. And fire doesn't alter gold. The people throw most of you away and step on you. And the bits they eat, they spit out. And the spittoon is emptied down the toilet.
>
> Qat scoffs: You say I come out of the mouth into a spittoon. It is a better place than the one you will come out of![14]

Qat has the last ribald word here, but its high standing did not stop Imam Mutahhar's father, the great Sharaf al-Din, issuing a fatwa against it in 1543, commanding that all qat trees in his domains be immediately uprooted and burnt. He had taken fright at the reported ill-effects of the plant after discovering some of his closest entourage stumbling around his palace, slurring their words, claiming that *halal* [permitted by the Koran] qat, rather than *haram* [forbidden by the Koran] wine, was to blame. The chronicler of this tale piously protests the Imam's harsh outlawing of his people's main solace, noting that 'God, realising that qat was utterly blameless, allowed some qat shoots to survive under the earth until the downfall of this dynasty, when they shot forth again, by means of his Grace. He the Creator par excellence!'[15]

Qat has had the whip hand over coffee ever since in Yemen, but it was never and will never be the enriching export commodity that coffee once was. Its defenders will point out that it is neither as mind altering nor as harmful to the health as alcohol, and forcefully argue that if not for its nation-wide popularity, if not for the fact that one in every seven Yemenis is involved in the cultivation, distribution and sale of qat, much of rural Yemen would be deserted. Its more numerous detractors will contest that it is both disgraceful and dangerous for Yemenis to be growing so much qat, that it represents a ruinous waste of money and time and, most importantly, water. There are those, however, who quietly reason that, if not for the passive consolations of qat, many more young Yemeni males than is presently the case would be eagerly resorting to the more active consolations of jihad.

## ZAYDI HOME RULE

On an expedition out of Sanaa to Mutahhar's northern highland fastnesses of Thula and Kawkaban, I stood on a lofty rocky promontory scanning the wide view over a bare plateau, here and there sparsely dotted with neat rows of qat trees and the odd fortress of a local administration building. Behind me, the village of Kawkaban was almost deserted and strewn with rubble. It was easy to imagine how the Turks had first failed and then lost interest in conquering such places, but it was even easier to identify the most crucially enduring fact about Yemen's political geography. In order to survive in their harshly inhospitable refuge, the northern highland tribes have had little choice but to turn their only asset, the threat or promise of their organised fighting potential, to their material advantage.

The attitude of defensive desolation I was sensing in Thula and Kawkaban had first struck me on a visit to another part of those highlands, the land of the Beni Shaddad, a clan belonging to the powerful

Khawlan federation, an area barely an hour's drive east of Sanaa. Along fifteen kilometres of unmade-up track only navigable by four-wheel drive, my Khawlani tribesman friend drove, climbing higher and higher, around rocky crags, past the range of seven high peaks on which beacons used to be lit as a signal for the clans to gather in preparation for war, past village after tiny village in which many of the mud brick multi-storey homes were collapsing into ruins or still bore the scars of 1960s civil strife, in which there was no sign of any economic activity whatsoever, not even a small qat plantation. At last we arrived at his home village, a loose cluster of mud brick or stone dwellings, some disintegrating, some already reduced to a pile of dust, and a small vineyard. A crowd of children gathered to welcome us, but there was no sign of any other life or activity. I learned that the village had neither electricity nor enough water to extend the vineyard into a commercial venture, that my friend's brother-in-law counted himself lucky to be working at transporting lorry-loads of stone to Sanaa for the building trade, and that I was the first foreigner to visit the place for more than thirty years.

People in such remote areas have always distrusted any intruders, preferring to remain, as in Imam Muttahar's day, a tribal law unto themselves. If, in the sixteenth and seventeenth centuries, the sweeteners paid to tribal sheikhs by the Turks had to be more and more generous to secure the tribes' loyalty, after the Turks departed a home-grown imam in Sanaa – his position was secured by the customs dues paid by foreign coffee merchants – continued to buy the support of those sheikhs by paying them regular stipends and rewarding them with gifts of fertile land outside their unproductive highlands. The majority of the most powerful Zaydi northern tribal dynasties today established themselves during the relatively stable period of northern Zaydi home rule that followed the Turks' departure.

The role of the Zaydi highland tribes in Yemen's failure to thrive as a modern nation state, complete with functioning and respected institutions, is easier to understand once the character of the Zaydi imamate is understood. First, a Zaydi imam could only derive from one of an aristocracy of *sayyid* families whose entitlement to special treatment – having their hands kissed and meriting the protection of tribesmen, for example – was based on their claim to be directly descended from the Prophet himself via his daughter and son-in-law. Lacking a divine right or a popular mandate to rule, an imam was more referee than ruler and entirely reliant on the armed support of the tribes for his maintenance in power. He lived in the knowledge that he was only imam for as long as his conduct and demeanour were deemed worthy of his office. The highland Zaydi tribes would not shrink from withdrawing their support since the violent overthrow of an unjust ruler was a specifically Zaydi religious duty. If those mercenary tribesmen could be kept in line with carrots and sticks – with gifts, but also frequent resort to taking a member of a troublesome sheikh's family hostage – an imam also had to be expert at dividing and ruling, at watching for rivals and plotting in an atmosphere of permanent and chronic insecurity and suspicion. Like 'dancing on the heads of snakes', ruling Yemenis called for a light and nimble touch, and an acute apprehension of danger.

An octogenarian early eighteenth-century imam whom the French coffee-merchant Jean de La Roque encountered in 1709 – a relatively prosperous era when, as he put it, it was 'easy to see that the consumption of coffee was never so great as it is at present'[16] – was particularly anxious to know how France was governed. The news that Louis XIV ruled in reasonable safety and by divine right must have awakened his envy as well as his interest. After accepting a gift of a mirror, Imam al-Mahdi Muhammad 'look'd himself several Times in it, as did all the Grandees of his Court' while quizzing the Frenchman long and hard about 'the Qualifications and Personal Vertues'[17] of his sovereign. In return for a generous gift of coffee, an alliance, and permission for a French trading post with preferential customs duties to be opened in Mocha, he requested a short history of France, a picture of the Sun King's most magnificent palace and a portrait of him with his family.

The modest appearance and lifestyle of that early Qasim imam impressed de La Roque. 'Going with his legs and feet bare and wearing slippers after the Turkish fashion', he was at least as much religious leader – 'Priest or Pontiff of the Law of Muhammad' – as king. The Frenchman described the main event of his week, Friday worship, which revealed him to be at least as much a military as a religious leader. Accompanied by a thousand foot-soldiers, two hundred members of his personal guard, camels and horses adorned with black ostrich feathers and a small army of drummers, with a son on either side of him, the Imam rode a white horse towards the large tent that served as his mosque. One of his cavalry officers held a vast green damask umbrella, with an eight-inch-long red and gold fringe and a 'globe of silver gilt' on top, over his head while in front of him another cavalry officer carried a Koran in a red cloth bag and behind him another carried his sabre, symbolising the distinctively Zaydi twinning of Islam with the pious duty of rebelling against an unrighteous imam. Emerging from the tent an hour later, the man the Zaydis revered as the rightful caliph of the entire Muslim *umma* was greeted by volleys of celebratory gunfire. Finally, a display of stylised skirmishing awaited him back in his palace courtyard.

Enriched and therefore empowered by the proceeds of the coffee trade, those early Qasim imams succeeded in extending their rule over what might now be called 'Greater Yemen'. Along with Aden in the south, they took Hadhramaut in the east and Dhofar, now a part of Oman, as well as Asir and Najran in the north-west, which are two southern provinces of Saudi Arabia today. There was a price to be paid for this success, however. Military campaigning coupled with the ceaseless game of dividing and ruling the tribes while showering them with gifts were always more pressing priorities than living up to the claim to be an ideally just Muslim ruler. When the mid-eighteenth-century Danish scientist explorer Carsten Niebuhr was travelling around Yemen, astonishing every Yemeni he met with his new-fangled microscope and cures for impotence, the imam of the day had a rotten reputation for 'perfidious cruelty'.

Niebuhr took the trouble to record a story that highlighted 'several particulars illustrative of the principles of the imam's government'. A good, loyal sheikh named Abd Urrab had speedily obeyed when told by Imam al-Mahdi 'to demolish the castles of some neighbouring lords', but his zealous obedience backfired on him. One of those targeted 'lords' took his revenge by convincing the Imam that Abd Urrab was getting above himself, plotting to raise a rebellion and depose him. The credulous, possibly paranoid, Imam sent an army of 3,000 to besiege Abd Urrab in his fortress for eleven months, but without success. When the abused Abd Urrab finally did turn against the Imam and succeed in capturing Taiz, the Imam had no choice but to acknowledge the conquest and offer an alliance. The agreement was duly sealed – 'confirmed with seven oaths'. Two sheikhs stood as its guarantors. The too trusting Abd Urrab then accepted a courteous invitation to visit the Imam in Sanaa. On arrival he was 'seized, bedaubed on the face and hands with red paint . . . placed on a camel with his face to the tail, and conducted through the streets' while his distraught sister 'sprang from the roof of a house and fell, dead at his feet'. But even this tragic gesture could not spare her brother the ignominy of being hurled onto a dung hill and beheaded. The two guarantor sheikhs did not hesitate to express their outrage. One, whom Niebuhr identifies as the head of the Hashid and Bakil tribal 'mercenaries', was instantly thrown into prison and beheaded, while the other was invited to a meeting with the Imam and swiftly despatched by a cup of poisoned coffee. 'Since that time', notes Niebuhr, the Imam had been constantly troubled by tribesmen encroaching on his dominions and burning 'several cities'.[18] Niebuhr guessed he would soon be deposed and/or murdered.

Yemen's best-known tribal federations today – the Hashid (east and north of Sanaa) and Bakil (west and north of Sanaa) – come out of this story well, as proud upholders of truth and honour. The Imam, meanwhile, is revealed as a ruthlessly vengeful villain, as a brazen flouter of tribal law, as illegitimate a ruler as any Ottoman Turk had ever been.

Generally, the eighteenth-century imams were not as competent as their predecessors, and the less competent they were, the more land they forfeited. Having lost Hadhramaut and Dhofar by 1680, they were forced out of Aden by the southern Abdali tribe in 1727. They also flouted another important qualification of their rule by copying European monarchs, starting to hand their office straight on to their sons between 1716 and 1836. A son became imam apparent as soon as he was appointed governor of Sanaa and he, along with all his brothers, gained the title *al-Sayf al-Islam* [the Sword of Islam].

The gap between the ideally qualified imam and the reality was widening all the time. 'He was more like a king than a caliph,' wrote one Yemeni chronicler about the imam who succeeded the one de La Roque had met. Although sufficiently modest never to wear silk, this imam only pretended to be learned, 'He inclined to the scholars, talking with them and imitating them . . . So the scholars in his court would help in this [pretence], both out of desire and fear.'[19] Al-Mansur Ali, imam from 1775 until 1809, was neither a brave military leader nor a just ruler; 'his habit was to seclude himself and to cavort with free and slave women', in a palace filled with 'gold and silver and all kinds of clothes, precious stones . . . weaponry, medical implements and vials, and trunks full of musk, amber and clocks'.[20] In 1823 he invited Robert Finlay, a doctor attached to the British trading post in Mocha, up to Sanaa to cure him and his family of various ailments. After presenting the Imam with gifts that included a 'double-barrelled percussion gun', Finlay treated him for a fever in a room stuffed full of horse tack, bales of cloth, weapons and no fewer than six ticking gold and silver watches. Unimpressed, Finlay reported back to London that there was 'nothing dignified or commanding in the Imam's countenance; he is extremely passionate and constantly changing and disgracing in the most shameful manner, by putting in prisons and in irons, his principal servants and favourites, then restoring them again to their former rank'. Fearful of *sayyid* rivals, his current closest favourites were 'a former watch mender and a tailor from the bazaar'.[21]

Finlay formed no better opinion of the highland tribes, dismissing them as 'an idle uncivilised race, constantly quarrelling with each other and committing robbery'. Their sheikhs, many of them bribed by the Imam not to 'plunder his subjects', inspired no respect in him because they looked 'just like their men, simple in blue cotton, all of them chewing kaat [qat], drinking kishr [a tea made from the husks of coffee beans]'.[22] He mentioned what the Ottomans had long ago discovered to their cost and what remains broadly true today, that the most independent sheikhs were 'those who inhabit the highest and most precipitous mountains'.[23]

Such an unfavourable report might have convinced Lord Palmerston that the southernmost tip of the Arabian Peninsula could safely be ignored, but Britain's mounting rivalry with France had compelled him to take an interest in the region.

## A FIRST JEWEL FOR QUEEN VICTORIA'S CROWN

With the French threat to India seen off, Britain was only looking for one thing at the far end of the Arabian Peninsula by the early 1800s – somewhere her speedy new steam ships could refuel on the long journey from Suez to Bombay, a coaling station.

A first plan to requisition the island of Soqotra, closer to Somalia on the Horn of Africa than to Yemen but always a Yemeni possession and now a valuable eco-reserve, had to be aborted in 1834 when its ancient blind ruler, most of whose territory was situated in the easternmost Mahra province of today's Yemen, told the British naval officer charged with the task of acquiring it that he refused to sell so much as the distance between his thumb and his little finger. The island, he explained to Captain Stafford Bettesworth Haines of Britain's Indian Navy, was 'the gift of the Almighty to the Mahras'.[24] A subsequent attempt to seize it failed, when much of the expeditionary force died of malarial fever.

The following year Captain Haines turned his attention to Aden, hoping for better luck. The situation was becoming urgent. Doing business in Mocha had become almost impossible thanks to newly independent America having developed such a taste for coffee it easily dominated all trade there. Still worse, as far as Lord Palmerston was concerned, was the news that the coffee business had excited the greed of Egypt's Muhammad Ali, who after invading Tihama had seized Mocha and now had his sights trained on Aden. Accordingly, in 1835 Captain Haines was despatched to Aden with instructions to negotiate its swift purchase. Detached from the imams' dominions for almost a hundred years, Aden had decayed into 'a sort of international colony for Indian Ocean pirates',[25] but was still nominally a possession of the Abdali tribe. In 1835 the sheikh of the Abdalis, the self-styled Sultan of Lahej, was a tricky character whom Captain Haines at first judged 'indolent, almost imbecile'. But Sultan Muhsin turned out to be motivated by a mixture of pride and greed, a potently unpredictable brew that played havoc with all Haines' rational attempts to strike a deal. Haines was not discouraged. In an era in which the Great Powers of Europe considered it their bounden Christian duty to impose their values and mores on the rest of the world, Haines did not consider giving up.

If Britain was ever to get its coaling station, he and his superiors in Bombay and London decided, they would have to wait for an international incident of sufficient seriousness to warrant a forceful retaliation. In January 1837 just such an incident occurred. Spying the *Duria Dawla*, an Indian sailing ship flying British colours that had run aground a short distance to the east of Aden, Yemeni tribesmen had wasted no time in boarding her and plundering her valuable cargo, before mistreating her *haj*-bound passengers, fourteen of whom were drowned. Still more scandalously, they grossly dishonoured some wealthy Indian matrons by parading them naked on deck, like slaves in a market-place.

Almost a year passed before Captain Haines arrived back in Aden to avenge the insult. Although Sultan Muhsin strenuously denied any part in the episode, Haines soon spotted some of the plunder on sale in his warehouse, and bullishly demanded 12,000 Maria Theresa dollars* by way of compensation. A compromise sum was reached and the old subject of the sale of Aden reopened. The moment favoured the British. Sultan Muhsin was well aware that if he did not sell Aden to Britain, Egypt's greedy Muhammad Ali would come and grab it for nothing, so he wasted no time in signing and sealing a pledge to transfer Aden to the British for the sum of 8,700 Maria Theresa dollars a year. The business might have been smoothly concluded if a significant obstacle had not arisen, if Sultan Muhsin had not suddenly insisted that he must – as a matter of personal honour and dignity – retain responsibility for the port's few hundred Arabs and Jews. Haines would not hear of it. In order to be able to guarantee the security of her coaling station, Britain had to exercise full control over all the inhabitants residing in the fifteen square miles of land she was purchasing – Arabs, Jews, Indians and British. Negotiations stalled. Sultan Muhsin's hot-headed son, Hamid, gathered a tribal following that was adamantly opposed to any land sale, and hatched a plot to kidnap Haines. It was foiled. Downcast but still not defeated, Haines sailed away to consider his next move.

A combative letter from young Hamid greeted him on his return to Aden in October 1838 and thereafter negotiations were carried on in an increasingly angry style. 'You write of the British Government as if you were speaking of some petty Shaikhdom,' wrote Haines. 'Undeceive yourself – they are powerful and will not be trifled with. Would you play with a lion, as with a cat?' Bullied by his son, old Sultan Muhsin gamely blustered back that Haines dreamed of becoming 'Sultan of Aden' but never would be, 'until the sword is at our throats'.[26] Haines held his nerve and insisted on the legal validity of the original agreement they had made, until Hamid's Abdali tribesmen fatally upped the ante by firing their matchlocks at a British vessel. Haines and his immediate superiors in Bombay, exasperated by months of dealing with 'such

* The preferred currency in most of Yemen from the late eighteenth century until 1970 was a silver dollar coin embossed with a bust of Empress Maria Theresa of Austria and the date 1780.

a tone of arrogant superiority followed by such a series of uncalled for violence',[27] concluded that the time for force had arrived at last. A small, heavily armed army of some five hundred mostly Indian sepoy troops were loaded aboard four ships that set sail from Bombay in December 1838 and arrived at Aden a month later.

It took a mere two hours – from 9.30 until 11.30 on the morning of 19 January 1839 – to disable the mostly Ottoman-era guns on what was then Sira Island but is now a part of the mainland and to deal with some brave but chaotic tribal resistance. The order was then given to storm the beach nearest the town and plant the British flag. Advancing from the beach up into the tiny town, to the huddle of dwellings clustered in the crater of an extinct volcano, the invaders encountered no resistance because its inhabitants had all taken refuge in the mosque. A Muslim cleric greeted the invaders, and was told that no one would be harmed, that everyone should stay in the mosque, and that all weapons were to be collected. The last order resulted in some desperate rearguard action; heinously dishonoured by the confiscation of their *jambiyah*s, some tribesmen revolted and stabbed a Serjeant Major of Artillery. In the ensuing mêlée twelve Arabs were killed: 'Had it not been for this unfortunate occurrence, so deeply to be regretted,' wrote one of the officers, 'the loss of life would have been very trifling.'[28] The British counted a total of fifteen either killed or wounded, the Arabs at least 139.[29] Three captured guns were despatched back to Britain as a gift for Queen Victoria. One of them, a Turkish bronze cannon dating back to the mid-sixteenth century, still graces the river front outside the Tower of London.

As the new territory's Political Resident, Haines set about controlling what happened in and around Aden by building up an efficient intelligence network of Yemeni Jews. He guessed that while the merchants of Aden – mostly Jews and Indians – were more than happy to be ruled by mercantile Britain, the surrounding tribesmen would not be so easily reconciled to the loss of the port, so he ordered its fortifications swiftly rebuilt and had his troops keep a round the clock watch for attacks. He also guessed that if he cancelled the debt still owed him as compensation for the plunder of the *Duria Dawla* and paid Sultan Muhsin the agreed price for the purchase of Aden, if he graciously let bygones be bygones and even paid the tribes surrounding Aden regular stipends in exchange for their recognition of Britain's right to rule the port, all would soon be very well. But he was too optimistic, and had made a serious mistake. Perhaps too accustomed to Indians to understand quite how different Arabs were, Haines did not understand the extent to which the traditional role of sheikh or sultan or imam in southern Arabia differed from that of rulers whom the British had so efficiently co-opted into the smooth running of their Indian possessions. Sheikhs were not absolute rulers, able or willing to take full responsibility for their tribes; off the field of battle they were little more than wise conciliators, fountains of trickle-down wealth and trusted authorities. Haines did not see trouble up ahead when old Sultan Muhsin, hoping to trap the British into guaranteeing his continued hold on power, pleaded, 'Will you treat me and my children as you do many of your Indian rajahs?'[30]

Arabists have pointed out an important clue in the Arabic translation of the western concepts of 'ruler' and 'government': the Arab idea of rule is contained in the stem word *hukm*, which suggests wisdom, arbitration and justice. The Arabic words for governance, government, court house, ruler and even referee are all derived from this single stem which conveys no hint of absolute power, whether divinely, dynastically or democratically granted. A British officer who saw fifteen years' service in Aden before and during the Second World War learned that Yemeni tribesmen 'didn't appear to understand the word "rule"'. They were in fact shy of ruling. When one talked of strengthening their power they made excuses, changed the subject or looked the other way, as if one had said something indecent.'[31] A former British colonial officer posted to Aden in the last years of British rule believes the early and persistent failure of the British to discern the true character of sheikhly authority first hampered and then fatally blighted Britain's achievements in southern Arabia. By treating the petty sultans as absolute monarchs in their territories, by reinforcing their dynasties and propping them up in power according to how willing the individual was to toe the British line, rather than according to how just and wise and skilled at arbitration they were, Britain alienated the rank and file.

Haines also reckoned without a variety of native thinking that the foremost historian of the capture of Aden, Gordon Waterfield, calls 'the eternal surge of Arab optimism'.[32] For the seven years until his death in 1847, Sultan Muhsin surfed that 'surge', never abandoning hope of recapturing Aden and expelling the infidel. Not all the tribes were so persistent. The Yafai tribe, for example, took its stipend and kept its promise to be peaceful, as did the Aulaqi tribe. But, by buying the support of the Fadhli tribe whose lands lay east up the coast from Aden, Sultan Muhsin and his Abdalis were able to launch a full-scale attack on the British in November 1839.

Well aware that if all the tribes had made common cause their 15,000 to 20,000-strong force would have overwhelmed his garrison, Haines counted himself lucky. Thanks to his intelligence service, he was forewarned of a revenge attack plotted for the following month, and evaded assassination in the spring of the following year. While the Sultan of the Fadhlis proclaimed jihad against the European infidel, declaring that any who fell in battle would be 'rewarded by our Prophet Muhammad in the next world',[33] Haines' superiors in the Bombay government refused his pleas for reinforcements and began to have doubts about the wisdom of the enterprise, telling him that 'if Aden cannot be made a valuable acquisition without entering into aggressive warfare with the Arab chiefs of the interior, the sooner the place is abandoned or surrendered for a consideration, the better'.[34]

In May 1840 an alliance of Abdalis and Fadhlis made a second attempt on the port and two months later yet another, and a year later Fadhlis murdered one of the British army interpreters. Every incident resulted in numerous Arab casualties and stopped stipends. Again and again, pledges of good behaviour were made, the payment of stipends restored, and promises broken again. Eventually Haines so shamed Sultan Muhsin with examples of his lies that the old man agreed to Haines taking two of his sons hostage and unbuckled his *jambiyah* in the traditional tribal gesture of utter submission. 'Now kill me or forgive me!' he declared, but he never handed over his sons and the plotting did not stop. In 1851, in the same month as another attempt on Haines' life, a British officer, a guest of Sultan Muhsin's successor on a bustard-hunting expedition, was killed while asleep in his tent. The Fadhli sultan gave the murderer sanctuary and, when challenged over his 'scurvy conduct', defiantly reiterated his objection to the presence of 'Franks' in his country.[35]

References to these incidents and others, including one which culminated in the corpse of a tribesman being hung in chains from a post *pour decourager les autres*, appear in the journal of a Scottish officer who spent 1851 and 1852 in Aden. Marvelling at 'the aspect of desolation which pervades the place', he described a hellishly noisy Aden – the armies of 'Herculean Africans' shovelling at the 'immense heaps of coal' for the steam ships, 'the Babel' that accompanied newcomers from the port to the new Prince of Wales Hotel, 'the howling of wild dogs and the shrill note of the little Arab cocks which crow at all hours of the day and night'. The broiling, clammy heat was at least as irksome: 'I cannot attempt to describe the misery of the nights in camp during the hot weather,' he wrote. Soldiers slept outside, on their parade ground, and woke sweating to head straight into the sea to cool off. Their lives were miserable. Although they had a library and even a theatre of sorts, sand ruled out their 'favourite pastimes' and all were prey to 'lowness of spirits, loss of memory and loss of appetite', not to mention 'prickly heat and indolent boils'.

The sort of action they saw was demoralising too – sporadic and inglorious. There were frequent false alarms of tribal attacks and the frustration felt by any military facing a guerrilla campaign, of knowing 'we could have held Aden against any Army they [the tribes] could muster, but the knowledge that your life was in danger from lurking vagabonds was very unpleasant'. The knowledge that 'according to their creed [Islam], any of them who can prove that he has taken the life of an unbeliever is ever after honoured, and looked on as an especial saint' was at least as bad.[36] Aden was never a prestige posting. A Viceroy of India at the turn of the twentieth century, Lord Curzon, used it as a punishment station for regiments that disgraced themselves. As late as the inter-war period, the army was sending any officers 'who had got themselves into matrimonial difficulties'[37] to Aden.

On the other hand, Captain Haines' private vision of a town thriving on trade diverted from Mocha was being marvellously realised by 1854, when he was suddenly recalled to Bombay, to face charges of embezzlement. No one in Bombay was thinking of abandoning the Aden enterprise by the time another anonymous observer reported that under British rule Aden was so relatively safe and prosperous that Arabs and Africans and Indians were 'flocking in with cheerful countenance, exclaiming "*Angrazi zain! Angrazi zain!*" – Oh, the Good English!' He added that 'cheap goods of the newest patterns' were being sold 'at a handsome discount for ready money' and that everyone was doing business 'in a fair and liberal style and to their entire satisfaction'. The opening of the Suez Canal in 1869 and the resulting increase in traffic through the nearby Bab al-Mandab* and up and down the Red Sea made Aden's fortunes. With its 'cafes and cabarets' in which the colourful cosmopolitan mix could be heard 'proclaiming that Arrack [brandy] cures the gout, the colic and is of all things the very best physic',[38] Aden was a lively, unbuttoned place to be – unless you were a tribesman still smarting from the loss of land to the infidel.

In the forlorn hope of putting a stop to the tribes' 'frequent paltry squabbles' which they dismissed as the product of 'ignorance and bigotry',[39] the British opened a school for the sons and nephews of sultans in 1858. Although it was free, only sixteen out of the sixty-eight pupils of the first intake were Arab and the rest were Indians. The stated Arab

* The Gate of Tears, the strait at the lower end of the Red Sea, the closest point between the Arabian Peninsula and Africa.

objection to the place turned out to be a reasonable one: the absence of the Koran from the curriculum. Less than two years later it had closed. More than a decade was to pass before the Bombay government reluctantly concluded that Britain's best hope of securing the coaling station from tribal attack was to build on what Captain Haines had started by formalising alliances bolstered by stipends and 'gifts' with each of the so-called rulers of the nine tribes surrounding the port, thereby establishing a protectorate, in spite of Prime Minister William Gladstone's objection that he could see 'every imaginable objection' to such an arrangement because 'it binds us to support those over whose conduct to others we have no control. It threatens to impair, and most chronically, our good understanding with Turkey, which is necessary to the peace of the East.'[40]

Like the Turks in the sixteenth and seventeenth centuries, Britain would find herself paying a high price for Aden in terms of time, effort and money. By the time the First World War broke out, her sphere of influence had extended still further inland with the signing of another twenty-three treaties. In 1937 Aden's tribal hinterland would be divided into the Eastern Aden Protectorate (EAP), which comprised Hadhramaut with its Qaiti and Kathiri sultanates and the Mahra provinces with the island of Soqotra, and the Western Aden Protectorate (WAP), in which the Abdali, Fadhli, Yaffa and Aulaqi tribes predominated. By 1954 there would be a total of ninety treaties in existence, for a population of less than a million inhabiting an area that was almost the size of Britain.[41]

## THE SECOND OTTOMAN OCCUPATION

Gladstone had good reason to fear that enlargement of Aden's defensive buffer zone would only serve to revive Ottoman interest in the area because, two hundred years after departing from Mocha, the Turks were back in Sanaa – initially as invited guests.

By the 1840s the lands of the Zaydi Imams had become so deeply plunged into what Yemeni historians remember as the 'Time of

Corruption' on account of their declining coffee fortunes and the chaos caused by competing imams, that a group of Sanaa notables – merchants and clergy – had despairingly penned an invitation to the Porte to come back and impose some order. Although presumably well aware the request did not guarantee a warm welcome from the highland tribes, the expanding British presence in the south was dictating a correspondingly 'forward policy' on the Ottomans' part. They also persuaded themselves that their occupation of Yemen was a charitable endeavour. As a Turkish journalist wrote at the time, 'The Arab is our teacher whose nerves have been harmed through the disorder and turmoil of ages past . . . Now we are going to assist them in rescuing them from the state in which they find themselves.'[42]

In 1849 a first Ottoman attempt to enter Sanaa with a force of 1,500 was thwarted by tribesmen who, incensed by the invader's demand that Friday prayers be dedicated to the Sultan rather than to their own imam, slaughtered a hundred of them. Just as they had in the mid-sixteenth century, the peaceful Sunni Tihamans made the Turks welcome, and even the southern highlanders tolerated them but, once again, not the Zaydi northern highlanders. A mightier army, whose transportation to Yemen was greatly hastened by the new Suez Canal,* fared much better in 1872 and was greeted by the merchants of Sanaa with roars of 'Victory to the Sultan!', as well as with open-mouthed amazement at the 'order and tidiness and magnificence, splendour and display of the imperial forces'.[43] For a time, even the northern highlands were subdued and the ruling imam thrust into what one historian terms 'subsidised obscurity'.[44] But before long, the highlander tribes started clamouring for stipends and mounting a fierce insurgency that would cost the Ottomans dearly in time, materiel and manpower for almost the next forty years. Still vivid folk memories of the last occasion they had ventured into the northern highlands plagued them. Recruits for their army in Yemen sometimes had to be chained and

* Opened in 1869, the Suez Canal linked the Mediterranean to the Red Sea.

physically carried on board troop ships, so great was their dread of almost certain death in those desolate mountains. An old Ottoman folk-song captures the dismay and misery surrounding the very name of Yemen in the empire's heartland:

> Yemen, your desert is made of sand
> What did you want from my son?
> I don't know your way or your sign
> I am just missing my son
> O Yemen, damned Yemen . . .[45]

The Ottomans' efforts to rule Yemen as they did any other part of their empire met with dismal failure. Even an admission that the population's backwardness forced them to administer the place directly, as a colony, as a *muslemleke* rather than a *vilayet*, brought no improvement. For example, after abandoning attempts to recruit Yemeni tribesmen into their own multi-national army, they tried to instil some discipline by following the British lead in India and establishing a native army. But, although the tribesmen were smartly kitted out with a specifically Yemeni uniform of white *futa*, black shirt and brass badge bearing the Ottoman state emblem, the force was unruly and unreliable and had to be disbanded after only three years.

Determined as ever to milk Yemen of whatever riches it had and recoup losses incurred by ceaseless punitive military expeditions into the highlands, the Turkish pashas did not follow the British lead in the protectorates by forbearing from taxing the tribes. Instead, misguidedly priding themselves on their sensitivity to local custom in giving the tribesmen a chance to put up a face-saving show of resistance, they sent out military expeditions to demand payment. Although they could be said to be making improvements – a road from Sanaa to the port of Hodeidah, a telegraph, some schools and sturdy stone administration buildings in Sanaa, Taiz and Hodeidah – taxation swiftly re-emerged as a main source of dissatisfaction with this second period of Turkish rule.

Sheikhs to whom they farmed out local administration soon found themselves having to pay for their posts and resorting to extortion in order to recoup their outlay. With the Turks in charge, Yemen's Time of Corruption can be said to have extended itself into the second half of the nineteenth century and on, into the first decade of the twentieth.

By 1890 Turkish rule was so hated that rival claimants to the title of imam had ceased their feuding and coalesced around one Imam al-Mansur, who promptly established himself in the north-western Zaydi stronghold of Saada and terrified the Turks by organising a guerrilla army of tribesmen to carry out hit and run raids. Al-Mansur's tribesmen dismantled telegraph poles, blew up municipal buildings and attacked Turkish homes and by 1892 there were 70,000 of them laying siege to Sanaa. The Turks tried to bribe the Imam into submission with an offer of a high position in their administration and a generous stipend in return for his lifting the siege, but al-Mansur was launched on a traditional Zaydi uprising against an unrighteous ruler, gathering fervent support by railing against the Turks' homosexuality, their European style of dress, their trousers and their fezzes, their love of alcohol and their absence from the mosque. If not to the merchants of Sanaa then to many Yemenis, their Ottoman oppressors seemed to have strayed so far from the true path of Islam that they could properly be reviled as *kuffar* [unbelievers] and still worse, as *nasara* [Christians].

Constantinople despatched a commander named Ahmad Feyzi Pasha at the head of a 4,000-strong army to break the siege and quash al-Mansur's uprising, which he managed to do by holding out to the famine-stricken rebel tribesmen the promise of a daily meal, a reward for any of their severed heads, and a general pardon. Locating the main source of trouble in the Hashid federation of highland tribes, Feyzi Pasha also took a leaf out of the British book by showering the Hashid sheikhs with gifts. But the Imam remained at large and on the offensive, pursuing Ahmad Feyzi Pasha's army to Sanaa and on south, as far as Taiz. Ottoman supply lines broke down and the Syrian troops mutinied over having received only one year's pay after several years' service in Yemen. Losses of manpower were running at over a third when, thanks to yet another fresh influx of miserably underpaid and disheartened troops, Feyzi Pasha, who was in his seventies and himself begging to be allowed to retire from a place already renowned as the 'graveyard of the Turks', gradually managed to turn the tide.

His back to the wall at last, Imam al-Mansur wrote to the British authorities in Bombay, begging for help. Wisely, Britain passed up this chance of extending its tribal protectorates around Aden north to the highlands. But still the jihad sputtered on, even spreading as far as the usually docile Tihama. By 1900 a team of foreign specialists surveying the route for a Turkish railway linking Sanaa to the Tihaman port of Hodeidah required a 350-strong armed guard to go about its business. In the same year an American visitor to the country detailed what he judged to be the baneful effects of Ottoman rule: 'The peasantry are robbed by the soldiers on their way to market, by the customs collector at the gate of each city and by the tax gatherer in addition,' he noted. 'No wonder we read of rebellions in Yemen, and no wonder that intense hatred lives in every Arab against the very name of Turk.'[46]

Al-Mansur's son, Imam Yahya, succeeded him, largely because a powerful Hashid sheikh threatened to slaughter all those involved in the selection process unless they chose Yahya. The memory of having briefly lost control of their highlands in the early 1870s made the Hashid tribes especially keen to fight the Turks. Under Yahya those tribes renewed the jihad in 1905, mounting probably the worst siege Sanaa has ever experienced. More than two thirds of Sanaanis starved to death while the remainder held out for the three months of the ordeal on a hideous diet of straw bread, dog, cat, rat and human flesh. The city's 8,000-strong community of Jews was especially hard hit. On a visit to Sanaa a few months after the siege had been lifted, the British diplomat Aubrey Herbert reported that the city's ghetto 'was like the dream of some haunted painter. Many of the men were still skin and bone, and the crowd of dark faces with cavernous cheeks, half-hidden by twisted, black elf-locks that hung on either side, begging eyes and clutching hands, were horrible.'[47] Described by one foreign visitor in 1900 as the 'most impressive city [in the Ottoman Empire] after Baghdad', filled with Greek shops selling European goods, whose Turkish quarter boasted billiard rooms, boot-blacks and a brass band,[48] Sanaa had been reduced to dusty savagery. It was estimated that no fewer than 8,000 of the 10,000 besieged Turkish troops had died too, the vast majority of sickness.[49] Another reckoning states that of the 55,000 Turkish troops that disembarked at Hodeidah, 6,000 were killed in the siege but 9,000 died of typhoid.[50]

Once again, Feyzi Pasha had mustered a mighty force to throw off the siege but, pursuing Imam Yahya to yet another Zaydi mountain fastness – this time to Shahara, half a day's journey by car to the north-west of Sanaa – he was forced to concede defeat after two months. There were 50,000 Turkish troops in Yemen at the time, but still the northern highlands resisted Ottoman colonisation and by 1911 they were ready for a fresh offensive. Arthur Wavell, an intrepid British army officer, happened to be in Sanaa that year. The only other European in town, an Italian merchant and spy named Signor Caprotti, had weathered the sieges of 1892 and 1905 and so warned Wavell that he should lay in supplies because another was in the offing.

The first shots were heard in January, and by the end of the month Wavell was observing a 'sudden great increase in the number of camp fires visible by night around the town'.[51] The Turks were rumoured to have two years' worth of rations in store and plenty of ammunition, but the tribes, outnumbering the Turks by a ratio of three to one, were also well armed with Mauser rifles captured or bought from their enemy. Guns of all sorts and every vintage, Wavell observed, were far cheaper in Yemen than in Europe. Scaling ladders were being prepared, but still the tribes hesitated. Popular belief had it that Sanaa enjoyed God's special protection, that anyone storming the city was doomed. At last, the siege began. For the first two months of its three-month duration only qat was in short supply. Cigarettes, lamp oil and cooking oil ran out eventually, but qat was available by the time it ended and anyone with money never went as hungry as they had in 1905.

Nevertheless, the Turks acknowledged that, once again, they had been bested by the highland tribes. Decades too late, one Ottoman official stated the blindingly obvious: 'To keep them [Yemenis] down unjustly will take much money and many troops. Conscientiousness and justice is what we expect from our administrators. Yemen has become now the graveyard of Muslims and money.'[52] Even a perceived duty to guard the southern approach to the holy places at Mecca and Medina and ever-mounting pressure to compete with the European empires failed to outweigh the crippling cost of maintaining a patchy control of Yemen. As well as the Sanaa siege, the Turks had an unrelated Italian-backed uprising in the Asir region of the country (now a part of Saudi Arabia), to say nothing of unrest in the Tihama to contend with in 1911.

A new pasha was sent out with instructions to come to terms with Imam Yahya, which proved easy enough. Yahya had long argued that he was only rebelling against corrupt Turkish officialdom, not against the Ottoman Sultan, and only on behalf of Zaydis who were, he claimed, the rightful rulers of all Yemen – the highlands, Aden and its tribal hinterland, Tihama and Asir – since the third century of the Islamic calendar. He had, he insisted, 'no desire save to "order the right" [a key Zaydi concept] and extirpate what is loathsome and reprehensible, to establish the shari'ah, set straight him who strays and advise the ignorant'.[53] In exchange for formal recognition of his control over the Zaydi highlands he could agree to dispense with the titles of Caliph and 'Commander of the Faithful' which had hitherto placed all Zaydi imams in direct competition with the Ottoman sultans. In return, he would be free to replace Ottoman with sharia law in his domains, to select his own judges and collect his own taxes. The Turks would remain in control over Tihama and much of the southern highlands including the city of Taiz and retain responsibility for Yemen's external defence.

Although Yahya faced numerous challenges to his rule, because there were many among his tribal supporters who thought he had conceded too much, the last few years of the Turkish presence in Yemen, until the end of the First World War and the collapse of the Ottoman Empire, were comparatively peaceful, the Turks less heavy-handedly controlling. 'Tact is the order of the day, and laissez faire', observed one British visitor to the region in 1912 of Ottoman rule at the time, '. . . the writing is on the wall'.[54] The game was up long before the Turks left Yemen and the stain of failure lingered long after their departure. More than a decade after his exit from Sanaa the last Ottoman pasha to administer the truncated province was still smarting at the memory: 'in my opinion, this is what happened, from the day we conquered it to the time we left it we neither knew Yemen nor did we understand it nor learn [anything] about it, nor were we, for that matter, able to administer it'.[55]

For the second time, Yemen's northern highland Zaydi tribes had expressed their objection to outside rule, even when that rule was by fellow Muslims, even when that rule was imposed in the name of uniting the Muslim *umma*. Together, the ancient memory of being a persecuted and dissident Shiite minority hounded out of what is north Iran in the ninth century, and more recent mistreatment and exploitation at the hands of foreigners, acted as a powerful prophylactic against any outside interference whatsoever.

Yahya stood by the Ottomans during the First World War but steered clear of taking on the British, refusing to fight shoulder to shoulder with the Turks outside Aden in early 1915, for example. When the Ottoman Empire collapsed in 1918 he was therefore well placed to fill the vacuum left behind, extending his rule west to the Tihama and south to the borders of the British protectorates. As the historian George Lenczowski puts it, after the First World War Imam Yahya emerged as the ruler of the first independent state on the Arabian Peninsula 'largely by default, inasmuch as there was no power ready and willing to assume imperial responsibilities in the area'[56] – as the French and British were then doing in other former Ottoman possessions that were being reconfigured as Syria, Palestine, Trans-Jordan and Iraq. Outside powers, whether Muslim or Christian, had learned a lesson. None of them cared to waste their time or their money trying to subjugate the Zaydi tribes.

## CHAPTER TWO

# REVOLUTIONARY ROADS (1918–1967)

### IN IMAM YAHYA'S PALACE

A search for traces of Imam Yahya, for some vestige of the man who ruled the north-western portion of Yemen for longer than anyone before or since, turned up only two reliable results in Sanaa.

Just outside the old city, behind the national museum, at the far end of an unmarked alley leading off September 26th street, is what could be one of the capital's biggest visitor attractions, but is not. All that remains of Yahya's palace compound is distinguished by a tatty signboard reading 'Government Property Office'. An old and once ornate wooden gateway, missing a few planks and warped out of shape, looks like the entrance to an abandoned junkyard. Beyond it a mess of plastic bags, rusting machinery and weeds rots in the shade cast by the old royal buildings, a cluster of sagging mud high-rises with broken windows. On closer inspection, scraps of filthy fabric doing duty as makeshift curtains suggested that some of the floors were still inhabited. A crowd of children who had gathered to stare at a rare foreign visitor confirmed that the squalid squat was their home. They seemed to know its special history, helpfully pointing out for me rusting iron rings once used for tethering the Imam's horses, and a bare space on the gate from which an Islamic inscription had recently been stolen. A short walk back and on along September 26th street and down another unmarked alleyway between houses brought me to a small untended Muslim cemetery where the largest gravestone standing among overgrown thorns, discarded plastic bags, cigarette packets and crumbling humbler graves belonged to Imam Yahya. The list of his proud *sayyid* genealogy, carefully inscribed on the stone, filled two pages of my notebook and ended with a simple statement of the fact of his killing in 1948.

Imam Yahya is utterly out of official favour in today's Republic of Yemen for refusing to rise to the challenge of updating the imamate, for retarding his country's development, for being an elitist aristocrat and a tyrant. But, in fact, his style of ruling was patriarchal rather than tyrannical. His motivation was not so much to restrict and control as to conserve and protect. He believed that as a true *sayyid* descendant of the Prophet he was doing God's will by shielding the land and its people from the perils of modernity and infidel foreign contagion. In an effort to return the country to a mythical golden age it had supposedly enjoyed under the Qasim imams, Yahya closed it down. Administering his expanded realms as if they were his immediate household, he occasionally tempered his authoritarianism and love of hoarding silver with a gratuitous sweetness towards children or beggars, charming his family of Yemenis with his modest and pious lifestyle and his reputation as a miraculous healer. Almost everything that concerned each of his subjects – from their education, to their health-care, to their relations with their neighbours, to their travel abroad, to their land disputes, to their choice of a spouse – required his say-so or sanction. Advice was only acceptable to him if it forbore from criticism, remained a secret and was presented in poetic form. One such poem, penned by an eminent *qadhi*, began, 'Take the stand of adviser towards the caliph/ Do not take the stand of a faultfinder/ Be gentle, don't exaggerate in reprimanding him.'[1]

The seat of Yahya's government was a chaotic room in his palace whose floor was strewn with papers and whose battered furniture contained drawers stuffed with more paper, some of it inscribed by a minute hand in tiny concentric circles to avoid waste. One visitor witnessed a servant entering the room with a tray piled high with silver Maria Theresa dollars which, after showing them to the Imam, he poured onto an existing pile on the floor. Yahya's response to a message announcing the death of a soldier was to mark and sign 'the document with a formula tantamount to giving the already deceased warrior permission to die'[2] astonished him more. Another visitor watched Yahya resolve a complaint about a neighbour's donkey kicking a wall with a command that the animal be chained from dawn until dusk. A fellow Arab, the Syrian American, Amin Rihani, saw the Imam deal with a request from one of his sons for the use of a car for a day. But Rihani gave credit where he felt it was due, judging Yahya to be 'of all the Arab rulers of today [the late 1920s] the nearest to some system in conducting the affairs of State. He has the head of a man of business, and his one-man Government, with all its rusty gear, could not, under the circumstances, be run better by the president of an American corporation.'[3] Yahya was well respected as both a ruler and a scholar in the Arab world. The scene outside his palace however, in the courtyard where he kept a caged leopard and hyena, was not so impressive. Scribes employed in writing petitions for the illiterate jostled with supplicants so desperate for their grievances to be heard and alleviated they set fire to their headcloths to draw attention to themselves.

Imam Yahya travelled around his capital either by a nineteenth-century horse-drawn carriage with outriders and a bodyguard singing and dancing alongside or in a black Ford the British presented him with early in his reign, as a goodwill gesture. The highlight of every week was his visit to the mosque. If commendably friendly to the environment, his Sanaa may have been a pungent place; the walls of many houses displayed traces of sewage passing on its long open-air drop down to ground level and one visitor discovered human excrement being sold by the donkey-load for heating the water in the city's *hammams*. The stink of that merchandise might account for the fact that many Sanaani women wore sprigs of basil or flowers dangling off 'two hat-pins poked like carpenters' pencils behind their ears', to hold their veils out in front of their faces to a distance of two or three inches.[4]

Traces of Turkish rule lingered on, though sadly not in the form of a large girls' school, which Yahya immediately closed. He had requested that the Turks leave behind some cooks and some of their German-trained military musicians to teach Yemeni soldiers how to play German marches, which they adapted by speeding up the tempo and adding an accompaniment of clapping and stamping. Yahya's attempts to introduce sharia law were not as much appreciated. Sanaanis complained that sharia was like a mountain, 'a magnificent monument of past ages but a terrible and overwhelming disaster to those on whom it falls',[5] and one foreigner observed that the capital's inhabitants spent far too much of their time 'watching for minute contraventions in the hopes of paying off old scores'.[6] In general, the old Ottoman law had proved more practical.

Although the quintessence of a righteous Zaydi ruler – brave, physically fit, well-versed in Koranic learning, pious – it took Yahya a good decade to establish himself firmly in his land. Always sympathetic, the Syrian-American Rihani detailed Yahya's chronic insecurity: 'He is at war openly with the Idrisi [Asir], at war secretly with Shawafe [Shafai Muslims of Tihama]; at war periodically with the Hashid and Bakil [the main Zaydi tribes]; at war politically with the English – also with those Arabs around Aden who enjoy English protection [the colony's tribal hinterland] – to say nothing of the Saiyeds [*sayyids*], his cousins, who aspire to his high place.' Rihani concluded that 'Not at all soft is the royal couch.'[7]

The most warlike tribesmen of Tihama, the Zaraniq, were not neutralised until 1925 and the Marib desert region to the east of Sanaa not secured until the 1930s. In 1925 Yahya had conquered the north-western Asir region, which had been thriving under the charismatic rule of the chieftain Muhammad al-Idrisi since 1909, but went on to lose it in a war with Saudi Arabia in 1934. The tribes accounting for the bulk of the Zaydi highlands, the Hashid and Bakil federations, sporadically rebelled until 1928, even treacherously allying themselves with al-Idrisi in Asir from time to time. Yahya forbore from taxing them and treated them as honoured allies when they co-operated with him. These means, and the old resort to carrots (bribes) and sticks (taking sheikhs' sons hostage), eventually brought a semblance of peace to the northern highlands. By the late 1920s he was reputed to have rounded up 4,000 boy hostages,[8] some of them under lock and key but many of them receiving an education that would instil in them a proper love of the imam. There are some who say that the man in Yahya's shoes today, President Salih, has had to dispense with this highly effective, if cruel, means of keeping Yemen's more troublesome tribes in line, but it has left him with only two unsatisfactory levers of power; either he can dance on the heads of snakes and run the risk of not ruling at all, or he can emulate his old friend, Saddam Hussein, by relying on brute force and terror.

For all the hardness of his 'royal couch' Yahya developed into a strong and confident ruler. His repeated forays into Aden's tribal hinterland to lure the tribes away from British protection with offers of guns and gold made him an aggressor as well as a defender. Those incursions were only temporarily halted when the British retaliated with cross-border air-raids. It was 1928 before Yahya agreed to respect the border that the Turks and British had agreed in 1914, but still he did not relinquish his early eighteenth-century-based claim to be the rightful ruler of all Yemen – Aden included.

Other external relations were more easily managed, generally by keeping them to the barest minimum. French offers to revive Mocha, to buy lots of coffee from Yahya and sell him lots of guns, were rebuffed. There could be no cosying up to Britain while she still occupied Aden, of course, or to America, Britain's close ally. Proudly suspicious of any outside interest in his realm, he once asked the Dutch explorer Daniel van der Meulen what his queen wanted from Yemen – 'gold, or other minerals, the white gold of oil perhaps?' Reassured to hear that she only wanted a friendship treaty, he confided that an American mining company had recently offered him two million dollars for the right to prospect for oil. When van der Meulen asked if he had accepted such an advantageous offer, Yahya's firm negative was couched in a rhetorical question: 'can you tell me how many millions it would cost me to be rid of them again?'[9] The Ford Corporation's offer to build Yemen an entire network of roads, in exchange for Yemen importing only Fords, was similarly rebuffed.

Without the services of a venerable Ottoman diplomat known as Raghib Bey the grandly named Mutawakkilite Kingdom of Yemen* would have remained utterly isolated until after the Second World War. Raghib Bey understood post-First World War realities and, given that the European powers remained intent on carving up the world between them, how best to position the new state on the world stage. The best an impoverished and insignificant country like Yemen could hope for, he calculated, was an alliance with anyone prepared to offer material assistance with no strings attached.

Imam Yahya did not always appreciate his efforts. On one occasion, during negotiations with an American envoy in 1947, Yahya drove Raghib Bey to the point of resignation. The American visitor witnessed a scene which seemed to 'out-Hollywood Hollywood'.[10] Negotiations had reached an impasse after seventeen days because the Imam had seen fit to replace Raghib Bey as chief negotiator with one of his sons who knew nothing of diplomacy. Sobbing and gesticulating, almost grabbing the Imam by his beard, Raghib Bey berated Yahya in the most disrespectful terms for ruining the 'international masterpiece' of diplomacy he had worked so hard on. Convinced that the old Turk was about to harm his master, Yahya's bodyguard reached for his *jambiyah* and

* Mutawakkilite refers to *al-Mutawakkil*, which means 'he who depends on God'. The Kingdom was formally declared by Yahya in 1926.

tiptoed up behind him, awaiting Yahya's signal to cut Raghib Bey's throat. But Yahya gave no such signal. Instead, smiling in a fatherly fashion, he merely told the old man, 'Do not upset yourself, Raghib Bey; things will come out all right.'[11] The Turk often bitterly regretted his decision to stay on in Yemen, once complaining to a foreign visitor that he felt 'surrounded by ruffians who had no conversation and filled their endless hours of laziness with that stupid, animal-like habit of chewing qat'.[12]

With Britain and America both off the menu of possible alliances, Raghib Bey had no choice but to steer Yahya in the direction of the rising totalitarian powers. After one of Yahya's sons and his foreign minister travelled to Rome to meet Benito Mussolini in 1927, a few Italian airplanes arrived in Sanaa and a small flying school was opened. Soon after that two more German planes arrived, but Yahya's aeronautical enthusiasm waned when the latter pair collided with each other, killing the two German pilots and two *sayyid*s. With the advent of a handful of Italian doctors the following year, Yahya acquired a lasting taste for Italian health-care. The mid-1920s witnessed the arrival of a large Soviet mission, chiefly composed of aviation experts and doctors. By a treaty of 1928 the Soviet Union recognised Yemen as an independent kingdom, paving the way for a one-way trade in Russian grain, sugar and soap. A sizeable Soviet mission was housed in politically incorrect luxury in the old Turkish quarter, but only functioned for a decade, until 1938, when Stalin recalled and 'purged' all but two of its members. A year earlier, Mussolini's envoy, the Fascist governor of Eritrea, had visited Sanaa to sign a treaty of friendship, and Hitler's Germany had despatched 50,000 rifles – which the Poles had already rejected as faulty – to Yahya for payment in gold. Commercial links with Japan were so good throughout the 1930s that the Imam sent his eldest son all the way to Tokyo to attend the opening of the country's first mosque.

By the time he was eighty, Yahya had buttressed his waning powers, not with well-trained and reliable professionals, but with a handful of his own sons whom he appointed to some rudimentary ministries and foreign embassies. His defiantly independent stance had looked noble and brave while most of the Middle East was still ruled by the western powers or their proxies, but in the era of imperial implosion it was starting to look dated, and there were other signs that his time had passed. Whether or not with the encouragement of Raghib Bey, he made two bad mistakes. For all his conservatism and wariness of ever being called a king, he was king enough to flout Zaydi tradition by declaring his son Ahmad his favoured successor and permitting him to be known as the Crown Prince. He was also king enough to establish his own army instead of trusting to tribal support to secure his rule. Both innovations mightily offended two pillars of the Zaydi order: the *sayyid* families who dreamed of replacing him and the northern highland tribes whom he was making redundant. The brains and the brawn of Zaydi Yemen were restive.

But it was a pair of non-*sayyid* young men who managed to receive an education in Cairo where they were influenced by the Muslim Brotherhood* who began taking practical steps to press for reform and foil Yahya's plan for a dynastic succession. The Sanaani poet and Zaydi member of the *qadhi* class Muhammad al-Zubayri tried convincing the Imam of the need for reform by intellectual argument, but the attempt landed him in prison for nine months. A switch in strategy, an attempt to win Crown Prince Ahmad for the reform cause, met with similarly discouraging results, so the movement's leaders – al-Zubayri and the Sunni southern highlander Ahmad Numan – were forced to flee to Aden, where they could rely on funding and support from the 25,000 or so Sunni migrant workers from Yemen's southern highlands, as well as take advantage of the colony's relatively free press.

In 1943 a Free Yemeni Party was born with Numan as president and al-Zubayri as director, but it failed to flourish. On the one hand Imam

* The Egypt-based Muslim Brotherhood was working to establish cells all over the Arab world during the 1940s, aiming at establishing Islamic states. The religious and isolated nature of Imam Yahya's Yemen made it an ideal target.

Yahya wreaked a terrible revenge by hurling hundreds of Sunni southern highlanders who were in any way connected with Numan in jail. On the other, the British would not support the movement because, just at that moment, Aden was relying heavily on food imported from Yemen to feed vast numbers of troops transiting through the colony to and from the different theatres of the Second World War. Only with the establishment of the newspaper *Voice of Yemen* in 1945 did the Free Yemeni movement begin to gain real traction, so much so that when Crown Prince Ahmad visited Aden the following year he vowed to kill Numan and al-Zubayri. They both fled the city for the duration of his stay and gained some excellent publicity by the episode, but events soon took an even better turn when Imam Yahya's ninth son, the thirty-year-old Ibrahim – a whisky drinker who had spent years in one of his father's jails – pretended to be in urgent need of foreign medical expertise in order to defect to Aden and join the movement. The bagging of so important a Zaydi to counterbalance the majority Sunni membership was a significant success.

Meanwhile the rudiments of a clandestine opposition movement had been taking shape in Sanaa too. It comprised some respected Sunni southern highlanders from the Ibb region who had prospered under Zaydi rule as judges and administrators. Sections of the *ulema*, army officers whom Yahya had risked sending to Iraq for training and some leading tribal sheikhs were likewise inclined to sympathise with the Free Yemeni movement. But it was a grandson of the imam who had preceded Yahya's father in the late nineteenth century, a former close adviser of Yahya's as well as a friend of Numan's, a *sayyid* named Abdullah al-Wazir, who finally emerged as a suitable alternative to Yahya. After spending eight years in Cairo al-Wazir judged himself fit and willing to rule 'on the lines now followed by the most advanced nations in the civilised world',[13] to be a constitutional imam, in other words. He and a handful of others – members of his own family for the most part, but also an Algerian merchant member of the Muslim

Brotherhood named al-Fudayl al-Wartalani, and a young Iraqi army captain named Jamal Jamil – hatched a plot to assassinate the Imam.

On the morning of 17 February 1948 the frail Yahya was being driven a short distance south of Sanaa to inspect a new well. With him were his prime minister, a couple of soldiers and four of his grandsons. Characteristically, the Imam had pared down his escort to save on expense. The plotters had employed a tribesman who had lost an eye and most of his nose to smallpox and been jailed by Yahya twenty years earlier to lead the attack. At a narrow point in the road Yahya's tiny convoy was strafed with gunfire. It was said that no fewer than fifty bullets found their marks in Yahya's frame.

Some 150 kilometres to the south, in Taiz, Crown Prince Ahmad acted fast on hearing the news from a brother who was Minister of Communications and therefore equipped with his own radio transmitter. Seizing as much gold as he and his retinue could carry and leaving a sister in charge of holding Taiz in his name, Ahmad fled to the Zaydi heartland north-west of Sanaa, towards the mountain fortress of Hajja, to bribe the northern tribes into rallying to the defence of his succession. To a polite condolence letter from al-Wazir, offering him 'position, respect and peace' in exchange for his stepping aside, Ahmad replied with a defiant missive, branding al-Wazir a 'wretched and despicable traitor' and warning of his warlike advance against him 'with God's helpers'.[14]

Delighted by the gold on offer but also disorientated by the sudden end of Yahya's long rule, some 250,000 northern tribesmen rallied to Ahmad. Yahya's assassin was soon caught and his one-eyed scalp tacked to Sanaa's main gate, *al-Bab al-Yemen*. Within a month, five more members of the al-Wazir clan had been rounded up and executed and the would-be imam's severed head hurled on a rubbish tip. Sanaanis bore the brunt of the tribesmens' wrath. Their blood up and discipline lax, they gleefully and vengefully set about punishing the liberal urbanites of Sanaa for their disloyalty to Ahmad by sacking the capital for a week. Like a plague of locusts, they stripped it of anything they could remove – jewellery, furniture, food stores, livestock, even doors and windows.

Wisely, given his ultimate responsibility for this heinous orgy of destruction, Ahmad moved the capital to the southern highlands, to Taiz where he had been governor, barely setting foot back in Sanaa for the ensuing fourteen years of his reign.

## IMAM AHMAD'S HORROR SHOW

In spite of their dramatic topology the southern highlands around Ahmad's capital, where crusts of stone villages cap every precipice, give the impression of being as densely populated as south-east England, a world away from their bleak northern counterparts. A visitor immediately recognises this verdant central region as united Yemen's natural centre of gravity, as its real engine room and heartland, but a hunt for traces of Imam Ahmad in Taiz throws up little more than a search for his father in Sanaa.

A military policeman sitting on a low crumbling wall outside the museum that was once his palace, spooning broad beans straight from a can to his mouth, grudgingly admitted me to the first floor lobby of the museum. Its shabby green walls were dotted with blurred photographs of the public beheadings that had taken place in Ahmad's reign, including one of a sword used for the purpose. No amount of pleading with the unveiled woman sitting idle at an empty desk could induce her to admit me to the rest of the museum, the cumulative effect of whose treasures a previous visitor had so invitingly described as being 'rather like stepping into the imam's living room with all the favourite possessions and souvenirs on show'. I was sorry to learn that neither I nor anyone else would ever again see Imam Ahmad's bizarre collection of 'hundreds of identical bottles of eau de cologne, Old Spice and Christian Dior, an electronic bed, a child's KLM handbag, projectors, films, guns, ammunition and swords . . . passports, personalised Swiss watches and blood-stained clothes'.[15] The entire exhibition, a unique hoard that decisively linked Imam Ahmad to some of his similarly magpie-minded predecessors, had recently been dismantled in an even worse act of bureaucratic vandalism than the slow neglect of his father's palace in Sanaa.

The missing display spoke volumes about the manner in which Imam Ahmad spent his reign debasing rather than updating the imamate. His version of the still venerable institution was a luridly burlesque imitation of his father's, almost a parody. Gratuitously cruel rather than harshly just, extravagantly degenerate rather than frugal, paranoid rather than wary, Ahmad relied on base trickery, assisted by minor products of modern technology and his people's credulous love of magic, to clothe himself in the charisma his father had earned by real piety and learning. With the aid of a pair of binoculars he could amaze the people of Taiz with his uncanny foreknowledge of a visitor's arrival. When a lioness given him by Haile Selassie died, Ahmad had her stuffed and set on the wall of his palace to scare bystanders. Before a beheading he would carefully enhance his already prominent eyes with an extra application of kohl and slather so much cream on his dyed black forked beard that it stood out rigidly, 'as if he had his finger in a light socket'.

One eyewitness recalled Ahmad losing his temper after a beheading because people came jostling too close around him. Thundering at them to back off, he drew his sword: 'The screech of grating steel echoed across the square and all of us in the crowd recoiled, collapsing onto our backs like dominoes one on top of the other. No one drew so much as a breath until the Imam had safely departed.'[16] He was said to have drowned his dwarf court jester for a joke and then, overcome with remorse, to have fasted, prayed and played with an electric train for a fortnight. Ahmad's murder of four of his nine brothers and his frequent and lengthy absences from public view on account of depression, only enhanced his supernatural image and earned him the grim sobriquet, *al-Djinn* – the Devil. A gigantic portrait of him, framed in neon lights, graced the square outside his palace.

As far as his style of ruling went there was little change to report. Just like his father, he micro-managed the kingdom – dealing with 200 telegrams at one sitting, sanctioning a school's purchase of ten inkwells, deciding the daily schedule of the national airline, authorising the internment of a sheikh's son – in the belief that to have done things any differently would have detracted from his dignity. Various brothers and a son formed a 'Royal Cabinet' of ministers answerable only to him, but he kept a tight personal hold on the treasury which one foreigner recalled as 'a profusion of money sacks, each containing 1000 [Maria Theresa] thalers, as well as an enormous safe full of foreign currencies, tins of petrol, tinned goods, spare parts for motor cars and filters for drinking water'.[17] Two councils, one of merchants – described by an American diplomat as 'elderly individuals with hennaed beards, dirty clothes, several endemic diseases (notably malaria) and a complete distrust of all foreigners' – the other of religious elders who were 'more conservative than Ahmad'[18] ensured that time stood almost as still in 1950s Yemen as it had in the 1920s.

Unsurprisingly, given the manner of his accession to power, Ahmad's relations with the northern tribes were closer than his father's had been, but he followed Yahya's lead again, neutralising any rival by never promoting talent. Under Ahmad 'informality and improvisation' remained the 'cornerstones of government'.[19] Defiantly trumpeting his responsibility for keeping Yemen as isolated and pure as it had been under his father, he early in his reign told a gathering of schoolteachers that he could have 'opened the gates to [Yemen's] enemies and told them, "Enter and extract the country's fortunes and minerals"' and have given them in return for this Yemen's 'religion, dignity, land and bravery'. 'Do you want this?' he asked them. 'No, no, no!'[20] they shouted back.

Nevertheless, with the aged Raghib Bey's assistance, he did open up the country a little, while ably maintaining it on the geo-strategic course it had embarked on under his father and has not deviated from since. Anyone prepared to grant Yemen material or financial aid while demanding nothing in return was a valued friend and ally. Given the Cold War superpowers' determination to infect other peoples with their ideological rivalry, there was no shortage of generous offers, the majority of them from Marxist countries. Some 2,000 Chinese arrived to build a 250-kilometre modern road from Sanaa through the mountains all the way down to the port of Hodeidah. An American *Time* reporter observed them labouring in the heat and dust alongside Yemenis, 'singing the great ballads of the Chinese proletariat, e.g., "We Will Not Allow United States Imperialists to Ride Roughshod over the People" '.[21] On the edge of Sanaa, a small cemetery, with some fifty Chinese graves and a pagoda-style monument, still marks the start of the road.

In the hope of ending Yemen's humiliating dependence on British Aden's port facilities, Russia weighed in with some 300 technicians to develop Hodeidah, at a cost of 15 million dollars. In 1957, generous shipments of Soviet weaponry arrived – thirty T34 tanks, fifty self-propelled guns, twenty aircraft, seventy armoured troop carriers, a hundred pieces of field artillery and a hundred anti-aircraft guns.[22] Sceptical of his people's ability to work such new-fangled weaponry, the Imam stashed some of their vital parts under his bed for safekeeping. A Yugoslav engineer arrived to oversee the construction of a Yemeni radio station, for Ahmad's personal use. Not to be upstaged by 'the Reds', the United States weighed in too, building another road from Taiz to Mocha* and a water supply system for Taiz. Although he turned down a $5 million American development programme, Imam Ahmad was not averse to having 'a squad of US Army and Air Force dentists' secure his dentures with 'US-made magnets'.[23] An American doctor who took up residence in Taiz to tend the Imam recalled Ahmad as a '300lb heroin addict' with a thirty-five-woman harem, as a sick old man who worried that if he failed to consummate his marriage to the thirteen-year-old

* The Chinese are back in Yemen today, involved in building the planned ring road around Sanaa, the president's new mosque, the new Foreign Ministry and the Parliament.

daughter of a sheikh, the latter would consider himself dishonoured, 'get mad, come down and raid the town and kill everybody'.[24]

But the Cold War warriors of East and West were wasting their time and money in Yemen in the 1950s. Much more appealing to all Yemenis than either the West's capitalism or the East's communism, and an influence Ahmad would prove powerless to counteract, was Egypt's Gamal Abdul Nasser's non-aligned Arab nationalism, thrillingly disseminated by the new-fangled and portable transistor radios that were finding their way from Aden's duty-free port to Yemen by the mid-1950s. One Yemeni recalled for me that while his educated *qadhi* family tuned in to the BBC for news, they looked to Cairo's *Voice of the Arabs* for entertainment, 'for excitement'.

Imam Ahmad played for time. Instead of combating the new 'ism' head on, as neighbouring Saudi Arabia was doing, he hastily espoused the fashionable creed, resolving to turn it to his own advantage. In 1958 Yemen became the third Arab state to join Egypt and Syria in Nasser's pipe-dream of a United Arab Republic (UAR). Less than four years later, when Syria pulled out, thoroughly disenchanted by Nasser's controlling style, Yemen followed suit. Ahmad felt empowered to broadcast a powerful verse salvo inquiring of Egypt's ruler why he 'pollute[d] the atmosphere with abuse' and 'shout[ed] over the microphone with every discordant voice',[25] reminding him that the nationalisation of property was a crime against Islamic law. Nasser's *Voice of the Arabs* retaliated with a rich diet of anti-imam propaganda. The ludicrously anomalous inclusion of Yemen's theocracy in the UAR in the first place had probably played a part in its failure to attract a larger membership.

UAR or no UAR however, the inspiring example of Nasser's Egypt was forcing Yemenis to confront the reasons for the pitiful state of their country. They were beginning to wonder if rather than Ahmad in particular, the institution of the imamate in general was to blame. Discontent spread, especially after Ahmad foolishly fell into the same trap as his father by nominating his son Badr as his heir. His over-taxation of the Tihama was another sore grievance, and his almost pathological cruelty yet another. Ahmad had hundreds of dissidents slung into horrible fortress jails in Hajja, Taiz and Sanaa where many were beheaded. Occasionally, one might be reprieved and cast into exile. One Yemeni woman described to me how her grandmother, 'a power in Ahmad's palace' on account of her beautiful renditions of religious songs, was forced to go down on bended knee to beg for the lives of two of her dissident sons: 'Please forgive them,' she pleaded with the Imam's wives, 'in recognition of the bread we have eaten together.' Her sons were permitted to flee to Aden rather than be executed.

Plots to remove Ahmad multiplied. In 1955 his own brother and foreign minister, Abdullah, led a coup aimed at forcing Ahmad to abdicate in his favour. With the backing of a small group of army officers Abdullah seized Taiz and imprisoned the ailing Ahmad, before telegraphing the news of regime change around the country. For two weeks no one reacted, not even Cairo's *Voice of the Arabs*. Then came the news that Crown Prince Badr was heading, like his father before him in 1948, up to the northern highlands to rally the tribes. Ahmad's captors trembled at the vengeance they knew to expect. Relaxing their guard, they allowed Ahmad to seize one of their Bren guns and overpower them all and, by the end of the day, he was back in charge.

Three years later the ailing Imam allowed himself to be persuaded to travel to Rome with his harem, a good deal of antiquated weaponry and plenty of gold bullion, in order to have his morphine addiction treated. Left in charge, Crown Prince Badr – a young man of reformist leaning who was thrilled by Nasser's Arab nationalism – clumsily upset his father's fragile equilibrium by raising the wages of the army and the stipends of the tribes and announcing a programme of reforms. An uncommonly wide assortment of merchants, intellectuals, army officers and even tribal sheikhs supported him, daring to hope that Ahmad was on his death-bed at last, dreaming of turning Yemen into a republic with Badr as a figurehead president perhaps. Most important among the tribal leaders was Hamid al-Ahmar, the son of the paramount sheikh of the Hashid tribes, Hussein al-Ahmar. Hamid al-Ahmar imagined a role for himself as prime minister in the forthcoming republic. But all those high hopes were dashed when Ahmad returned from Italy refreshed after four months away, furious at his son's manoeuvrings, suspicious of Egyptian meddling and thirsty for vengeance. 'There will be some whose heads will be cut off . . . and there will be others whose heads and legs will be cut off',[26] he promised. The two al-Ahmars were among those he beheaded, a mistake that in the longer term was to prove as serious as any Yahya had ever made.

Although there were reportedly seven attempts on Ahmad's life in 1961 alone, the last one cemented his reputation as *al-Djinn*. In the spring of that year he travelled to a hospital in the Tihaman port of Hodeidah, home to the only two X-ray machines in Yemen, for a check-up. There, while he lay helpless on a trolley, a hospital worker and his accomplices shot him three times at point blank range. Although astonishingly Ahmad survived by rolling onto the floor and pretending to be dead, the rest of his life until his peaceful demise in Taiz in September the following year was spent in a morphine-fuelled fug.

To Imam Badr he bequeathed a country less developed than any other on the Arabian Peninsula. By 1962 coffee exports were less than half what they had been before the Second World War and the country could no longer feed itself. The Mutawakkilite Kingdom of Yemen had no native doctors, no factories, a single paved road (thanks to China), and a handful of secular schools for boys but only one for girls, run by the wife of the American chargé d'affaires in Taiz.

## ONE DARK NIGHT IN OLD SANAA

The fuse of revolution was finally efficiently lit in Sanaa a week after Imam Ahmad's peaceful demise. On the night of 26 September 1962,

Imam Badr, and the centuries-old imamate with him, were overthrown in a military coup d'etat.

It was an intimate, treacherous affair. A forty-five-year-old Colonel Abdullah al-Sallal – described by two French reporters as looking 'absolutely like a comedy villain; smouldering coal-black eyes, bristling eyebrows, hard profile, sombre and distrustful'[27] – a man who had twice been jailed by Imam Ahmad, once for seven years, but had recently been rehabilitated as chief of Badr's personal bodyguard and trusted confidant – emerged as the president of the new Yemen Arab Republic (YAR). It was typical of Badr, a well-meaning but naive man with a pronounced fondness for foreign travel and whisky, that he failed to suspect that his friend's military training in Iraq* might have inclined him towards republicanism after that country experienced a military coup against its Hashemite monarchy in the summer of 1958.

Al-Sallal who, at the age of thirty, had never slept in a bed and was so confused by the first pair of trousers he owned that he wore them as a shirt, was one of around 400 Yemeni army officers who had been infected with Republican ideals while receiving training abroad, in Iraq or Egypt. In the words of a fellow member of the clandestine Free Officers movement, he had long dreamed of being 'the hope for our nation' and rescuing it from 'backward and dirty rule'.[28] Yemen's most famous living poet of the revolution, Abdul Aziz al-Maqaleh, a venerable old man today, was a member of an equally clandestine civilian organisation made up of intellectuals who all shared al-Sallal's dream and had managed to avoid being hurled into jail for dissidence. Al-Maqaleh fondly recalled how they had all drunk qat tea together – 'qat was cheap back then, and the tea had the same effect' – and how literature served as an excellent cover for their activities and 'a great bond', how 'even the army officers' used to write poetry and enjoy

* In about 1948 Imam Yahya had permitted a first small batch of officers to leave Yemen for military training in Iraq.

Shakespeare. Officers and intellectuals were also supported by some powerful sheikhs; Imam Ahmad's execution of the al-Ahmars, father and son, in 1955 was still crying out for vengeance. If the average Yemeni remained in the dark as to what the Arabic word for republic, *jumhouriya*, actually meant – there are tales of tribesmen assuming from the word's feminine gender that it must be a woman and descending in their hordes on Sanaa after the coup for a glimpse of a ravishing beauty – the likes of al-Maqaleh were soon whipping up excitement and enthusiasm for the new order over the airwaves. Almost half a century later, the elderly poet still basked in the memory of having been responsible for composing the declaration of revolution for broadcast on the morning after the coup.

Imam Badr's account[29] of events of the night of the coup suggests a surprising capacity for trust. After a late meeting of his Council of Ministers in his palace, Badr had been heading back to his living quarters with his father-in-law when one of al-Sallal's men had tried but failed to shoot him in the back. The rifle's trigger had temporarily jammed, but he had proceeded to shoot himself in the chin the instant another guard moved to arrest him. Not much alarmed by their lucky escape, the Imam and his father-in-law had repaired to the palace's top-floor *mandar** to relax, agreeing that the failed assassin must have been sick or just drunk. Less than an hour later the lights had gone out, which was not a remarkable occurrence either since power cuts were common in Sanaa, but, when Badr picked up the phone to find out when the power would be restored, the line had gone dead. 'By the light of another match, my father-in-law and I looked at each other for a long moment, then, without speaking, we both turned and walked across the room to the verandah, opened the French window and stepped onto the balcony.' The city was silent, until they had heard the 'rumbling noise'[30] of three or four tanks heading towards the

* The light top-floor room in traditional Sanaa homes, furnished with low cushions along the wall, low tables and carpets, where discussion and qat chewing take place.

palace. With the telephone exchange already under their control, the revolutionaries were seizing Sanaa's radio station and the airfield, and Colonel al-Sallal overseeing operations from the city's military academy.

Hurrying downstairs to the third floor of the palace because the lower floors were shielded by surrounding buildings and so out of range of tank fire, Badr and his father-in-law had called for Bren guns and rifles. Just in time. Within minutes the *mandar* they had occupied a moment before was crashing down into the garden and the narrow lane behind the palace. After sending some loyal guards out through the firing line in search of any remaining loyal officers, the Imam had organised others to fetch sandbags, douse them with petrol, set them alight and hurl them down onto the tanks, while he and his father-in-law manned the third floor balcony with their submachine gun.

The strategy worked. The terrified tank crews deserted their vehicles and the palace was not stormed. But the coup-plotters controlled the radio station so the news that the Imam had been killed in the assault on his palace was confidently broadcast through the land and, by early the following morning, eager revolutionaries were wreaking a terrible vengeance. Forty-six men, among them two of Badr's uncles and his entire council of ministers were hauled to the main square and killed. Some were shot, some tied to army trucks by their feet and necks, some hacked to pieces with knives. Others were executed and their severed heads nailed to the city walls.

In the space of a single night the backward and isolated theocracy that had been the Mutawakkilite Kingdom of Yemen for the past forty-four years had leap-frogged over the British-ruled southern portion of Yemen into the modern world.

## BRITAIN'S 'FORWARD POLICY'

The Age of Empires was ending but, far from loosening her grip on Aden, Britain had been tightening it since the end of the First World

War. Among the factors dictating London's new energy in the region was Imam Yahya's loudly and constantly reiterated claim to be the rightful ruler of a Greater Yemen that included Aden, and his dispensing of free rifles and Maria Theresa dollars to any protectorate tribesman willing to betray the British infidel. One former tribal ruler told me he had been sorely tempted in the 1940s and had accepted a rifle, 400 rounds of ammunition and 400 Maria Theresa dollars from Yahya before thinking better of it and wasting all the ammunition on shooting birds, and all the cash on a battery charger for his radio.

For decades, if not centuries in the case of the British, the rulers of both parts of Yemen had been enjoying precisely the same sort of 'carrots and sticks' relationship with their tribes. In each case, carrots involved stipends, tax exemption and 'gifts' of guns. Anyone who dared to question the morality of Britain exercising a protectorate over an area it was arming to the hilt was asked if he would prefer to see a military occupation of Aden's hinterland, and 'if so, how many divisions of troops?'[31] Britain was not about to fall into the trap the Turks had fallen into, so flooding the area with weapons – an arms race with the Imam, in effect – was the lesser of two evils.

One important aspect of Britain's more proactive inter-war style of securing the colony was the appointment of 'political officers' who were usually young single men posted up-country to live among the tribes in order to keep them out of the Imam's clutches. While doing their best to ensure that the roads were kept open and safe and the occasions for inter-tribal fighting reduced, they tried to encourage a respect for the law and the spread of education. A member of one tribe's ruling famly retains to this day his own less rosy memory of the role of a political officer: 'They [political officers] were the real rulers – they kept saying "I advise you" and "If I were you, I would do such and such." If we didn't *have* to take their advice then, of course, we didn't. But if we had to, then we had to.'

The real reason why the deployment of British political officers in the Aden protectorates constituted a big stick was that, as early as 1928, a refusal to do the British bidding was liable to bring down the destructive wrath of an RAF bombing raid on their villages and crops. Resort to this controversial, if economical, means of control was one which successive administrators of Aden were always at pains to justify: 'The Arabs are a proud race and rate personal bravery highly, as highly as they do prestige,' explained a 1950s governor of Aden, 'and frankly, that is far too high. They will not give in to an inferior force, but will shoot it out to the end. They are unlikely to give in to a slightly superior force, but they will give in to an overwhelming force and often be secretly glad to do so.'[32] Owing to the fact that the raids were provoking outrage back in Westminster over thirty years later, in 1961, my father, the BBC correspondent in South Arabia at the time, accompanied one to the Lower Yafai Sultanate, and reported back in some detail, explaining how many advance warnings were given to move humans and livestock out of the area and how carefully pinpointed the targets were and concluding his despatch with: 'This is a highly exacting task and the RAF rightly resents any suggestion that bombs are being scattered carelessly or lives endangered.'

On occasion tribal custom served far better than a bombing raid to bring an end to an inter-tribal war over water or land rights. A political officer advising the Fadhlis in the early 1960s recalled accompanying the Fadhli sultan to one tribal battlefield where some10,000 tribesmen had been fighting all day, with only a short break for a lunch brought to them by their womenfolk because both sides had determined that only an even score, deadlock, would resolve the matter. Alarmed by the mounting death toll, the officer called in British armoured cars to shoot over the combatants' heads and then Hawker Hunter planes to rocket the hillsides, but to no avail. At last, a religious leader of a neutral tribe arrived to lead his tribesmen in a formal procession down the middle of the battlefield, parting the combatants to either side. The gesture swiftly ended hostilities because tribal law dictated that no one would harm anyone of the neutral tribe for fear of setting off yet another cycle of vengeance. The injured were ferried by helicopter to hospitals in Aden, leaving each side with twelve deaths to mourn.

It may be that an important reason why the British and southern Yemenis co-existed as well and for as long as they did in south Arabia was not just that the British conceded so much ground to the tribes by playing by many of their rules and forbearing from collecting any taxes, but that the two races shared an exuberantly boyish sense of humour and a love of derring-do. Recalling his years spent in the West Aden Protectorate,* one political officer wryly observed that 'not many people have had the privilege of being paid to play cowboys and Indians when they were grown up'.[33] The tone had been set before the First World War by mettlesome adventurers like George Wyman-Bury, alias Abdullah Mansur. On one occasion Wyman-Bury had ascended with a posse of soldiers to the mountain stronghold of a 'miscreant sheikh', boldly demanding that he descend to Aden to pay his respects to the *Wali*, the British Resident there. 'It is not our custom to visit strangers until they call on us,' the sheikh replied, to which Wyman-Bury retorted, 'Does the lion seek the mountain fox? Will you call on the *Wali* as a chief of your house should, with safe conduct and respect, or will you visit him lashed to the back of a gun mule?' and pressed home his point with a wounding jibe, 'Is this your tribal hospitality?' Instantly, 'the tension relaxed at this allusion to a national virtue'.[34]

The tribes of the protectorates and the British amused and greatly interested each other. A political officer posted to the Western Aden Protectorate in the late 1950s recalled a conversation with the son of a Yafai sultan: 'I don't understand,' said the young man, 'I've seen your country now. I've seen so many strange things that I could never have dreamed of, cities so big that one could spend one's whole life without knowing all the people, full of cars and great houses. I have seen fields there, and the grass, and the many, many fine trees. I have seen that the cattle and the horses and sheep are fat and nearly double the size of

* In 1937 Aden was officially designated a Crown Colony and its hinterland protectorates divided into the East and West Aden Protectorates – EAP comprising Hadhramaut and Mahra.

ours. With all this, tell me, why do you come here to work? Here, where it is too hot. . .'[35]

Aden's efforts to wean the tribes away from their weapons and wars by educating the sons of sultans remained an uphill struggle. Thirty-six sons of sheikhs and sultans, 'political pupils' funded out of the British Resident's entertainment allowance, had begun to attend school in the colony in 1928, but the arrangement had soon proved impracticable. First, the education was not perceived to be a special training in the art of ruling, so that only six of the thirty-six had been sons of sultans. Second, there had been no suitable boarding facilities so that boys were mixing 'with undesirable persons in the town'; two, aged fourteen and eight, had had to be expelled for contracting venereal diseases. A boarding school, the 'Aden Protectorate College for the Sons of Chiefs', was opened in 1935 but Aden's colonial masters were disappointed by the number of chiefs who deigned to contribute 'even a few rupees from their stipend' towards its running costs. A signed portrait of King George VI hanging in the hallway and the claim that the Emperor was taking a 'personal interest in the college', did little to remedy the lack of enthusiasm; the college boasted ten staff but only seven pupils when it opened.[36]

Aden's twin civilising strategy of educating the sons of the sultans and backing up the efforts of political officers with punitive RAF bombing raids could be said to have worked best in the East Aden Protectorate. But that had a good deal to do with the fact that the Wadi Hadhramaut, a deep and fertile canyon carved into a high, barren plateau known as the *jol*, happened to have a dominant non-tribal elite of Sunni merchant *sayyid*s with whom the British found it easy to do business.

The wadi's fabled inaccessibility meant that it was almost *terra incognita* as far as the western world was concerned until the early twentieth century. In 1918 the British in Aden had been 'protecting' Hadhramaut for over thirty years, but only a handful of explorers and not a single British official had taken the trouble to venture beyond the coast. The traffic was all the other way. Since as early as the tenth century *sayyid* Hadhramis had been descending from their wadis to the port of Mukalla on the coast to travel east to south-east Asia as well as west across the Red Sea to East Africa to spread their distinctively Sufi brand of Sunni Islam. Generally welcomed on account of their *sayyid* claim to be descendants of the Prophet and their great learning, they soon settled among the higher echelons of their Muslim host societies and prospered.

Where *sayyid* Hadhramis led, non-*sayyid* Hadhramis followed, to trade and do business and make fortunes. In British times, Hadhrami boys as young as twelve and of all classes migrated to join whichever of their relatives had blazed the most lucrative trail, to learn a trade from the ground up, goaded into money-making by sayings like 'Be as industrious as an ant and you'll eat sugar' and 'If there is a benefit to you in the arse of a donkey, stick your hand in it up to the waist.'[37] By the end of the nineteenth century there were thriving communities of migrant merchant Hadhramis scattered over much of the southern hemisphere. Often, they remained in *al-mahjar* [place of emigration] for decades and intermarried with the natives, sometimes maintaining a wife and establishment back in Hadhramaut as well. Mixed-race Hadhramis are still a common sight because they always sent their foreign-born sons home to *al-Balad*, as they called it, at the age of seven to imbibe the moral purity of their beloved ancestral homeland.

Just as it is hard to imagine a people with a narrower and more parochial tradition than the northern highland tribes of Yemen, so it is hard to imagine a people with a broader outlook and more experience of the world than the Hadhramis. Their hard-headed thriftiness and an exclusivity that was often interpreted as arrogance gradually superseded their earlier reputation for holiness and learning, earning them a reputation not unlike that of the Jews in pre-Second World War Europe. Hadhramis are often referred to as the Jews of the Arab world, and a still popular joke against them goes, 'If a Hadhrami had a place in Heaven he would rent it out and go and live in Hell.'

Hadhramaut remained a well-kept secret in the outside world until, at some point in the 1910s, a fabulously wealthy Hadhrami, the founder of a property empire in British-ruled Singapore, imported the first motor-car to the Wadi Hadhramaut, undeterred by the fact that there was not a single road in the region. Once disembarked at Mukalla, the precious vehicle had to be carefully dismantled and loaded piecemeal on the backs of camels to be ferried the 200 miles up from the coast, up to and across the baking *jol* plateau and down the precipice of the wadi wall. Lovingly reassembled in the city of Tarim, it was set to work every Friday for almost the next thirty years, ferrying its owner along the region's single, tiny stretch of road he had constructed between his home and the mosque. Only in 1932 did Aden get around to endowing its future East Aden Protectorate with a few landing-strips, one of which proved useful the following year when the romantic dream of retracing Arabia's ancient frankincense route tempted the British explorer and travel writer Freya Stark to brave Hadhramaut's pulverising heat, insanitary conditions and lack of roads. The effort almost cost her life. After weathering the long donkey ride across the bleak *jol* and reaching the sweltering lushness of the Wadi Doan she was felled by an attack of measles and dysentery. At death's door, she had to summon the RAF to airlift her from Shibam back to Aden.

In the early 1930s Abubakr al-Kaff, a member of the same family that had imported the first car, invested over a million pounds of his own money in a first road up and out of the wadi, onto and across the *jol*, all the way back down to the coast. Without any surveys, its builders relied on ancient camel tracks to indicate how wide and steep the hair-pin bends up the wadi wall should be. With the magnate's money, the builders paid off the tribes through whose land the road passed. It was almost finished by the time Freya Stark visited. As soon as it was, the camel drivers who had been plodding the eight-day-long route for centuries realised that it spelt doom for their livelihoods. They wasted little time in obstructing it, forcing the British to broker a compromise between the old and the new; some goods were restricted to carriage by camel, others by lorry.

Difficulty of access was one excuse, but the British had had other good reasons not to investigate Hadhramaut too closely. The region's tribes were as restive and quarrelsome as those of the West Aden Protectorate but, thankfully, sufficiently distant not to threaten Aden. It was shortly after Freya Stark's ill-starred expedition and Mussolini's invasion of Abyssinia in 1935 that Aden turned her attention to Hadhramaut. Once it had been ascertained that its two rulers, the Qaiti and the Kathiri sultans, were incapable of ordering their lands and securing the trade routes, a British colonial official named Harold Ingrams was despatched to the region to introduce it to the benefits of a Pax Britannica.

Energetic, ambitious and deeply committed to the task in hand, Ingrams succeeded in persuading an impressive total of 1,400 different tribal leaders to sign up to an agreement that put a stop to the warfare which had even been impeding work in the Wadi Hadhramaut's date groves and fields. At least three factors seemed to have secured what is still remembered in Hadhramaut today as *al-sulh* Ingrams – 'The Ingrams Truce'. First, Ingrams was backed by the inexorable force of the RAF whose bombing raids he called in reluctantly but effectively, and with some approval from the natives. 'What do a few lives matter if we're all gong to have peace?' one wealthy migrant Hadhrami reassured him, 'And anyway it is nothing to do with you – it is from God.'[38] Secondly, and more importantly, because he and his at least equally impressive wife Doreen both held enlightened views about how to treat with Arabs, they went as native as they possibly could. Taking up residence in Hadhramaut, they learned Arabic, dressed in the local style and did not begrudge hours, days and months spent cajoling and reasoning and arguing with Hadhramis, she with the women, who proved largely receptive to the message of peace, he with the men who were more distrustful. Instead of behaving like a typical British colonial officer, Ingrams strove to conduct himself among the Hadhramis in the manner of the wisest of native sheikhs but the strain of the job must have told on him; while staying with the couple in Mukalla in 1937, Freya Stark noted how, with his mop of fair hair and pale blue eyes, Ingrams looked 'like an angel whose temper has been tried rather often'.[39]

In the end, Ingrams' mission to Hadhramaut succeeded where those of his fellow political officers in the Western Aden Protectorate failed for two reasons. The Hadhrami custom of migrating in search of work and wealth to places as far-flung as British-ruled Singapore or Malaya and Dutch-ruled Indonesia had given enough of the natives, essentially those of the educated *sayyid* class, a cosmopolitan and even western outlook. Quite apart from developing a taste for European cars and bicycles and gardens and telephones, for both Indonesian and British Raj architecture, they had thrived under colonial rule abroad and seen at first hand how peace and order might promote prosperity in their own land.

The wealthy *sayyid* al-Kaffs, who had made their fortune in Singapore* by the end of the nineteenth century, were sufficiently influential by the time Ingrams arrived in Hadhramaut for a German explorer to dub them 'the Medicis of the Hadhramaut'[40] and Freya Stark noted that, 'they run the Sultans, the schools, the trade, the army – in fact, all that there is to run'.[41] Without Sayyid Abubakr al-Kaff's enthusiastic support and active co-operation, without the large amounts of his money needed to sweeten the pill of compliance with the truce, Ingrams' efforts would certainly have been in vain. Although much impoverished by the Japanese capture of Singapore during the Second World War, Sayyid Abubakr al-Kaff proudly accepted a knighthood for his services to the British Empire from a girlish Queen Elizabeth II on a visit to Aden in 1954, but only once a special dispensation had been granted him. On the grounds that a Muslim was

* Like other important Hadhrami families in Singapore, the al-Kaffs had first arrived in Indonesia to trade in spices. The founder of Singapore in 1819, Sir Stafford Raffles, designated a large part of the new colony as an Arab quarter for Hadhramis.

forbidden to abase himself before anyone but God, he had refused to kneel before Her Majesty.

By the early 1960s, however, when my journalist father visited the Wadi Hadhramaut, to stay at Sayyid al-Kaff's comfortable palace with its grown English garden and swimming pool, al-Kaff was disillusioned with the British. Like the Dutch explorer of the Hadhramaut, Daniel van der Meulen, who discovered that 'the thorny subject of the Palestinian troubles' was familiar 'even in the remotest corner of Arabia',[42] my father was treated to a bitter tirade against Britain's sponsorship of Israel. Like many Hadhramis at the time, the old *sayyid* also resented Britain's failure to capitalise on the famous truce with more investment in the region. The sad fact was that the ravages of a mid-1940s famine had undone much of his good work. Hideous privation had helped to turn many against the colonial power that had proved incapable of alleviating their suffering and the names of both Ingrams and al-Kaff had become tarnished in the process.

But Hadhramaut, labouring under the yoke of *sayyid* supremacy as well as that of British rule, had long been showing signs of blazing a trail that would eventually, by many twists and turns, lead to them casting off both these burdens. Restricted by *sayyid*s and British rule and yet more exposed than Yemenis of any other region to different ways of thinking and being, it was logical that the first stirrings of a movement for political reform and independence in the region should have sprouted among émigré Hadhramis, even before the First World War. Irritated by the stranglehold that the more established *sayyid* Hadhramis were exerting over economic opportunities, non-*sayyid* Hadhrami émigrés in the Dutch East Indies were the first Yemenis to organise themselves into a political movement, Irshad. A bitter contest between *sayyids* and non-*sayyids* erupted into violence on Java in 1933 when a crowd of *sayyids* barged their way to the front of a mosque, asserting their inalienable God-given right to occupy pride of place; the resulting clash left two *sayyid*s and six members of Irshad dead, and the mosque scattered with knives and stones and sticks. By the time

Freya Stark was roaming Hadhramaut, the émigré schism was being powerfully felt back home. The *sayyids* she encountered were voicing their distrust of Irshad, and successfully misrepresenting the movement to the British in Aden as a dangerous Bolshevik threat to Aden and the British Empire.

In time, the British realised that they were being manipulated by Hadhramaut's *sayyids*, that treating Irshad members' calls for improved access to education and equal opportunities as criminal offences was unfair and counter-productive.

## FALSE FRIENDS

In the dimming light of her declining empire and shrinking resources, Britain would be forced into a good many more about-turns in South Arabia.

Reluctant she may have been to acquire the protectorates, but Aden itself was an entirely different matter. Strategically situated from the point of view of British oil interests in the Gulf, with its Khormaksar airfield soon handling more traffic than any other RAF base in the world and its harbour receiving more ships than any other except New York and Liverpool, Aden remained a valuable jewel in the British crown, one worth making concessions to keep.

Accordingly, the colony acquired a parliament, the Legislative Council, in 1947, although not until 1955 was permission granted for four of its eighteen members to be elected. Permission to establish trade unions had been granted in 1942, but unions which crucially emphasised their members' group identity first as industrial workers and then as Yemenis (whether guest-workers from the north of the country or local Adenis), rather than as members of a particular tribe, did not appear until the early 1950s. The first to organise were employees at Britain's gigantic joint forces base in Aden. Aden Airways workers, led by the softly spoken Abdullah Majid al-Asnag, soon followed suit. Al-Asnag's first meeting with Aden Airways' British management did not go well, as he recalled: 'We were all scared to death as we sat, numbed and silent, opposite the management. For three minutes, we were too terrified to speak but glanced from one to the other, waiting for someone to pluck up the courage and break the silence. Finally, the Labour Commissioner rose to his feet and said: "You called this meeting, Why don't you get up and speak?" '

He soon learned to use the weapon in his hand. By 1956 some 20,000 workers – the majority of them disenfranchised* northern Yemeni guest-workers plugging the labour gap created by Aden's rapid expansion – were organised into twenty-one different unions, demanding better working conditions but also loudly championing Egypt in the Suez War of that year, fired up by Nasser's pan-Arab gospel. Their frequent strikes, especially at the new BP oil refinery and the port, threatened the colony's prosperity to such an extent that by 1960 the British authorities were insisting that every dispute be referred to arbitration by an Industrial Court ahead of any strike action. The ruling had an unintended consequence; the unions' growing dynamism was channelled into a political activism that aimed at an end to colonial rule. Before very long, the independence party had split in two. Al-Asnag and his ATUC became the face of Arab nationalist and Nasserite anti-imperialism that wanted the British out of Aden and longed for union with the brand new Yemen Arab Republic. Hassan Ali Bayoomi, meanwhile, led a faction that wanted to continue doing business with the British while slowly preparing for independence. Mindful of Aden's economic interests, Bayoomi was prepared to countenance Britain's unpopular plan for an arranged marriage between Aden and the protectorates.

Little by little, from 1950 onwards, Britain had been trying to rid herself of her colonial stigma while securing her stake in the region with a plan to bind the protectorates and Aden into a new country

* The colony's Indians, Pakistanis and Somalis were given the vote on the grounds of their belonging to the Commonwealth. There were added qualifications of income, property and length of residence in the colony.

called South Arabia. In its first phase, the myriad mini-sultans and sheikhs of both protectorates were encouraged to join forces in a federation strong enough to face down the rising Arab nationalist tide, which was threatening their interests as much as it was Britain's. A useful majority of Western Aden Protectorate sultanates was duly toeing the line by 1961, though not the Hadhramaut's Qaiti and Kathiri sultanates which both dreamed of a sudden oil find that would make Hadhramaut's independence a viable proposition.

The next phase of the plan, to marry this federation to Aden, was trickier because, in the words of an Adeni novelist, it seemed to have come straight from 'the corporate brain of Whitehall'[43] rather than from any on-the-spot feasibility study. The former protectorates, the British argued, would be enriched and developed by closer links with Aden, and Aden, in turn, would feel more secure if it could rely on the physical protection of the tribes. But from a practical and emotional point of view, the plan was anathema to both parties. The tribes distrusted and scorned the cosmopolitan bazaar cum army camp that was modern Aden, while Adenis, for their part, both feared and despised the archaic and xenophobic tribesmen who encircled them. The more thoughtful among the British in Aden were sympathetic to Adenis' distaste for the project. One political officer wittily compared Aden to 'a neurotic maiden being cajoled and prodded into wedding a virile though retarded cousin'. The colony's governor, Charles Johnston, one of its keenest advocates, later acknowledged that the scheme was about as workable as 'bringing modern Glasgow into a union with the eighteenth-century Highlands of Scotland'.[44] Far removed from the scene, and perhaps ignorant of the gulf of civilisation dividing the protectorates from Aden, Prime Minister Harold Macmillan insisted in his diary that the real problem Britain faced in Aden was 'how to use the influence and power of the Sultans to help us keep the Colony and its essential defence facilities'.[45]

The old mistake of fatally over-estimating the power and authority of the sultans whom Britain was subsidising – to the tune of £800,000 a year by that stage – tripped Britain up. The assumption that the tribes led by their sultans represented a constituency that was at least as solidly pro-British as the merchants of Aden, for example, was badly mistaken. Most Aden officials, let alone Macmillan, had no conception of the extent to which Nasser's thrilling radio propaganda had penetrated the remote wadis and mountain fastnesses, or of the increasing antipathy felt by tribesmen towards many of what Cairo called their 'puppet' sultans. Instead, charmed by a world they judged still unadulterated by modern politics, one governed by bravery and honour and personal loyalty, many British officials greatly preferred the protectorates to the brashly materialistic mongrel mix that was Aden. Especially in the wake of north Yemen's revolution, when Conservative Britain was convinced that Nasser was a new Hitler, this predisposition towards the sultans and their tribes meant that their interests came to take precedence over those of Aden's merchants and the preservation of the British base. In the later estimation of a British diplomat, 'the tail had been allowed to wag the dog'.[46] The extent to which the still impoverished and under-developed protectorates were able to set the agenda seems astonishing now. While they were of no strategic interest whatsoever to anyone except perhaps north Yemen, Aden – so ideally situated between East and West – was the whole world's transport hub.

Still, Britain was confident it was getting things more or less right, convinced that the tribes would remain friendly and Aden a thriving port for decades to come. A few months before the start of the Suez Crisis, in May 1956, Selwyn Lloyd, Under Secretary of State for the Colonies, had flown into Aden to inform the colony that 'Her Majesty's [Conservative] Government wish to make it clear that the importance of Aden both strategically and economically within the Commonwealth is such that they cannot foresee any fundamental relaxation of their responsibilities for the colony'.[47] Almost a decade later, after Britain's defeat in the Suez Crisis, after the strikes of the ATUC, after the revolution in north Yemen, that official line remained unaltered. The ruinous effects of ATUC's strikes had been neutralised by a threat to break all strikes by inviting the sultans and their tribesmen into town to do the work that needed doing. A few months before the revolution in Sanaa, in early 1962, a Ministry of Defence White Paper had confidently designated Aden the 'permanent' headquarters of Britain's Middle East Command* and Defence Minister Harold Watkinson had flown in to preside over a week of festivities. A few months after Yemen's revolution a £3.5 million contract for the construction of new married quarters and army workshops was signed and a year later, a further contract – for £20 million worth of investment, spread over three years – was in place.[48]

There still seemed to be ample grounds for optimism. In January 1963, lured by some solid constitutional reforms designed to pave the way to full political independence, Aden's Legislative Council's reluctance to accede to a federation with the protectorates was overcome at last. Sultans and Adenis were hastily herded into the government of a brand new political entity called the Federation of South Arabia. A daringly complicated new flag was designed – a black stripe for the mountains, two yellow ones for the desert, a green one for the fertile lands and a blue one for the sea, all overlaid with a central white crescent moon and a star – and a South Arabian national anthem composed:

> Long live on this Arab land
> By the people's wishes planned
> Live in pride and dignity, upright men with conscience free,
> All adversity withstand;
>
> Long live, with wills aflame in pursuit of lofty aim,
> Valiant in freedom's name:

* Aden became home base therefore to all three services – army, navy and air force – operating to the east of the Suez Canal.

> Men who've won the right to fly the Federation's flag on high
> Now the Arab South proclaim.

A similar note of dogged optimism informs one of my father's reports about the prospects for the new Federation: 'If you want to see exactly how the proposed merger between Aden and the Federation of South Arabia is going to work, you have got to read through a big blue book with 297 pages.' Less than four years later, the last High Commissioner of Aden, Humphrey Trevelyan, the man who presided over Britain's hasty withdrawal from the colony, did not care how the merger would work. He never bothered to read the big blue book because 'it was obviously never going to come into force'. On arriving in Aden in May 1967, Trevelyan noted, 'the only question of importance was whether the country would hold together or be submerged in anarchy'.[49] By then his residence, Government House at Steamer Point, boasted 'two perimeter fences, lights, barbed wire and police, alarm bells behind the bed . . .'[50]

## TO THE BITTER END

What had gone so wrong in the intervening four years?

Less than a year after the joyous proclamation of the Federation of South Arabia, in October 1963, a tribal uprising in Radfan – a mountainous region north of Aden, not far from the border with the brand new Yemen Arab Republic – could have alerted the British to the fact that for all their careful manoeuvrings the tide in southern Arabia was turning to their permanent disadvantage.

The British did not understand that the restive Radfanis were not just over-excited by developments across the border or letting off steam against British sponsorship of an unpopular local ruler. No useful intelligence had apprised Aden of the fact that some 7,000 Radfanis – renowned for their sharp shooting – had been converted to the dream of independence and organised into a reasonably efficient guerrilla force by the very best activists of a new guerrilla movement called the National Liberation Front (NLF)* that had been organising with Egyptian encouragement north of the border, in the Yemen Arab Republic. Thoroughly committed to two key aims – violent rather than merely political struggle, and mobilising the tribes of the protectorates rather than merely the workers of Aden – the NLF was a broad church, open to anyone prepared to take up arms against the British. Its strategy in Radfan was to mobilise the tribes to harass and exhaust the British military with hit and run raids, to wage a war of attrition in which the enemy's superior technology and even manpower were no real advantage.

By the end of the year, the British had manifestly failed in their aim of 'convincing the tribesmen that the Government had the ability and will to enter Radfan as and when it felt inclined'.[51] Worse still, the violent struggle was being taken to Aden. In December, a hand grenade hurled at the then High Commissioner, Ken Trevaskis, who was a former political officer in the Western Aden Protectorate and the main brain behind the unpopular Federation plan, kicked off what became known as 'The Aden Insurgency', provoking the British authorities to impose the first of a series of states of emergencies. The new year brought an all-out three-month effort against the Radfanis. Operation Nutcracker employed three battalions and air-strikes but failed, largely because the British discovered they could not rely on the native Yemeni troops in the new Federal Army. By the spring it was clear that only a massive push by 2,000 fresh troops, flown straight out from Britain and backed up by helicopters, tanks and bombers, would do the trick. The cost to Britain in bad publicity was gigantic, but still there was no understanding that everything had changed with the advent of the NLF, no idea that the NLF even existed.

Radfan was subdued at immense cost, but for those with eyes to see the battle lines were already clearly drawn. On the one hand were the rebellious Radfan tribes and Aden's army of disenfranchised but unionised and

* News of the NLF was first broadcast from Sanaa four months earlier, in June 1963.

mainly north Yemeni workers and disgruntled intellectuals who had picked up nationalist, socialist and even Marxist notions while studying in Cairo. None of these groups cared twopence for the arduous forging of a new Federation of South Arabia that might one day be independent, because it was so obviously the creature of the colonial imperialist power they were intent on expelling. On the other side were the British, the majority of Aden's middle class which was dominated by Indian and Jewish merchants, and the sultans of the protectorates, all of whom were still hoping against hope that the Federation of South Arabia's transition to independence could be managed without detriment to their interests.

The ugly experience of Radfan and the start of the Aden Insurgency forced a change of British tone in 1964. At last, the question of whether there was any point in trying to hold onto Aden was being raised, both inside and outside Parliament. A Chatham House essay entitled *Imperial Outpost – Aden: its Place in British Strategic Policy*, delicately pointed out that 'there are undoubted military difficulties inherent in trying to cling on to a base which at present depends upon a large Arab labour force, in the face of strong and possibly violent opposition'.[52] It went on to draw the still widely unpalatable conclusion that 'British defence policy in Aden is at the mercy of Arab events which the United Kingdom has no power to control'.[53] The installation of Harold Wilson's first Labour government in October that year might have generated a greater willingness to swallow that hard truth, and abandon for good any vestige of imperial self-regard, especially since money was tight, but Wilson was unexpectedly firm. Although with Labour at the helm there was not so much bullish talk of defending Britain's oil interests in the region or of keeping the Soviet-backed Egyptians at bay, Wilson boldly announced: 'I want to make it quite clear that whatever we may do in the field of cost-effectiveness . . . we cannot afford to relinquish our world role which, for shorthand purposes, is sometimes called our "east of Suez" role.'[54]

The Aden Insurgency moved up a gear, albeit in an amateur fashion at first. One insurgent destroyed himself and an empty club room by wiring his explosive wrongly; two more blew themselves up; another hurled the pin of his grenade instead of the weapon itself, and blew off his feet. But in December 1964 the sixteen-year-old daughter of a British air commodore, Gillian Sidey, was killed by a hand grenade hurled into a teenage Christmas party. Another grenade which landed on the dinner table of an officers' mess terrace wounded six, and two forces' open-air cinemas were attacked. The NLF also got busy in Aden; one of their training manuals for insurgents, entitled *How to Disturb the British*, lists eight different actions to be undertaken, including 'rendering their air-conditioners useless', 'pouring sugar or earth in the petrol tanks of their cars', 'puncturing their tyres with nails', 'setting fire to their cars, NAAFIs, petrol, and arms stores, and anything British which is inflammable'.[55] It was often a game of cat and mouse: the rebels threw grenades at British Land Rovers; the British responded by throwing nets over their tops; the rebels attached fish hooks to the grenades; the British replaced the nets with metal covers; the rebels hurled their grenades into the centre of the vehicles' spare tyres; the British covered the tyres with dustbin lids. A strict injunction to British troops not to offend the locals by entering mosques, which often doubled up as useful arms caches, combined with school children's support for the insurgency and their use by the insurgents as cover, and a fresh rash of strikes, rendered the job of suppressing the unrest intensely frustrating. Both Aden and its hinterland were awash with weapons whose flow the British proved powerless to restrict: women helped with gun-running, the ranks of the native army and police forces were being steadily infiltrated by insurgents and their sympathisers.

By 1965, the battle lines were not looking quite so clearly drawn because al-Asnag of the ATUC, frustrated at his friends in the new Labour Government's refusal to change tack in his favour of independence for Aden, had regretfully abandoned his non-violent stance, broken off links with the British TUC and formed the Front for the Liberation of South Yemen (FLOSY) which was closely supported by

Egypt. This should have meant easier and closer relations with the similarly Egypt-supported NLF for whom violent struggle was a *sine qua non*, but it did not, in large part because, by then, the NLF had moved far to the left in its politics. By 1967 FLOSY and the NLF would be at each others' throats, battling for power among themselves, rendering the soon to be departing British no more than an irritating obstacle, virtually irrelevant.

But in September 1965 there was still no real question of a British withdrawal. Five British schoolchildren, about to fly back to London after their summer holidays, were badly injured by a grenade attack. When, in the same month, the generally liked and respected Speaker of Aden's Legislative Council, Sir Arthur Charles, was shot dead, it was clearly open season. Another state of emergency was declared and direct rule imposed. Panicking at last by the end of the year, wondering if Britain's declared aim to retain her military base at Aden might lie at the root of the insurgents' dislike of the Federation solution, if that might be the real reason why they did not trust the promise of independence, Wilson's government devoted nineteen meetings and two weekends at Chequers to the production of another Defence White Paper in February 1966. It declared that Britain would evacuate her base in Aden, cancel all her defence treaties with Aden and the protectorate sultans, and allow her former colony to achieve its independence no later than 1968.

The volte-face was shocking. The American consul in Aden easily spotted the bomb in the pudding, reporting to Washington that London's decision to cancel her security guarantees to her former colony amounted to 'throwing the Federation to the wolves',[56] and to losing South Arabia for the West in the Cold War. A British colonel clear-sightedly noted: 'The fact is, that having encouraged the rulers [sultans] to take an anti-Nasser line and having turned them into "imperial stooges" hated by the Arab world, we are now about to go back on our word and desert them.'[57] Robin Young, the senior political officer in the West Aden Protectorate at the time, noted in his diary: 'We are clearing out lock, stock and barrel, leaving our friends high and dry and apparently London does not care a hoot what happens thereafter. I was hit for six. I felt as if my tummy had suddenly been removed.'[58] One of the protectorate sultans confided his fear of 'being murdered in the street'.[59]

Far from calming the situation, the 1966 White Paper only inflamed it. While the loyal Federation government was distraught at being 'thrown to the wolves', the insurgents did not trust Britain's promise to depart; why would London be abandoning such an important defence base, such a booming port city as Aden, without a real fight, they reasoned. The British responded to the continued unrest with toughened security measures. Crater, the over-crowded heart of old Aden where rumours flew and insurgents plotted, buzzed with angry tales of shopkeepers shot for displaying a portrait of Nasser, of poor people arrested for breaking curfews when they had nowhere but the streets to sleep. Starved of reliable intelligence, the British were also resorting to torturing suspects in interrogation centres, until one appalled soldier sent a letter of complaint to *The Sunday Times*, an eye-witness account of a British soldier beating an Adeni 'about the head and prodding him in his midriff and genitals, a second soldier hitting him with a tin mug, before a third' used his fists, which rendered the man unconscious and in need of reviving with a fire hose for a further beating.[60] The Red Cross and Amnesty International complained; questions were asked in the House of Commons and Britain's standing in the world reached a new nadir.

By March 1967, when the date for the British withdrawal looked firmly set for November, anxious discussions were being held about the wisdom of letting some four hundred children of services families come out to Aden for their Easter holidays. It was eventually decided that a ban would dangerously lower morale. But in June, within a couple of weeks of Aden's last High Commissioner arriving in the embattled colony, Israel's lightning victory in the Six Day War triggered a wild speeding up of developments. Britain's leading role in the establishment of Israel after the First World War meant that she was blamed for this latest and most resounding humiliation of the Arab world. 'A bullet against Britain is a bullet against Israel' was the new slogan accompanying stepped up attacks on the British and on Aden's synagogues. The colony was daubed with the acronyms of the competing nationalist movements – FLOSY and NLF – who, while slugging it out between themselves, continued to attack the British.

While London was still tinkering ineffectually with its Aden policy, backtracking on removing all security guarantees, and postponing departure until January 1968 on the advice of Saudi Arabia's King Feisal, far more decisive events were in train. The Radfani tribesmen were up in arms again, imprisoning an unpopular sheikh in his own prison, successfully signalling that the time had come for the tribes of both the protectorates to throw off Britain's 'stooges', their sultans. A mutiny in the Federal army, caused by Britain's clumsy misjudging of tribal politics and promotion of an unpopular officer, revealed that the army of the fledgling Federation was unwilling to or incapable of either maintaining order or defending the federal government.

In Crater meanwhile, NLF-directed Arab police mutinied, ambushed a British military patrol, brutally slaughtered three Argyll & Sutherland Highlanders, and seized control of the area. This capture of Crater, the heart of the Colony, with the result was the first good piece of news the Arab world had had since its defeat by Israel that Arab celebrations lasted almost a fortnight until, enraged and shamed by the insurgents' barbarous treatment of his dead men, a Lt.-Col. Colin Mitchell marched his battalion of impressively piping Argyll & Sutherland Highlanders back into Crater and retook it without any British and only one Arab casualty. 'Mad Mitch', as he was admiringly dubbed by the British tabloids, proceeded to re-impose order in a manner that was, by his own clipped boast, 'extremely firm and extremely mean'. The American consul in Aden reported grimly back to Washington that in the space of less than a year 'British handling of terrorists has evolved from efforts to take them unharmed, to summary justice in the streets'.[61] The suspicion that Mad Mitch had contravened his orders in his manner of retaking Crater – especially as he later admitted that the task had required 'as much smoke and subterfuge and haze to be directed at the people behind me as the people in front'[62] – led to his speedy ejection from the army. The episode added up to little more than a heroic but hopelessly archaic echo of Britain's nineteenth-century colonial past. It was far too late to turn any tide.

The sultans, the backbone of the new Federal government, were desperately trying to come to terms with FLOSY, a lesser evil than NLF, they calculated, but without success. Some of them took British advice and flew off to Geneva in the hope that the United Nations would be able to help negotiate decent terms for them with the NLF, but the NLF seized the opportunity of their absence to overrun their sultanates, setting up its headquarters in the Fadhli tribe's capital of Zinjibar, only thirty miles from Aden. Although FLOSY insisted it had the upper hand, it was the NLF that was toppling the sultans, making headway in Aden, efficiently winning over Hadhramaut and the more remote sultanates of Mahra and even the island of Soqotra. On 7 November the Federal Army hammered the last nail in the Federal Government's coffin by coming out in support of the NLF.

Ten days before the last British troops left Aden on 20 November, London at last recognised the NLF for the sizeable organisation it had become, as the de facto new power in the land. The interim, until the 30 November departure date, was spent parleying with its representatives at the UN headquarters in Geneva, about how little aid Britain could get away with paying; the promised £60 million was meanly pared down to £12 million.[63] Oliver Miles, a Foreign Office aide to Aden's last high commissioner, has eloquently recalled how bewildered the British were by the pace and nature of events by late 1967, how irrelevant they had become:

> The end was a mystery. The Front for the Liberation of South Yemen, absurdly known as FLOSY, the darling of Cairo, of the United Nations and of a great part of the British Labour Party . . . was blown away in a few weeks by a mysterious organisation known to us as the NLF, the *Qawmiyin*. Who were they? How did they do it? How was it that when we eventually sat down with them for our hasty handover negotiations in Geneva, we recognised more than one face we had known in the Federal Army or the armed police, people of whose true purpose we had known nothing?[64]

The last thousand British troops departed by 1500 hours on 29 November, just eleven hours before the birth of the 'People's Republic of South Yemen' at midnight on 29–30 November. In the brief, bleak words of one British official in Aden at the time, 'it was not a moment to bring tears to any eyes, or lumps to any throats'[65] – unless you happened to be one of Aden's thousands of middle-class Indians, for example, or a sultan of one of the former protectorates, humiliated and furious at Britain's betrayal of her treaties.

# CHAPTER THREE
# TWO YEMENI REPUBLICS (1967–1990)

## EGYPT'S VIETNAM

In the space of only five years – between late September 1962 and late November 1967 – the two parts of Yemen rid themselves of both the imams and the British. In theory, the northern Zaydis' old dream of unity and independence, which had become that of most Yemenis under the influence of Nasser's Arab nationalism, was attainable at last. In practice, any chance of it had evaporated within days of the Sanaa coup.

Contrary to popular report, Imam Badr had not perished in the botched tank assault on his palace. After withstanding a siege in his crumbling palace for twelve hours, after running out of cigarettes and low on ammunition, after a fierce argument with his father-in-law about what to do with their families, Badr had decided that if he could only escape Sanaa, he could do what he had done for his father in 1955: make for Hajja in the north, break open the royal arsenal there, and rally the Zaydi tribes to his defence. Badr, in other words, was down but not out.

At noon on 27 September he and his father-in-law slipped out of the crumbling palace, into a back lane, and knocked on a friendly neighbour's door. The woman of the house swiftly surmised that they stood a better chance of getting out of town alive if Badr was relieved of his priceless *jambiyah* and dressed as a common soldier in her husband's uniform of *futa*, khaki shirt, turban and cheap *jambiyah*. Armed with two sub-machine guns, a rifle and a pistol, the pair were soon safely outside the city walls and headed north. Day and night they trudged, stopping off here and there to eat, snatch a few hours' sleep and some cigarettes, and gather support. By Saturday, 29 September, word was spreading that he was still alive and soon he could count on 3,000 supporters. But his luck changed. With recent injuries such as Imam Ahmad's execution of the al-Ahmar sheikhs still raw and smarting, many highlanders were relieved to see the back of the imamate and welcomed the revolution. Hajja could not serve as Badr's loyal heartland because it was already won for the new republic. With a loyal remnant of only 250 followers, the fugitive monarch kept heading north and at last crossed the Saudi border, where he called a press conference.

The sure proof that Badr was not only alive but willing and, more importantly, able to fight for his inheritance thanks to generous financial backing from the Saudi royals who easily detected their Egyptian arch-enemy's hand at work in Yemen's revolution, helped secure another switch in his fortunes. Many of the more pragmatic and mercenary highland tribes, the Bakil tribes and much of the Hashid federation, now rallied to his cause. Basing themselves in caves in the highest mountains of some of Yemen's remotest reaches, Imam Badr, his uncle Hassan who had been Yemen's ambassador to the United Nations in New York, and a handful of younger relatives embarked on an unwinnable but also unlosable guerrilla war for his restoration. Just as the Saudis, not to mention the British in Aden, had feared, Nasser was pouring troops into Yemen to bolster the new republic.

For the next five years, Saudi Arabia, Britain, France, Jordan, Iran and even Israel* tried to counteract the Egyptian push onto the Arabian peninsula by funnelling cash, know-how and arms to the Imam and his Royalists. Alarmed for the safety of Aden and convinced since the national humiliation of the Suez Crisis that Nasser was Hitler reincarnated in Middle Eastern form, Conservative-run Britain was at least as determined as Saudi Arabia that Yemen's new republic must fail. Prime Minister Harold Macmillan briefly lamented that it was 'repugnant to political equity and prudence alike that we [British] should so often appear to be supporting out of date and despotic regimes and to be opposing the growth of modern and more democratic forms of government',[1] but the prospect of Nasser establishing a puppet regime in north Yemen and from there heading south to threaten Aden was a great deal more repugnant than championing Imam Badr and his Saudi backers.

With the tacit approval of first Macmillan's and then Alec Douglas-Home's Conservative governments and the active encouragement of MPs known as 'the Aden Group',† mercenaries were despatched to the region, flush with Saudi money and arms, to bolster the Royalist war effort by means of 'keeni-meeni' – undercover operations like mine-laying, sabotage and gun-running. While Aden played its part by organising arms, intelligence gathering and cash transfers over the border, the plucky Imam's David-like resistance to the Egyptian Goliath caught the imagination of the British public, generating plenty of eye-witness reporting from war zone. One account described Imam Badr's HQ in a deep cave in a high mountain near the Saudi border, its entrance protected by an arrangement of 'elaborately cemented stones

---

* After an approach by a British SAS officer, Mossad agreed to mount two operations – 'Porcupine' and 'Gravy ' – to supply fourteen planeloads of weaponry to Yemen's Royalists between 1964 and 1966 (*Ha'aretz*, 20 October 2008).

† Neil (Billy) Maclean MP; Julian Amery, Minister for Aviation; Duncan Sandys, Secrretary of State for the Colonies and Commonwealth Realtions; David Stirling, founder of the SAS; Colonel David Smiley.

and boulders', its 'royal privy, artfully contrived between the rocks', its 'open-air kitchen, over which a cheerful Egyptian prisoner presided as chef'[2] and its infestation of mosquitoes and scorpions. Apparently, it was not as comfortably appointed as a previous residence that had taken the reporter seven hours to reach by mule. Another correspondent described being received by Prince Hassan in 'a roomy cave'[3] richly furnished with carpets and cushions and a hubbly-bubbly pipe, just as graciously as he would have been in the prince's suite at the New York Plaza Hotel. Imam Badr never succeeded in reclaiming his ancient inheritance and removed himself to Saudi Arabia in 1967. Hurt and angered by his hosts' formal recognition of the Yemen Arab Republic in 1970, he left for Britain, where he died, aged seventy in 1996, in the south London suburb of Bromley.

The legacy of Nasser's intervention in Yemen's revolution was to prove far more durable. The poet of the revolution, Abdul Aziz al-Maqaleh, insists to this day that the coup d'etat of September 1962 had needed no 'outside push' from Egypt, but the speed with which Egyptian military arrived in Sanaa, let alone Badr's credible claim that the conspirators had been in close touch with Egyptian diplomats in Sanaa,[4] have considerably muddied the picture. What is certain is that Nasser moved swiftly to exploit the opportunity Yemen's revolution offered him to restore a prestige that had been badly battered by the collapse of his United Arab Republic (UAR) a year earlier. The establishment of a republic in Yemen was just the new boost his pan-Arab project needed. It was also a deliciously hard punch in the eye for his arch-rival, Saudi Arabia, not to mention a likely means of extending his sway onto the Arabian Peninsula, up towards the Saudi Kingdom's oil treasure, and down towards the British imperialists in Aden.

Within three days of the coup, while Imam Badr's fate was still not certainly known, Anwar Sadat, then the Speaker of Egypt's National Assembly, was already on a plane bound for Sanaa. There he discovered the freshly promoted Brigadier al-Sallal desperately trying to secure the wavering support of the tribes by welding the four separate tribal armed forces bequeathed him into a useful Republican army. Only twenty-four hours later he was back in Cairo, confidently opining that Yemen's revolution badly needed Egyptian reinforcements. Convinced of the inexorable might of his country's forces, Sadat boasted to a Yemeni, 'we train every soldier to eat serpents. Who in Yemen can face them or stand in their way?' and was deaf to the Yemeni's wise warning that Yemen's tribes were 'solid as a rock, carved out of the mountain itself . . . [people] who, in some areas, regard serpents as delicious fruit'.[5] Within a fortnight of the coup a hundred Egyptian troops were on the ground in Yemen. A week or so later Nasser believed that a bodyguard for al-Sallal, a regiment of Special Forces and a few fighter bombers would suffice, but within a month he was committing another almost 5,000 troops to the fraternal struggle.

Nasser might have hesitated if he could have imagined the extent and likely duration of the chaos in Sanạa. A former Yemeni prime minister has recalled his bitter disappointment at the way things were already turning out: 'It was obvious that chaos, offhandedness, recklessness, ambitions, competition and the rush to jostle for positions and power were dominating the new political arena in Yemen.'[6] Within a month of the coup my father, thrilled and fascinated by his first visit to Sanaa, was filing a more colourful report:

> There's still no pattern to the piecemeal efforts of the reformers to change a way of life centuries old . . . Inside the Republican Palace where the antique gilded chairs of royalty are rapidly being scratched into junk-shop condition by submachine guns and rifle-barrels, there is a ceaseless coming and going of sheikhs and their followers indescribably clad in what looks like the wardrobe for a wide-screen production of the Arabian Nights. They contrast oddly with the returned expatriate Yemeni officials in their natty suiting and two-tone shoes bought in Cairo or Aden . . . Then there are the Egyptian officers with banks of gaudy medal ribbons

> and shovel peak hats and two Soviet diplomats in slate-grey lounge suits . . . The new Minister for Justice who, oddly enough, is a slim hawk-faced aristocrat in traditional white robe, turban and with an immense curved dagger at his belt sits down for a moment beside me for a cup of coffee and a chat. 'What sir,' I ask, 'are your plans for the reform of justice in Yemen?' 'There is nothing to reform,' is the reply, 'What we have to do here is to create.'[7]

Outside the palace plastered with posters of al-Sallal and Nasser and teeming with foreigners ineffectually trying to order the chaos to their advantage, were clamouring crowds of ordinary Yemenis desperately trying to get their needs attended to in the only way they knew, by scribbling petitions about taxes, crops, infirmities and land disputes for the ruler to solve, utterly oblivious to the wider geo-strategic power game suddenly being played out in their backwater of a country. After an interview with al-Sallal that was 'cut short by the steadily mounting tribal chorus in the yard below', my father emerged to find 'a bullock beheaded in a pool of gore and a couple of hundred tribesmen from a turbulent place called al-Gauf – looking none too pleased with life'.

Nasser soon conceded that the job of sustaining the newborn republic required a great deal more Egyptian assistance, not just military but civilian too; the project of modernising Yemen was indeed about 'creation' rather than 'reform'. Hundreds of Egyptian teachers, doctors and administrators were shipped in to set about fashioning a twentieth-century nation state from scratch, and still the fighting continued. At the end of 1962 some 10,000 more troops were shipped off to Yemen with their president's grandiose exhortation – 'We must, under all circumstances, defend our principles in the heart of the Arabian Peninsula against reactionism, imperialism and Zionism!'[8] – ringing in their ears. But within a year their number had doubled. Two years into the Yemen campaign, Nasser was thoroughly exasperated by the protracted chaos, but even more so by al-Sallal whom he introduced to Nikita Khrushchev on a Red Sea cruise aboard his yacht, before remarking, 'I just wanted you to see what I have to put up with.'[9]

Three years after the revolution, all Yemen's main ministries remained under tight Egyptian control. By the end of 1964 Egypt's troop commitment in Yemen had reached 50,000 and it had climbed as high as 55,000* by the end of 1965,[10] at the cost of approximately 5 million dollars a day.[11] By the time Israel launched its pre-emptive strike on Egypt's Sinai peninsula, triggering the Six Day War of June 1967, approximately half of Egypt's ground forces were still bogged down in Yemen,[12] very far from where they were needed. What had been conceived as 'a limited action comprising political, moral and material support'[13] had become what President Nasser himself ruefully described as 'my Vietnam'.[14]

He had only himself to blame. His troops were ludicrously ill-prepared for the task he had set them, in part, because they were stumbling into a country they knew nothing about beyond the fact that it bordered Egypt's rival for Middle Eastern hegemony, Saudi Arabia. They had expected to be fighting in desert, not mountains. A chronic lack of maps meant that, like the Turks before them, they were forced to rely on untrustworthy locals. Without suitable kit, Yemen's climate, which could veer between 130 degrees Fahrenheit on the coast to 18 degrees Fahrenheit in the mountains, was a horrible handicap.

Initially encouraged by the republican fervour of the Sunnis in Tihama, their generals had seriously underestimated the level of Royalist resistance they would encounter in the Zaydi highlands. Morale plunged. Many had expected to be fighting only a few die-hard Royalists and a lot of Saudis and Jordanians and were appalled to find that, in the absence of a Yemeni army worthy of the name, it was just them against tens of thousands of recklessly brave tribesmen who knew every inch of their treacherous terrain, and whose hit and run raids

* Some estimates put the figure as high as 70,000.

exposed the clumsy ineffectiveness of their own air attacks and tank assaults. The Egyptian forces were largely composed of conscripts from the Nile Delta area, men of sturdy peasant stock who knew little about fighting and nothing about the rigours of either cold or mountains, let alone fierce warrior tribes. Even today, one only has to mention Yemen to an Egyptian chef or businessman living in London, to elicit the same gruesome tale of a whole platoon of snoring Egyptians having their throats slit at dead of night by nimble, *jambiyah*-wielding Yemeni tribesmen. But Egypt's officer class must bear as much of the blame for the fact that Egypt's casualties in Yemen between 1962 and 1967 have been reckoned as high as 20,000. More interested in pocketing their enhanced salaries and trading in cheap electrical goods brought in from Aden than in fighting, they scandalously neglected the welfare of their men.

A revolutionary romantic like the poet al-Maqaleh is still grateful to the Egyptians, still convinced that without them the revolution would have been lost. 'The Egyptians' help, and that of Iraq and Syria, meant that the enemies of the revolution couldn't win – the Egyptians' mistakes here have all been forgotten,' he assured me. But there are many ordinary Yemenis with tales to tell of random Egyptian air-attacks that killed women and children. One highlander recalled for me being four years old in 1966, walking along a wadi near his home, with his mother, his grandmother, some other women from their highland village and some camels, when an Egyptian plane swooped down low over their heads. Instantly, his grandmother and mother threw him to the ground and shielded him with their bodies, causing one of their neighbours to berate them for cowardice. 'I remember looking up and seeing that plane, and a black hole at the back of it and something moving', he told me, 'and the noise of the bombs. And when the plane had gone and we all got up we saw the woman who had called us cowards was dead. All the coloured bracelets on her arm had been broken, so I took them to play with.'

Worse still, as early as 1963 the Egyptian air force was using chemical warfare against the Royalist tribes. Richard Beeston of the *Daily*

*Telegraph* scored a world scoop with the news that Nasser was the 'first person to employ chemical warfare since Mussolini used mustard gas on Ethiopian tribesmen during the thirties'.[15] Beeston travelled for three days from the Saudi border to a village in north Yemen named al-Kawma where he witnessed the 'pitiful coughing of the gassed villagers', saw the 'vivid yellow face' of one woman and a twelve-year-old boy's 'deep blister wounds' and learned that seven people had died. In January 1967 a greyish-green poison cloud drifting downwind over the village of al-Kitaf killed 200 villagers within fifty minutes of its descent. Four months later, over 300 more died in attacks on five different villages.[16] Only then did the Red Cross and subsequently the United Nations condemn Egypt for employing chemical warfare against civilians.

Dr Abdul Karim al-Iryani, a former foreign minister and prime minister of Yemen, was out of the country, studying in the United States in the 1960s, but is likewise in no doubt today that Nasser's intervention in Yemen's revolution was a costly disaster. 'For one thing, we never knew anything like secret police before the Egyptians came. The imams had just a few spies, but with the Egyptians terrible things went on – sodomising, torture, people having air pumped up their anuses.' And al-Iryani had a more general objection: 'Even if Nasser got fed up with him, al-Sallal was completely Egypt's man. Without showing any respect for our national identity or pride, the Egyptians came in here and practised "direct rule", just like Bremer* in Iraq. That was the biggest problem of all, because it lost us the very best of our revolutionary leaders.'

In 1965 two of the leading lights of the Yemen liberation movement whose activities dated back to the 1940s – the Sanaani lawyer and poet Mohamed al-Zubayri and Ahmad Numan – were neutralised (one by assassination, the other by retreat into exile) for daring to call for

* L. Paul Bremer headed the Coalition Provisional Authority in post-Saddam Iraq from 2003 until 2004.

Egypt's withdrawal. In the same year Nasser summoned al-Sallal to Cairo for a dressing down, permitting a General Hassan al-Amri to rule in his place. When General al-Amri, in turn, travelled to Cairo with around fifty more of the cream of Yemen's revolutionaries to beg that al-Sallal be prevented from returning and that the Egyptians loosen their stranglehold on the country, Nasser had the general and his entire retinue either placed under close house arrest or hurled into jail, while al-Sallal returned to Yemen.

One of those eminent dissidents, Yahya al-Mutawakkil, has recalled his freezing, squalid prison cell and the nights he spent scraping away with a belt buckle at the mortar in the wall between his cell and that of a friend:

> I managed to dislodge one of the bricks. I removed it every night after the final guard check so I could tell Ali about the films I had seen and Ali could recite poetry to me in return. In the daytime I would seal the brick back in place with cooking oil. So many flies swarmed on the grease that they were like a coat of black paint over the brick, so the guards never noticed that the mortar had been removed.[17]

The cream of Yemen's revolutionaries were not freed to return to Yemen until 1967, by which time Egypt had been defeated in the Six Day War against Israel and Nasser was offering to resign, admitting that his adventure in Yemen had been a mistake and would soon be terminated.

The root of the Egyptians' problem was not that all those tribes were thoroughly, nobly wedded to the enemy Royalist cause and the dream of restoring their Imam Badr. It was not even that Republican and Royalist tribes had eventually formed a powerful coalition against the foreign invader. It was the fact that many of them were inconstant in their affiliation, indifferent to any ideology, pragmatic and flexible, eager to prolong the hostilities indefinitely, happy to receive guns and supplies from anywhere and to continue fighting for whichever side would pay them the most. A Soviet *Pravda* correpondent, reporting on an abortive peace conference near the Saudi border in 1965, has described an almost shocking absence of hostility between the various Royalist and Republican tribes gathered for the negotiations: 'They hugged each other like old friends, kissed each others' hands, and, once the initial greetings were over, spent a good while strolling around the enclosure hand in hand, as is the local custom.'[18]

The tribes had rarely, if ever, had it so good. The case of a Bakil sheikh whose fortunes were immensely enhanced by the end of the war graphically illustrates the point. Very shortly after the revolution Sheikh Naji al-Ghadir declared himself and his following of 120 tribesmen for the Royalists, and was rewarded with Saudi arms and money via the Sharif of Beihan in the West Aden Protectorate. A year later he was being bribed by the Egyptians with 2,000 rifles, plenty of ammunition and 800,000 Maria Theresa dollars to bring all his Khawlan tribesmen out on the side of the Republic instead. He gave some of the booty to the Royalists, but he was in Saudi Arabia six months later asking King Feisal for more guns and money for 12,000 men. In 1967 he was boasting to a French journalist: 'At the moment I receive subsidies from King Feisal, from Sharif Hussein of Beihan, and from our sovereign (May God grant him a long life!) the Imam al-Badr.'[19]

Sheikh Abdullah al-Ahmar of the Hashid played an almost equally flexible hand. Initially inclined towards the republic on account of Imam Ahmad's cruel killing of his father and brother, he even served as Minister of the Interior and Tribal Affairs in the republican government, but he turned against the Egyptians and al-Sallal in 1965 and went into exile, while his tribesmen chose whichever side offered them the best pecuniary inducement. Representing the durable, pragmatic might of the northern highlands, al-Ahmar was the biggest winner of all, emerging as Yemen's chief power-broker, the speaker of the Yemen Arab Republic's Consultative Council by 1971. Almost without a break, he retained his pre-eminent position as power broker and *éminence grise* in Yemeni affairs until his death at the age of seventy-four in late 2007.

Like every unwelcome invader before them, the Egyptians had been seen off at last by Yemen's highland tribes. Field Marshal al-Amer, who masterminded the Yemen campaign and later committed suicide or was poisoned after his country's defeat in the Six Day War, bitterly regretted the way the Yemen adventure had distracted his army from preparing to face its real enemy. In terms eerily similar to those used by the last Ottoman Turkish governor of Yemen, he wrote about those five wasted years in Yemen: 'We did not bother to study the local, Arab and international implications or the political and military questions involved. After years of experience we realised that it was a war between tribes and that we entered it without knowing the nature of their land, their traditions and their ideas.'[20]

With the Egyptians gone after 1967, and al-Sallal finally fled into exile in Iraq after attending the fiftieth anniversary of the Russian revolution celebrations in Moscow in November that year, the Royalists were emboldened to mount a last offensive, a siege on Sanaa which lasted seventy days, from November 1967 to February 1968. Officers from the southern highlands whom the Egyptians had trained and encouraged as a useful counterweight to the Royalist northern highlanders played an important role in defending the revolution and finally throwing off the siege, but were soon deemed too dangerously leftward-leaning in their views to reap the rewards of their efforts. In effect, their more egalitarian outlook represented a threat to the Zaydi northern highlanders' traditional supremacy. General al-Amri, then in charge of the armed forces and effectively Yemen's ruler, but presumably still smarting from his humiliating treatment by Nasser, was as determined as sheikhs like al-Ahmar to purge the new Yemen of any taint of socialism. So the fighting and killing continued among the Republicans themselves. By the start of 1969 the desired purge had been achieved and a group of what the historian Fred Halliday calls 'tribalist republicans' – General al-Amri, President Abdul Rahman al-Iryani and Sheikh Abdullah al-Ahmar of course – were in a strong enough position to extend a conciliatory hand to the Royalists. In the end, it was far easier to do business with home-made highlander Zaydi Royalists than with foreign-made Socialists with Sunni backgrounds, especially since Saudi Arabia had made clear that it would only agree to stop funding the Royalists if the Yemen Arab Republic declared itself 'Islamic'.

When it came down to it, the Yemen Arab Republic was likely to get more aid with fewer strings attached out of Saudi Arabia than out of impoverished, demoralised and leftward-leaning Egypt. But, just as importantly, the Zaydis had reasserted their ancient right to rule north Yemen. Royalists and Republicans mingled easily at last in a new unelected National Assembly. The country, it was easily agreed, needed no political parties because it had its tribes and, in the words of President al-Iryani, parties only brought unwelcome foreign interference because 'people import political ideas from outside the country'.[21] But al-Iryani knew just what kind of a new Yemen he was presiding over. His politician nephew, Abdul Karim al-Iryani, told me that his uncle was perfectly well aware of the extent to which he, like any imam before him, depended on the support of the northern highland tribes, because he once told their principal sheikhs, 'If ever you want me out, you won't have to do anything to me. Just tell me to go and I'll go. There'll be no need to kill me.'

## WHO CAN RULE?

For four years, from 1970 until 1974, Abdul Rahman al-Iryani struggled to steer Yemen on a fair and steady course that put all its factions to work rebuilding a country on its knees after almost a decade of war and three years of drought.

A member of the *qadhi* class who had spent fifteen years in the imams' jails and narrowly escaped beheading by Imam Ahmad for his part in the 1955 coup plot, al-Iryani embodied the spirit of reconciliation.

He took steps to heal the old Zaydi/Sunni regional split. Sunnis from the southern highlands and Tihama were welcomed into his five-man Republican Council and well represented in his government of foreign-educated technocrats and intellectuals, some of whom were even moderately inclined towards socialism. But so were the appointees of the leading northern Zaydi tribes, whose stipends and access to lucrative posts in the rapidly expanding civil service cost Yemen very dearly, as did the army which was demanding heavy expenditures in weapons purchases. Yet, for all al-Iryani's strenuous efforts at establishing a new politics, for all his good relations with the tribes (he was close to Sheikh Abdullah al-Ahmar, having tutored him in one of the imam's prisons), for all his promotion of a new breed of urban technocrat and his laudable achievement of providing the Yemen Arab Republic with its first constitution and a vital Central Planning Organisation to power his reforms, there was no reconciling the clamouring demands of the disparate factions. The most serious obstacle was the tribes: accustomed as they were to stipends and exploiting the more productive Sunni areas of the country for their income, they did not take kindly to the threat posed by a new, modern order to their age-old hegemony.

Prime ministers came and went. One lasted less than four months in 1971, complaining that when the YAR was £75 million in debt and annual expenditure running at more than double its revenues, the tribal leaders were grabbing far too large a slice of the budget pie.[22] General al-Amri, the mighty defender of the country from the socialist contagion in 1968, lasted hardly a week in 1971, having lost his temper and shot a photographer who insulted him. Muhsin Alaini notched up four separate terms of office under al-Iryani, two of which lasted only a month. A boldly determined reformer, Alaini once tried to cancel all stipends to the tribes and was so embarrassed to be begging for international food aid while Yemenis spent what money they had on qat that he banned all government workers and military from on. In his autobiography, *50 Years in Shifting Sands*, Alaini details the miserable impotence of the Yemeni premiership: 'When the Prime Minister or one of his ministers "dares" take a decision that even slightly challenges the authority of those in power (be it tribal, religious, military or economic [note the order of interests]) his own position is threatened. Mediators may even have to intervene for him to be forgiven and pardoned.'[23] The time-honoured customs of respecting physical might and seeking direct access to the highest authority – preferably by winning an invitation to the president's afternoon qat chew – sabotaged the creation of an efficient government machine. The various powerful interest groups effectively rendered all governments as superfluous to the running of the country as they had been in the imams' day.

By mid-1973 the Saudis had come to al-Iryani's rescue with an agreement to cover the deficit in the YAR's annual budget, and made a first payment of $25 million, but there was a price to be paid for their help. The extent of Saudi leverage, not just financial but also political, would sink al-Iryani. Alarmed and infuriated by the establishment of a Marxist state in the formerly British-ruled south after 1967, Saudi Arabia helped to reopen old civil war wounds by encouraging an army of ex-Royalists from the north and ex-sultans from the former protectorates to invade the south. In 1972, with al-Iryani and the technocrats in his government looking on helplessly, a two-week war between the two Yemeni republics erupted, at the end of which the leaders of both parts of Yemen suddenly concluded a peace based on a reiteration of their commitment to the ideal of unity. Wise President al-Iryani had good-humouredly defused his Marxist counterpart's dogmatic stipulation that unity was impossible until the north had got rid of its bureaucracy and bourgeoisie, with 'I agree. But first you have to give me a bureaucracy and also give me a bourgeoisie. Once I have them, I can then discuss getting rid of them again.'[24]

Displeased with this truce, alarmed by the prospect (however dim) of a union of all Yemenis in a single state to rival their own, the Saudis increased their financial and political pressure on al-Iryani by boosting the influence and confidence of the tribes and the army with generous gifts. Al-Iryani first left for Syria in the summer of 1973 but chose a permanent exile there the following summer, after the sputtering war with the Marxist south, just as soon as he learned of a plot to oust him. He had told the tribes they would not need to kill him in order to be rid of him, and he was as good as his word. The only civilian president Yemen has ever had died peacefully in Damascus in 1998, at the age of eighty-nine.

Lieutenant Colonel Ibrahim al-Hamdi, a protege of General al-Amri, succeeded him. Al-Hamdi's military status meant that he enjoyed crucial access to the country's 'means of coercion' and he was of Zaydi highland stock, but educated and well travelled thanks to his family's *qadhi* class origins. 'Ibrahim', as he was popularly called, possessed the kind of charisma Nasser had once had; his oratory was grand and he was dark and stocky, and dressed down in the same short-sleeved military style that Nasser had affected. Frequently spotted driving his own battered VW Beetle around Sanaa, he rejoiced in the common touch. Generally perceived as a sophisticated man of the modern world who could dream up a three-year economic plan and a Supreme Corrective Committee to tackle corruption, and embark on a thoroughgoing legal reform and even try to improve tax revenues which only accounted for 10 per cent of the budget when he took power, he was also gratifyingly emotional about the dream of Yemeni unity. But he was careful not to cross the Saudis, at least at first. Sharing their mistrust and fear of the south's Marxist regime, he invited the Saudis to fund the spread of their Sunni Wahhabi schools as an ideological counter-influence, and appointed Abdul Majid al-Zindani – today branded a 'Specially Designated Global Terrorist' by the United Nations and the US Treasury Department – as the YAR's spiritual 'Guide', or chief religious authority.

Al-Hamdi was also sincerely interested in improving the condition of the countryside, having taken a lead in the emerging Co-operative Development Movement, *al-taawun*, the YAR's most efficient engine of modernisation. Hundreds of new local development agencies were sensibly building on the mutual self-help traditions that had long been a feature of tribal culture. In the words of the British anthropologist Sheila Carapico, who cites them as crucial evidence in her defence of tribalism against the charge of inactive backwardness, the Local Development Associations (LDAs) became known among foreign aid organisations as 'inclusive, non-government, non-profit, community-level services providers'.[25] Attracting funds from residents, migrant workers and foreign donors as well as the government, they promoted and supervised the building of roads, schools, clinics and irrigation projects. But perhaps most importantly of all, al-Hamdi was lucky. His period of rule – 1974 to 1977 – coincided with three years of excellent rains and a swift rise in living standards thanks to the hundreds of millions of dollars worth of remittances earned by Yemeni migrant workers in Saudi Arabia.

By the mid-1970s a spell of lucrative work in the Kingdom was almost a rite of passage for a huge number of Yemeni males. Unseen by their family and tribe, proud Yemeni tribesmen, for whom manual work was traditionally demeaning, could slave on building sites or in the oil industry or as a domestic servant for a couple of years and with the proceeds buy a gun, a cassette recorder, perhaps a diesel-powered water pump for irrigation as well as a car, loaded with gifts for all the family, and still be able to build a house. Those were halcyon days. Provincial towns gained electricity at last, the souks filled with imported foods, homes with basic household appliances and newly paved roads with pick-up trucks. Hitherto an expensive delicacy whose enjoyment was largely confined to the urban elites, qat became ubiquitous, swiftly supplanting food crops. In 1975 a north Yemeni finance minister comfortably mused,

> Few nations are as dependent as we are on abroad for their development, but what enables us to survive, while waiting for our agriculture to revive and perhaps for some happy surprises beneath our earth [Yemeni oil did not come on stream until 1986], are our emigrants. From Chicago to Kuwait, from Marseilles to Jeddah, they are 1,235,000 and each one sends us, on average, about one dollar a day.[26]

There was also plenty of aid from a West that had satisfied itself that the YAR was firmly in their Cold War camp, even if its army was entirely kitted out with Soviet-made weaponry thanks to Egyptian influence since 1962. Al-Hamdi, wrote the former American diplomat and historian of Yemen Robert W. Stookey fulsomely, was giving 'Yemen by far the stablest [*sic*] and most effective government the country has had since the 1962 revolution. Its single-minded devotion to economic and social development has produced impressive results and growth seems likely to continue.'[27]

Al-Hamdi is still remembered by Yemenis as a prince among presidents, as a real friend to the poor. In a Sanaa back street one afternoon in 2008, I came upon a battered old army jeep. Painted a startling gold, its bonnet adorned with a dented tin tea-pot sprouting flowers and its roof crowned with a megaphone, its back and sides were plastered with a collage of posters and yellowing newspaper cuttings covered in plastic to preserve them. Noting my puzzled interest, a passer-by pointed out the mobile number painted on the front of the vehicle and kindly offered to phone the owner of the vehicle whom he happened to know lived in the opposite apartment block. A rotund middle-aged man, his cheek bulging with qat and his eyes fiery, soon descended to street level to tell me that driving his mobile history class around the city for the past thirty-four years, since the year of al-Hamdi's accession to power, was his favourite hobby. Leading me on a tour of the vehicle, he pointed out a fading photograph of the boggle-eyed Imam Ahmad and another of a beheading in 1955, and various martyr revolutionaries, and a poster of the late Yasser Arafat, and another of the recently deceased paramount sheikh of the Hashid tribes, Sheikh Abdullah al-Ahmar, until we reached a torn newspaper image of al-Hamdi – 'Ah!' he paused theatrically, turning to address the cluster of children who had gathered to enjoy his history lesson, 'we all loved al-Hamdi best – he was so simple and honest.'

But those who knew al-Hamdi rather better than the doting masses, had their doubts. Out of the public eye, he was hot-tempered, too fond of alcohol and had a boorish habit of stifling the flow of conversation at afternoon qat chews by playing music cassettes. Far more worryingly, he was as chronically suspicious as any imam had ever been of anyone he considered a rival, so it was not long before he alienated some important constituencies. Determined to curb the power and greed of the tribes and re-channel the stream of Saudi money that was flowing directly to Sheikh Abdullah al-Ahmar, for example, into development projects and arms purchases, he was soon surrounded by disgruntled enemies among the leading highland sheikhs, the Hashid and Bakil. While Robert Stookey was happily applauding al-Hamdi's mission to 'gradually take power from the traditional leaders [in order to] place it in the hands of the new elites possessing technical skills needed for modernisation and enhancement of the people's material and cultural well-being', those northern sheikhs believed al-Hamdi was stripping them of their influence and concentrating all power in his own hands, not just in order to promote technocrats but to elevate lesser sheikhs in their place, a mark of unforgivable disrespect – utterly *ayb*, shamefully dishonouring.

The YAR's most powerful sheikh, Abdullah al-Ahmar, was out of a job as the Speaker of the Consultative Assembly when al-Hamdi abruptly dissolved that body. Turning his back on the president he retreated from Sanaa to his tribal stronghold of Khamir and, in the spring of 1977, there were serious fears that his Hashid tribes would march on Sanaa to subject the capital to another great siege and sacking. Increasingly isolated, with only his closeness to the Saudis and his popularity with the masses and the army rank and file to boast of, al-Hamdi finally managed to alienate the Saudis too by making peaceful overtures towards south Yemen. This, and the fact that his old comrade-in-arms and Chief of Staff, the ambitious Ahmad al-Ghashmi, was egging him on in his ill-judged confrontations with the most powerful sheikhs, sealed his fate. But a peaceful retreat into exile like his predecessor was not an option. His popularity among the military rank and file meant that his removal from power was guaranteed to involve violence.

On the day before he was due to fly down to Aden to meet his south Yemeni counterpart to advance the cause of unity, al-Hamdi and his brother Abdullah were murdered at his home in Sanaa. Two dead French women – some reports said they were Japanese – were also found at the scene but later revealed to have been planted there in a squalid little touch designed to confirm rumours about al-Hamdi's louche lifestyle. Al-Ghashmi, possibly in cahoots with Saudis determined to scupper al-Hamdi's rapprochement with the south, was reckoned to be the most likely perpetrator of the crime.

Scion of a sheikh's family hailing from Hamdan, near the Saudi border well to the north of Sanaa, al-Ghashmi was an uneducated soldier-tribesman who had none of his predecessor's charisma or way with words. Operating gloomily under a cloud of suspicion that he had killed the people's beloved 'Ibrahim', he spent much of his eight-and-a-half months in office rooting out any vestiges of al-Hamdi support and socialist dissent by means of brutal purges and executions. He also embarked on a rationalisation and consolidation of the army, which at the time of his accession barely merited the name, being a loose grouping of units generally led by powerful and independent-minded sheikhs whose loyalty to the new state could not be relied upon.

Otherwise, his accession to power caused few ripples and even brought some benefits. While he soon demonstrated little appetite or time for the great state-building and modernising project al-Hamdi had embarked upon, he understood that any dramatic change of al-Hamdi's reforming course would be bound to halt the torrent of western aid that the country was beginning to rely on as much as Saudi aid. Like the twentieth-century imams and al-Hamdi before him, he solicited and accepted any aid, from any quarter, as long as it came without strings attached. From the Soviet Union and its Eastern bloc allies came military advisers and training and weapons, from the West and international agencies came development aid and technical know-how.

With solid Saudi backing – he had immediately received $570 million in direct aid from the Saudis – al-Ghashmi had plenty of money to dispense. Shortly after a governor of Hajja turned down a job in his government and asked the president instead for the wherewithal to improve Hajja's roads and bridges, he was startled to receive a suitcase 'filled with several million dollars worth of Saudi riyal notes'[28] from al-Ghashmi. Even a twelve-year-old school girl who had played a starring role in a ceremony held to welcome the president of Algeria on an official visit to the YAR, found herself summoned to al-Ghashmi's home the following day to receive a Rolex watch and the equivalent of $1,200 for her pains. This kind of disarming open-handedness, plentiful largesse, dispensed in the traditional manner of a good sheikh, served to mollify many of his domestic opponents, but it could not shield him from becoming a pawn in the lethal domestic power game going on in the Marxist south.

Despite Saudi opposition to the idea of uniting the two Yemens, the old ideal remained powerful and important enough to Yemenis to ensure that the leaders of both parts of Yemen continued to make time for six-monthly unity talks. So it was that towards the end of June 1978, al-Ghashmi prepared to receive an envoy from his Marxist counterpart, Salim Rubaya Ali, in Aden. The most colourful account of what ensued is to be found in Khadija al-Salami's *Tears of Sheba: Tales of Survival and Intrigue in Arabia* (2003). Her version of al-Ghashmi's assassination relies on the eyewitness report of a newspaper editor, a close friend of al-Ghashmi, who had been entrusted with the task of meeting the Adeni envoy at the airport and driving him to the president's office. The editor noticed immediately that the southerner was nervous, distracted and very unwilling to be parted from his briefcase:

> I bent down to take the briefcase from him – just to be nice – and he jerked it away from me. But I was polite and insisted. I guess he felt confident I wasn't going to open it and he finally handed it to me. It was a beautiful briefcase, brand new, and when he wasn't looking, I tossed it up in the air, studied it in the light, spun it around to get a good look at the quality of the leather . . . I looked

at the guy and smiled and told him 'I'd like to have a case like this one.' I had hoped he might promise to send me one when he got back to Aden. But he didn't say anything; just stood there wiping the sweat from his forehead. I left him in the reception room and went to inform the President of his arrival.

'He has a briefcase with him,' I told al-Ghashmi, 'Should I open it before he comes in?'

'That won't be necessary,' the President said, 'Just show him in.'[29]

Why would al-Ghashmi – as suspicious as al-Hamdi, to the extent that he would barely taste food outside his own home for fear it was poisoned – waive the most basic safety measures in this case? One explanation of the event has it that he was not expecting any vital communiqué about unity from Aden, only payment for a consignment of qat which he had been regularly purchasing for his opposite number in a gesture of Yemeni brotherliness. While easily available in the north, qat – judged an opium of the people – had been restricted to weekend usage in most of the Marxist south and banned altogether in Hadhramaut. Al-Ghashmi may have waived the usual search for the simple reason that he did not want his guards seeing a briefcase stuffed with cash[30] and, putting two and two together and making five, spreading rumours that he was in the pay of southern Marxists. Noting that the envoy was not the southerner they had come to know on previous occasions, two of the president's guards moved to search him and his beautiful briefcase, but the editor impatiently shooed them away. Ticking them off for insulting a visitor, he ushered the southerner straight into the president's office and was still on his way out of the building when he heard the bomb go off. The booby-trapped briefcase killed both the president and the envoy.

Al-Ghashmi's demise was neither tragic nor noble. He was collateral damage in a war being waged among the leadership of the south. It seems that either the envoy or the briefcase, or possibly both, had been switched, probably at Aden airport, by supporters of Abdul Fattah

Ismail – a fervently pro-Soviet Marxist – who was intent on first blackening the name of and then replacing the more Chinese Maoism-inclined party chief, Salim Rubaya Ali. The transfer of power was smooth. In spite of its brevity, al-Ghashmi's term of office could be seen as marking the consolidation of the tribal military republic; al-Iryani's *qadhi*-run republic had failed and so had al-Hamdi's *qadhi* and military-run republic. The experience of the YAR's past thirty years has proved the winning formula to be the al-Ghashmi one, the military-tribal republic. In other words, the barely disguised traditional supremacy of Zaydi highland tribes in military costume.

Within a week a tribesman army officer was installed as the YAR's president. He was a member of the small Sanhan tribe belonging to the Hashid federation which paramount Sheikh Abdullah al-Ahmar headed, the man widely believed to have played an active part in al-Hamdi's murder thanks to being a close friend and protégé of al-Ghashmi. A handsome, bull-necked thirty-five-year-old military commander of Taiz in the southern highlands, a man rumoured to be heavily involved in the lucrative business of smuggling alcohol over the border from the Marxist south, he was Lieutenant-Colonel Ali Abdullah Salih. Few believed Salih would last any longer than his predecessor. In the summer of 1978, a year in which the YAR rejoiced in no fewer than three presidents, a good black joke was doing the rounds of Sanaa's afternoon qat chews: on arriving in heaven and meeting up with al-Hamdi, al-Ghashmi shrugs off his predecessor's angry complaint that he has forgotten to bring any qat with him, saying, 'President Salih has promised to take care of the qat – and he should be joining us any time now.'[31]

More than thirty years later they are still waiting for that qat. Within two months of his accession to power in July 1978 Salih had proved his mettle by scotching an attempt to assassinate him by die-hard al-Hamdi loyalists, and trying and executing its leaders within a matter of days. By early spring of the following year he had introduced compulsory military service and was fighting a war against the Marxist south. Because both Yemens had massed troops along their border in the wake of al-Ghashmi's assassination, it had not taken long for border tensions to boil over again. The United States, hitherto only interested in the affairs of the Yemen Arab Republic in so far as they affected its relations with Saudi Arabia, was galvanised into action, terrified that this border skirmishing, when viewed alongside the recent toppling of the Shah in Iran, was a sure sign that, via its proxy, south Yemen, the USSR had grand designs on the entire Middle East. An American aircraft carrier steamed into the Gulf of Aden and gigantic cargo planes flew in and out of Sanaa loaded with tanks and anti-tank missiles, paid for by Saudi Arabia.

For a couple of weeks it looked as if the line dividing the two Yemeni republics might be shaping up into an important Cold War front, but it was not long before the rest of the Arab world, desperate to maintain a show of unity after what they perceived to be Egypt's treacherous defection to the West at Camp David, exerted themselves to lower the temperature. In the space of little more than a month the crisis had passed. Just as in 1972 – peace was restored with pious mutual declarations in favour of uniting all Yemenis in one country one day.

Although no one could have guessed it at the time, Salih was embarking on a period of rule as long as (perhaps longer than) Imam Yahya's.

## ARABIA'S ONLY MARXIST STATE

If independent north Yemen was firmly under the rule of Zaydi military tribesmen by 1978, the south, under Marxist rule for the past decade, had been doing its best to ensure the word 'tribe' was never heard again.

Although all Yemenis continued to recall their ancient unity as a people and dreamed of being, as they thought of it, reunited, the leaders of the two Yemens were very far from agreeing on what a unified Yemen might look like. No real progress was made. In the south, increasingly dogmatic Marxists, the backbone of the old National Liberation Front (NLF), made aggressive attempts to spread their creed north, while the north never relinquished the old Zaydi imams' claim to Aden. Each side even supported armed dissident movements in the other, each hunted down and persecuted those dissidents, and demonised the other. Southerners were infidel atheists, hell-bent on destroying Arab customs and Islam with their imported infidel creed, while northerners were simply primitive barbarians, a bunch of lawless and greedy tribes. The financial need for both states to choose sides in the superpowers' Cold War was another polarising factor. While the YAR was mainly subsidised by Saudi Arabia and western aid, southerners were tackling the ambitious project of building the People's Republic of South Yemen,* the only Marxist state on the Arabian Peninsula, with mostly Soviet-bloc backing.

In 1968, the year after the British departed, the Soviet Union discovered to its delight that, without having to lift so much as a finger let alone mount a military expedition, it had made the first (and only, it turned out) Arab convert to its ideology, expanded its sphere of influence onto the Arabian Peninsula, and gained a useful port from which to conduct its Indian Ocean naval manoeuvres. 'We wanted to prove that a small under-developed Arab country, a former British colony, would advance with seven-league strides towards the bright future provided it was armed with the slogans of scientific socialism,' recalled one former Soviet ambassador to south Yemen.[32] Another Russian diplomat who served in Aden described his country's involvement in the furthest corner of the Arabian Peninsula to me with more world-weariness: 'South Yemen was a great asset to us at the time, simply because it proved our ideology was right, but we soon understood that we had to pay for this result.'

That payment was never enough as far as the Yemenis were concerned. Fraternal feeling towards Moscow was generally in short

* The PRSY was renamed the People's Democratic Republic of Yemen (PDRY) in 1970.

supply and the Kremlin soon tired of its little Arab brother's pestering demands. In the eyes of the Soviet leadership, the PDRY was never a fully-fledged 'Marxist' country, like Cuba or Vietnam, only ever 'a state of Marxist orientation', on a par with Nicaragua, Angola and Mozambique. As Yevgeny Primakov, a Soviet-era diplomat who served as Russia's foreign minister after the fall of Communism, recalls in his memoir, *Russia and the Arabs* (2009), 'the example of Southern Yemen showed the perils of making the "leap" to socialism without taking account of the country's socio-economic and political situation'.[33]

The Marxist NLF had inherited a country that was one-and-a-half times as big as the YAR thanks to Hadhramaut and Mahra, but with a population totalling only two million to the YAR's approximately five million. They had also inherited economic chaos, caused by a sudden impoverishment for which they were not to blame. The closure of the Suez Canal in June 1967 reduced traffic to the port of Aden to a quarter of what it had been in its colonial heyday and the dismantling of the British base had left 25,000 people out of work. The level of direct British aid to its former colony plunged abruptly from accounting for almost 70 per cent of its revenue to accounting for none at all.[34] But, unlike the YAR under President al-Iryani after 1970, the south's NLF leadership made little attempt to heal the divisions in the population by gathering together the most constructive elements in society, whatever their political colouring. There were more pressing concerns. Thanks to the cultural and economic gulf dividing Aden from the protectorates, the threat of the territory completely disintegrating was very real. A strong totalitarian state and the binding force of a brand new ideology had to be the priority, especially after the Maoist branch of the Hadhramaut NLF's early attempt to secede from the rest of the country.

Since Egypt's defeat by Israel in the Six Day War had taken all the shine off the glamorous figurehead of Arab national-socialism, it was soon abundantly clear that anyone opposed to the project of turning the new state into a laboratory for a hard-line Marxist experiment that took no account whatsoever of existing conditions and ancient customs, was more or less superfluous. An elderly Adeni lawyer of Muslim Indian extraction named Sheikh Tariq Abdullah recalled for me what the end of British colonial and beginning of NLF rule had meant for him. 'It took us about a year to start regretting the departure of the British.' Here and there one could still find faint traces of their presence, he remembered. The waiters at Aden's Crescent Hotel still addressed each other in English as 'Boy'. A small army of Somali women whom British forces families had employed as nannies begged in the streets, among the scavenging stray pets the British had abandoned. 'We all understood that the NLF was more violent than FLOSY; most of us educated Adeni intellectuals had supported FLOSY for that reason alone, but when the NLF took power we assumed they'd need us.' Sheikh Tariq recalled, 'I was personally naïve enough, unfortunately, to very much believe that every single educated person would be fully exploited, because there was such a shortage of such people with standing in the community.'

The former trades-union leader and leading light of FLOSY, Abdullah al-Asnag, was a lot less starry-eyed than Sheikh Tariq. Invited by his old school-friend, Feisal ash-Shaabi, to join the new government in 1969, al-Asnag joked that since he valued his life he would only accept the post of his country's ambassador to Mauritania. Thousands were slung in jail, thousands of civil servants – the sturdy backbone of the former colony – fled north where their British-honed skills were appreciated in the YAR's new banks and government offices. Salih Farid, a member of an old ruling family in the former West Aden Protectorate, returned from his scholarship studies in Britain in 1968 only to be jailed for four years for being 'a stooge of the imperialists', a 'semi-feudal bourgeois'. On his release he also fled north where, armed with a law degree gained by a correspondence course he had completed in jail, he soon arranged to leave for Saudi Arabia.

An estimated quarter of south Yemen's population – principally its educated elite – fled, meaning that the country was in no fitter state than its northern counterpart to tackle the nuts and bolts job of establishing a functioning modern state. 'People here are not even used to reporting facts and evaluating data,' complained a finance minister who had been trained in India.[35] The entire first year of the first three-year plan had to be devoted to planning. 'We educated Adenis all felt that the barbarians had taken over,' Sheikh Tariq recalled. Southern Yemenis learned to fear their new East German-trained security service and grew accustomed to their new leaders' alien mode of speech which was stripped of any references to Allah and his will but peppered with neologisms like *brulittariyah* [proletariat]. NLF stalwarts were soon gamely parroting variations on statements like: 'Making the Marxist revolution means transforming the existing social relations and installing revolutionary social relations, in other words, destroying the old state apparatus and building an entirely new one in its place'[36] and 'The compromising petty-bourgeois leadership in the epoch of imperialism is even more dangerous for the national popular democratic revolution than the explicit counter-revolutionary policies of the semi-feudal, semi-bourgeois alliance.'[37]

But there were plenty of advances too. After three years of independence the southern half of Yemen had leapfrogged over its northern counterpart again, at least in terms of the civil order and social development. The PDRY boasted more than double the number of clinics it had in British times by 1972, the 199 primary schools and eight secondary schools in existence when the British departed had been augmented by a factor of more than four; there were 910 primary schools, ten secondary schools and almost four times as many teachers.[38] School children were required to wear uniforms like those worn by children in the Soviet Union. There are tales of schoolboys hurrying to school in their *futa*s with pairs of trousers bundled under their arms, quickly changing at the school gates.

A universal literacy campaign involved thousands of women government employees and schoolteachers in supplementing their regular work with lessons in reading for adult women. Women organised themselves in a General Union of Yemeni Women, joined the NLF militias and demonstrated against wearing the veil. But, although a Family Law of 1974 substantially improved their status in divorce settlements (allowing them to retain custody of their children), regulated the payment of dowries and outlawed polygamy, their position remained glaringly unequal. There was always a yawning gulf between the law and its practical implementation. One woman complained to a visiting westerner: 'Here, too frequently, the progressiveness of some men in the Front [NLF] stops at their doorsteps. They still consider women as property. We don't blame men personally for this. We recognise it as an illness that pervades the whole society.'[39] Only one in five of those privileged to attend primary school were girls.

One did not have to venture far outside Aden to see the changes being wrought among the 'poor people'. On a visit to Lahej, just to the north-west of Aden, in 1972 a visiting American academic found one of the former sultan's palaces transformed into an agricultural college and watched men of all ages finishing their seven-hour shifts in a fruit farm and gathering for lessons in reading, writing and arithmetic. 'They are impetuous and eager and frustrated at this recent encounter with knowledge and the dignity which this whole act, this almost ceremony, confers',[40] he observed approvingly, mentioning that the walls of the local NLF headquarters were plastered with magazine photos of Lenin and Mao Tse Tung. What he was witnessing was the implementation of a nation-wide programme aimed at securing tribesmen's support for the new regime.

Because spending on the army was gobbling up half the state budget by 1971, it was decided that regional NLF centres should take the risk of establishing militias of armed tribesmen and just hope that they would not turn their guns against their political masters. Under the supervision of Cuban and Chinese advisers, tribesmen were required to undergo a three-month training period that included a crash course in literacy skills, basic Marxism and modern farming methods. Ideally, it was hoped, they would return to their villages and spread, not just their learning and know-how, but their freshly acquired grasp of Marxist dogma.

In practice, Yemeni tribesmen were not nearly as biddable as either Cuban or Chinese peasants; their loyalty to the NLF and Marxism was usually conditional on adequate tribal representation in the higher echelons of the ruling Yemeni Socialist Party (YSP, the renamed NLF), the government and the army. A Russian anthropologist who spent much of the 1980s in the PDRY described to me the way in which the southern tribes easily accommodated themselves to the new regime without ever troubling themselves with the philosophical implications of Marxism: 'If a tribesman settles successfully in the capital he constitutes a vanguard for other members of his tribe to follow and position themselves gradually in the economic, military and political spheres. It has nothing to do with individual success or any political ideology – it's just reinforcement of the overall position of the tribe.'

Despite concerted attempts to demolish the old tribal order by branding it 'sectarianism', it survived. From the start the NLF had promoted Yemeni and Arab nationalism and denigrated tribalism, and the country was speedily re-divided into six governorates whose boundaries bore no relation to the old tribal ones, but none of these measures eradicated millennia of custom. A five-year General Truce Among the Tribes in 1968, followed by the outlawing of tribal justice in the form of murder in 1970, only succeeded in curbing tribalism's more violent manifestations. Tribal divisions and loyalties continued to dictate the country's true political geography, a truth that would be brutally exposed in a coup d'etat in 1986, but one about which the thousands of Soviet military and civilian 'advisers' who poured into the PDRY within weeks of the British departure were always acutely aware.

Professor Vitaly Naumkin, now Director General of Moscow's Centre for Arab and Islamic Studies, began teaching history at the Yemeni Marxist Party school in Aden in 1972, a position that afforded him easy access to the PDRY's leadership, some of whom attended his classes and revealed themselves to be a good deal more dogmatic than he was. Salim Rubaya Ali, a former Radfan rebel with strong Fadhli connections who emerged as the Maoism-inclined leader of the country in 1969, was responsible for the most doctrinaire excesses. 'He was tribal,' recalled Professor Naumkin, 'very cruel and very devoted to the violent change of society.' Naumkin vividly recalled a meeting with Rubaya Ali at which he urged him to learn by the Soviet Union's mistakes and not set about nationalising every aspect of the country's economy, illustrating his point by extolling the virtue and value of a hard-working owner of a small bakery near where he was living. Rubaya Ali's response was immediate and unhesitating: 'We'll nationalise him!'

Dr Veniamin Popov, who served as the Soviet chargé d'affaires in Aden in the 1970s, observed, 'They understood that power was the important thing. Looking back now, I don't think we did them any favours by telling them how only 10,000 of our Bolsheviks were able to convert millions to their cause by means of good organisation and discipline. They listened to those kind of stories *extremely* attentively.'

Professor Naumkin was particularly close to the staunchly pro-Soviet Abdul Fattah Ismail who, fearing too much Fadhli influence over the running of the PDRY, was possibly behind Rubaya Ali's assassination in 1978. Ismail, whom Naumkin first encountered as a student in Cairo and who later worked at Aden's BP oil refinery, was 'a real intellectual, a mild person and a very good poet, in touch with other poets all over the Arab world, and very keen to belong to something bigger and better than fragmented little Yemen,' Naumkin recalled. 'His great advantage was that he was not a tribesman, or even a southerner. His roots were in the north, in Taiz, which meant that he could act as some sort of "honest broker" on occasion'. It was Ismail who consolidated the NLF and other left-wing forces into a semblance of unity by the creation of the Yemen Socialist Party (YSP), but in the long run his idealistic internationalism was too abstract for Yemenis.

He was ousted from his position as Chairman of the Party by a coup in 1980.

Islam proved at least as difficult as tribalism to extirpate in the quest for the 'new Yemeni man'. The nationalisation of all *awqaf* – religious trust property – in 1970 stripped Muslim clerics of much of their influence but came nowhere near uprooting ancient belief and religious custom. After a short period of excessive Marxist zeal in which tombs of Hadhrami saints were smashed and eminent preachers and scholars from towns like Tarim hounded, humiliated and even murdered, the regime refrained from trying to ban religious practice. A high-ranking member of East Germany's Marxist Party suggested a cunningly foolproof means of co-opting Islam to the Marxist cause: 'Why don't you say "We are against exploitative capitalism" and say at the same time "Our master Mohammed was against exploitative capitalism"? No *faqih* [religious teacher] or *qadi* will be able to find any Quranic verse or hadith to prove that Mohammed was in favour of exploitative capitalism since he was, in fact, against exploitation.'[41] Islam remained part of the school curriculum and its holidays were observed, though routinely downgraded by the media. Ramadan, for example, was marked by media exposés detailing epidemic rates of absenteeism from the workplace, lower productivity and increased food consumption. Similarly, the great holiday of *Eid al-Adha* was stripped of any religious significance and defined as just 'a good opportunity to strengthen ties among comrades'.[42]

The economic aspect of the PDRY's grand Marxist experiment was hobbled from the start by the fact that the country had no natural resources to seize back from the exploiting capitalist British – no mines, certainly no industry, and no agricultural wealth. Although less than 1 per cent of the land was arable, the doctrinaire leadership forged ahead with creating first collectives and then larger state farms, which proved as inefficient as they had already done in other eastern bloc countries. A Soviet anthropologist who worked in Hadhramaut explained to me: 'Large-scale land nationalisation couldn't possibly work in the PDRY because irrigation systems and their maintenance could only be organised on a co-operative basis.' Within five years of the establishment of state farms – between 1975 and 1980 – official wheat yields had dropped by almost two thirds. Like the YAR, by the end of the 1970s the PDRY found itself relying for 40 per cent of its GDP on remittances earned by some 200,000 migrant workers in the Gulf and Saudi Arabia, no matter that official rhetoric declared those countries the PDRY's arch enemies.

Isolated, hemmed about by enemy capitalist imperialist regimes, the leaders of the poor and unhappy PDRY consoled themselves with the moral high ground of constituting a Marxist vanguard on the Arabian Peninsula, and with their ardent backing for other revolutionary organisations in the area, especially the Popular Front for the Liberation of Palestine (PFLP) which opened an office in the centre of Aden in 1973. Members of the Baader–Meinhof group have admitted to receiving training in terrorism at camps in the PDRY[43] and Carlos the Jackal held a PDRY passport for a long time. Occasionally, there was money to be made from such associations. When the PFLP hijacked a Lufthansa flight bound for Athens in February 1972, the PDRY claimed a 20 per cent cut of the $5 million ransom paid by the airline in 'landing fees'.

Perceiving it to be their urgent duty to spread the good Marxist word north, it was the PDRY that instigated the cross-border tensions that led to the mini-war of 1979 that so alarmed President Jimmy Carter's administration. One of the PDRY's leaders admitted as much to the Soviet ambassador in Aden at the time, 'Yes, it's us who've started the war. If we win, we'll create Great Yemen. If we lose, you'll intervene and save us.'[44]

## COLD WAR BENEFICIARIES

The Soviet Union showed less inclination than the United States to fan the flames of war on a new Cold War front because, for all their different ideologies, by the start of 1979 there was little to choose between the two Yemens in the areas that really counted: finance and defence.

First, the USSR was arming both countries; the YAR continued to buy Russian arms and to describe itself as non-aligned in the Cold War because it was the best way of claiming a little breathing space in Saudi Arabia's 'tight hug'.[45] By the end of the decade both countries owed around 45 per cent of their entire national debt to the USSR, for military equipment.[46] Second, both countries were recipients of large amounts of aid from Gulf countries as well as from the West, and were hugely reliant for the rest of their income on remittances from emigrant workers.

In the YAR, the 1980s witnessed a steady process of centralisation that was greatly assisted by the aggrandisement of the army and the co-operation of powerful sheikhs. Favourites in the system of state patronage, the Zaydi tribes and the military and security forces in which they predominated became ever more closely identified with each other, and with commerce too. Prominent sheikhs were spending more and more time in Sanaa attending to business fortunes founded on lucrative monopolies acquired through licences for foreign imports (for Japanese bulldozers, or steel or lumber, for example) that they had been granted as rewards for their loyalty to the republic.

The top echelons of the military – dominated by members of the president's family and tribe – were permitted to expand their activities into the market-place too, under the umbrella of the Military Economic Corporation (MECO). From humble beginnings as the supplier of boots, uniforms and field rations to the army, MECO diversified into 'such unmilitary items as shower curtains and bathroom fittings'.[47] A member of the president's Sanhan tribe became the head of MECO and built himself a more than usually luxurious residence in Sanaa. Once commercially viable quantities of oil had finally been discovered in the YAR's Marib region in 1984, it was not long before MECO acquired 20,000 hectares in the area. MECO changed its shameless name to YECO but continued to expand into the real estate market, especially after the unification of the country in 1990 when there was land to be acquired in the former south. The proliferation of such dubious arrangements is what has led the leading American historian of Yemen, Robert D. Burrowes, to brand contemporary Yemen 'a kleptocracy – i.e., government of, by and for the thieves'.[48]

The Zaydi highlanders' strengthening grip on the country was most clearly seen in the fate of the Local Development Agencies (LDA) whose origins lay in Tihama and southern highlands of the country and whose promotion had secured President al-Hamdi's popularity back in the mid-1970s. They worked reasonably efficiently to improve the YAR's infrastructure until 1984 when the knock-on effects of the plunging price of oil meant that both the government and migrant workers' contributions to projects plummeted. The following year they were merged with regional and local branches of the General People's Congress (GPC) which, created by means of a thousand-man council in 1982, was soon shaping up into a ruling party to rival the south's Yemeni Socialist Party (YSP). Consolidated into new 'local development co-operative councils', the old LDAs became directly responsible to the Ministry for Local Administration in Sanaa and were robbed of all their energy.

A job, however menial, in the expanding government bureaucracy or the military or the president's party, the GPC, became most people's best hope of a steady income, however small, and a vital means of securing people's loyalty to the regime. Often, these posts amounted to a stipend, requiring neither attendance nor work, let alone efficiency from the recipient. Other ways of favouring the northern highlanders were found so that by 1989 it was reckoned that the southern highlanders and Tihamans were paying as much as five times more tax than the highland provinces of Dhamar, Hajja, Saada and al-Mahweet.[49] Small wonder that those over-exploited regions, especially the highly populated southern highland towns of Taiz and Ibb remained the focus of a political dissidence that had first surfaced in the year after the Egyptians left, when northern highland Zaydi Republicans battled with southern highland Sunni Republicans in order to retain their traditional supremacy.

The speedy and unregulated expansion of Sanaa in the 1980s was another reflection of the growing centralisation of power in a highland area that lacked sufficient resources – jobs and homes, let alone water – to sustain its exploding population for long. In the 1980s Sanaa overtook Aden as Yemen's largest city and, by the second half of the decade, it had spread as far south as the leafy Hadda whose trees made way for the high-walled palace fortresses of the newly enriched, adorned with lawns and swimming pools, buildings of the kind one sees in the Gulf and Saudi Arabia but would not expect to see in a country as generally impoverished as Yemen. With the discovery of oil these residences were joined by the equally grand headquarters of foreign oil companies and a luxury hotel. Sanaa was no longer among the hardest of hardship postings for any of the foreigners stationed there.

Konstantin Eggert, a Russian military translator stationed in the city in the mid-1980s, recalled for me the extent to which President Salih was succeeding, just like the imams before him, in welcoming assistance from whatever quarter as long as it had material rather than political strings attached.

> Sanaa was the Vienna of the Middle East – there were us [Soviets], and the Americans and the Iraqis, all there watching each other and advising Yemen's military. We Russians had to wear Yemeni uniforms, but without any insignia because we didn't want the Americans knowing who was a colonel, for example, but Yemenis respected the Americans more than us; there was a problem when we gave them a consignment of SAM missiles equipped with heating for Siberia instead of air-conditioning, and I remember a Sanaani shopkeeper once saying to me, 'You know what the problem is with you Russians? – you have no authorised dealers

> here to repair your Zil cars and your refrigerators, and when are you going to get round to producing screw top lids for your jars? Is that beyond the capacity of a superpower?'

Yemenis, he recalled, were always asking him why the USSR didn't nuclear-bomb America's main ally in the region, the source of the Arab world's humiliation, Israel.

Although most of Eggert's time in Sanaa was tediously spent translating into Arabic letters requesting immediate payment for weaponry delivered, he counted himself lucky to be posted to Sanaa, rather than Aden. 'I was paid in Yemeni riyals so I could buy things like jeans and cosmetics that I couldn't get back home. We'd all do anything to be allowed to stay there and get on with getting hold of stuff we wanted.' The one and only advantage of a posting to comradely Marxist south Yemen was far freer access to alcohol. The product of the Sira beer factory, a kind donation from East German comrades, was excellent.

The PDRY struggled on into the 1980s, mercifully rid of its most doctrinaire Soviet Marxist leader, Abdul Fattah Ismail, who retired in disgrace to Moscow in 1980, and the more pragmatic Ali Nasir Muhammad proceeded to concentrate all important state powers in his own person in order to preside over a loosening-up. Even the Kremlin, itself feeling the pinch, applauded his moves towards establishing better relations with the oil-rich Arab states and there was no more trying to export Marxism at gunpoint, either to the YAR or to neighbouring Oman. Ali Nasir, as he was known, also permitted the construction of private housing, issued farmers with certificates of title to their land and even invited an Italian company, Agip, to come and prospect for oil, while encouraging private enterprise and the appointment of educated, urban technocrats – whatever their ideology – to positions of influence.

Competence, not ideology, was now the order of the day, but before long he was facing mounting hard-liner hostility over his deviation from the Marxist path. His alleged fostering of a 'bureaucratic and bourgeois layer which has allied itself with the parasitic layers in society' was backed up by reports of the indecent wealth he and his cronies were enjoying largely thanks to 'making personal gains in dealings with foreign capitalist companies'.[50] He had, his foes complained, built himself 'a palace with gardens, swimming pool and satellite television' and a hotel that was a 'fortress of capitalism', and he was wasting precious water on a pond and fountain in Aden's public park.[51] One of his closest allies, the governor of Abyan, had squandered funds earmarked for social housing on building a bowling alley.

Judging Ali Nasir to be straying too far from the Marxist straight and narrow for comfort, Moscow encouraged Abd al-Fattah Ismail to make a comeback. In late 1984 the chief ideologist of the PDRY returned to Aden to wrest back control of the YSP and accuse Ali Nasir of being 'ideologically impotent'.[52] A lethal power struggle ensued,with Ali Nasir at the head of the less ideologically rigid tendency against Abd al-Fattah and the last remaining purist stalwarts of the original NLF leadership. As the two heavyweights confronted each other and tension mounted, each side hastened to organise support in the army, at last revealing that the split in the leadership was tribal, not ideological. Suddenly, all the structures of the modern state counted for nothing. The 'rightist' Ali Nasir, a member of the Dathina tribe in Abyan, looked to the Dathinis, the Fadhlis, the Aulaqis and Audhalis who had dominated the military in British times for his support. Abd al-Fattah and his purist 'leftists' was backed by the Lahej area, and Radfani, Yafai and Dhali tribes who had been well represented in the army since independence, as well as to Hadhramaut.

The president was the first to resort to violence. Declaring that his opponents were plotting to topple him, he seized the initiative on the morning of 13 January 1986 by sending his bodyguard to stand in for him at a meeting with members of his Politburo, the majority of whom were his opponents. According to a KGB officer serving in Aden at the time, the bodyguard entered the room, set a briefcase down on a chair, opened it, took out a machine gun and began shooting. Four corpses soon slumped to the floor. Others were wounded but survived. One of them, the man who would be the PDRY's last leader, Ali Salim al-Bidh, feigned death by dropping onto the floor and later escaped out of window down a rope made of curtains. Abd al-Fattah Ismail also managed to make a getaway, but his subsequent fate, according to his old friend Professor Naumkin, remains a mystery: 'It is most likely that friends tried to evacuate him in a tank and then, on the road from Tawahi [often called Steamer Point] to Crater it was shelled and he was completely burnt – no part of him was ever found.'

The event unleashed ten days of the bloodiest, over-armed, infighting either half of Yemen had ever seen. 'People behaved just like beasts in the field,' recalled Farook al-Hakimi, a supporter of Ali Nasir and a diplomat. 'There were pilots killing each other at the airport and shoot-outs in the corridors of the Defence Ministry, but our opponents, the "leftists", always had the advantage because they had the support of the tank brigade. Rockets fired from way outside the city, from the British forces cemetery in Silent Valley, blew up the weapons store in the Maalla district. By the end, there were so many dead they had to be cleared from the streets by bulldozers,' he remembered. A minor casualty was Aden's famous clock, the Hogg Clock Tower or Little Big Ben, a potent reminder of British times; its hands froze stopped at 10.20 on the morning of the first day of fighting.

Although suspected by western governments of stirring up trouble against pragmatic President Ali Nasir, the Kremlin – about to be swept up in Gorbachev's *glasnost* and *perestroika* – was genuinely surprised and embarrassed by the grisly goings on in Aden. Thousands of Soviet diplomats evacuated their wives and children and, holed up in their beachside embassy by the fourth day of fighting, tried their best to mediate a peace. Without success. 'Four of our embassy buildings were shot at – it was like a message to stay neutral,' remembered one Soviet official who also recalled merrily raiding the embassy shop for drink and tobacco, dodging snipers on his way to the lavatory, seeing corpses littering the nearby beach and a Georgian colonel being peppered with seventy bullets while begging fighters not to fire rockets on the city. It later transpired that the Soviet Embassy was located on an important tribal fault-line.

Four days in, with the fighting escalating and the Soviet ambassador to Aden proving incapable of mediating a peace, the time had come to evacuate all foreign nationals. The Kremlin agreed that the situation was serious enough to merit a loosening of the usual restrictions on western craft entering what were effectively their territorial waters. The royal yacht *Britannia*, sailing nearby at the time, recommended itself for the task of evacuation because she could easily be converted into a hospital ship. By 18 January she had removed 450 people, including many Soviet citizens, to safety. Beating a hasty retreat under shellfire, she sailed on up the coast and collected 200 more.[53]

Realising that his cause was lost without the support of the tank brigade, Ali Nasir first begged President Salih in the north for support, luring him with the promise of speedy unification and then, when no help was forthcoming, fled to the YAR* with some 30,000 of his supporters, which was a blessing in disguise since it meant that the clashes lacked fuel to spread outside Aden and become a full-blown civil war. But ten days were more than enough. Officially the death toll was reckoned to be 4,330, but unofficially it was put at far higher than that run up during the struggle for independence twenty years earlier. Officially the cost in damage to property and loss of military hardware was set at $120 million, but unofficially it was reckoned at nearer $140 million, a figure that matched the total amount of foreign aid received by the PDRY since independence.[54]

The toll on the PDRY's morale and international credibility was just as crippling. 'When are you people going to stop killing each other?' was all a weary Fidel Castro had to say to the 'leftist' al-Bidh, the Hadhrami who assumed the leadership of the YSP once the smoke of

* Ali Nasir later chose exile in Damascus where he remains to this day, still taking an interest in south Yemeni affairs.

battle had cleared, once the bulldozers had done their gruesome work, and new posters of the 'martyrs' been plastered on the bullet-pocked walls of the city.

The unification of the two Yemens had never looked less likely. With the hard-liners back in power in Aden, the project could be shelved and forgotten as far as the YAR was concerned. In that blood-soaked spring of 1986 no one could have dreamed that the two Yemeni republics would become one less than four years later.

## CHAPTER FOUR

# A SHOTGUN WEDDING (1990–2000)

### ESCAPING TO UNITY

On 22 May 1990, after more than 150 years of separation and the sharp frost that descended on relations between the two Yemens in the wake of the PDRY's blood-letting in 1986, the noble dream of unity at last came true. The speedy coupling took everyone by surprise. Only a few months earlier the US ambassador to Aden had confidently opined that unification was 'at least fifty years away'.[1]

Given the swift contraction of both political and economic Soviet influence in the region after Mikhail Gorbachev came to power, the YAR looked by far the sturdier of the two Yemens. Like other collapsing eastern bloc states, the PDRY was suffering underemployment and chronic shortages of everyday items such as fresh fruit, cigarettes, cars and spare parts. Southerners knew that, although ruled in the interests of the Zaydi highland tribesmen, northerners were wealthier and freer and their society a lot more dynamic than their own. If both Yemens were able to rejoice in the news that, at last, economically viable quantities of oil had been discovered in their territories, it was the YAR – with an energetic Texan oil company named Hunt Oil Inc. on its team – that had got off to a quicker productive start in the Marib desert east of Sanaa, in 1986. South of the border, further to the east, in Shabwa, the USSR's Tekhnoexport was begrudging investment and dragging its heels.

But President Salih's position was not as advantageous as it seemed. By the late 1980s he was sorely in need of a grand populist project to boost his support among almost everyone but the military and the bloated civil service. There had been a price to pay for the longed-for oil find; high hopes that Yemen might soon be as rich as neighbouring Saudi Arabia had excited the local tribes and led to flare-ups of feuding around the oil fields. Clumsy army interventions to protect the Hunt Oil installations and workers took dangerously little account of tribal custom, eroding Salih's support among the tribes and his control over the region. In other words, Salih's control over the all-important means of coercion was weaker than his counterpart's over the PDRY. Unlike the PDRY's Marxists, the YAR's military tribal republicans had never tried to disarm the tribes or to disabuse them of their belief in their sovereignty over their tribal territories. In effect, the northern tribes had been allowed to avoid explicitly signing up to the project of building a modern sovereign state. The anthropologist Sheila Carapico has argued that by the end of the 1980s the Yemens were 'each in their own way so flimsy, flawed and illegitimate that merger [unity] was each leadership's best option'.[2] A former PDRY and Adeni historian recalled that the rulers of the two republics 'escaped to unity' to save their skins.

Following the 1986 events, the best vehicle for a rapprochement between the two Yemens turned out to be oil. Both regimes were equally anxious to extract as much of it as possible in as short a time as possible from the large and desert Marib-Shabwa region straddling their border. A joint committee whose work on the production of a geological map of the area had long been a rare oasis of transparency and trust between the two states served, in the words of a PDRY deputy oil minister, as 'the guinea-pig for unification'. At a summit meeting in Sanaa in May 1988, after a bout of particularly serious cross-border skirmishing, Salih and al-Bidh seized on the new map and made it the basis for an agreement that 850 square miles of the Marib-Shabwa border area be demilitarised and declared a no-man's-land. In addition, a consortium made up of Hunt Oil Inc., Tekhnoexport, France's Total and Elf Aquitaine, and a Kuwaiti firm signed an exploration and production-sharing agreement with both governments.

By the early spring of 1989 enough excitement about oil had fuelled enough confidence in a peaceful future for unification to be back on the agenda on both sides of the border. President Salih must have assessed the risk of diluting his power and that of his northern tribal Zaydi highlanders by adding two million-odd more southern Sunnis to the YAR's already densely Sunni-populated southern highlands and Tihama. He certainly failed to convince either Sheikh Abdullah al-Ahmar, or the country's leading religious authority, that unification with an impoverished atheist state was a good idea, but these domestic doubts paled into insignificance when weighed against the demands of living in a neighbourhood increasingly dominated by Iraq.

Like Nasser before him, Saddam Hussein was dreaming the grand pan-Arab dream of uniting the entire peninsula under his rule. To that end he had set about promoting his country as the peninsula's main rival to Saudi Arabia and the Gulf Cooperation Council (GCC)* by creating a rival economic union, the Arab Cooperation Council (ACC). Jordan and Egypt as well as the YAR, all friends and supporters of Iraq in its recent war against Iran, joined the new ACC in February 1989, but it seemed to Saddam that the more Yemenis he could muster under his flag for the coming confrontation with Saudi Arabia, the better. A swift eradication of the border between the two Yemens would suit him very well. From Salih's point of view, Iraq looked like a far more attractive ally than Saudi Arabia. In the wake of Aden's 1986 blood-bath, the Saudis had enraged him by suddenly staking a territorial claim to

* GCC – Saudi Arabia, Kuwait, Bahrain, United Arab Emirates, Qatar and Oman.

Hadhramaut and to some of the PDRY oil region in Shabwa and even to a sliver of the YAR, as well as distributing Saudi passports to Hadhramis. It seems likely that Saddam Hussein managed to persuade Salih that the PDRY's Marxists were not nearly as serious a threat as he feared, and boosted his confidence by mentioning their common backgrounds (humble, tribal) and equally long hold on power (twenty years).

Whatever the exact truth, there is no doubt that by November 1989 President Salih was entirely won over to the cause of unity. He therefore seized an opportunity to advance the matter on a trip to Aden to attend the PDRY's anniversary celebrations of the British departure. According to his own account on his government website,[3] Salih was politely received at the border crossing by three PDRY leaders who joined him in his car. Not having been exposed to Saddam Hussein's pressure, they were not as convinced of the wisdom of unification as Salih. 'When we entered Aden, I was greeting and waving to the public whilst all three men accompanying me in the car remained silent,' Salih recalled. 'They were in shock to see the overwhelming support for unity.' Those PDRY leaders proceeded to erect every barrier they could think of to the merger Salih was asking for, even warning him that the Saudis would be so alarmed by the demographic threat of a united greater Yemen,* they would probably have him assassinated. A bullish Salih in turn warned them that they themselves might be slaughtered if they selfishly denied their people the chance to realise the noble dream of unity. Salih claims he insisted on union 'at all costs, including our lives, and even if we only get to experience it for a few days'.

Not until he and General Secretary Ali Salim al-Bidh reconvened later for a more private evening qat chew was any headway made towards Salih's suddenly declared goal of signing an agreement on unity that very night. Bending over backwards to make unity seem

---

* It is said that on his deathbed in 1955, the founder of Saudi Arabia, King Abdul Aziz, croaked, 'Never allow Yemen to be united'.

attractive, Salih acknowledged al-Bidh's fears that the PDRY, with a fraction of the YAR's population,* would be swallowed up by promising him that there would be jobs for all southern civil servants, a quarter of the PDRY's working population. In addition, the post of vice-president of the new state would not only be reserved for a southerner, for al-Bidh himself therefore, but would be equal in status and privilege to president. Furthermore, the prime minister of united Yemen would be a southerner and southerners would head the trade and oil ministries.

Reassured by these arrangements as well as by the promise of free democratic elections which he calculated his YSP could win with some support from the YAR's southern highlanders and Tihamans, al-Bidh was won over. But many of his colleagues still hesitated, complaining that there was no need to rush into a union, suggesting that a federation might be a sensible first step. One member of the PDRYs politburo even threatened to slaughter all his fellows if they agreed to Salih's plan. Another resorted to delaying tactics, claiming that there could be no signing ceremony that night because there was no hall available. President Salih stood his ground and issued a clinching ultimatum: 'Either we sign tonight, or I leave to Taiz and publicly disclose to the people the reality of the situation as it stands.'

Rushed and bullied was how many of the south's leaders felt by the end of 1989, as much by their own reportedly 'pig-headed' al-Bidh as by President Salih. And the new year brought no relief. President Salih met al-Bidh in Taiz and together they agreed that the process of merging the two systems, scheduled to take only a year, needed to be speeded up – in fact, crammed into only six months. Neither dared allow the opponents of union, who included the powerful Saudis, time to organise a coherent challenge. Furthermore, it was hoped that the presentation of a united Yemen at an ACC summit in Baghdad at the end of May 1990 would both enhance the image of the new

* Population of north c.11 million, of south c.2.5 million.

organisation and intensely irritate the Saudis who would find themselves suddenly encircled by a ring of more or less hostile ACC states.

Unification was rushed, but it was also bungled. No merger was achieved in the most crucial area of all, defence, because neither side was prepared to relinquish control of its armed forces. The best they could agree on was a half-hearted exchange of units. Nor was there any true merger of the two civil services, only a vague and unfulfilled direction to institute whatever in either regime had proved 'best practice'. A week before unification the lists of official appointees had only just been completed, while the constitutional committee had not finished its work. All this spoiled the excellent impression made by President Salih's offer to share out the government ministries and establish a brand new two-chambered parliament. And behind delays and logjams lurked a dangerous complacency. Both sides were convinced that the nuts and bolts of a fair-minded amalgamation did not matter too much since their own side's way of doing things would be bound to prevail in the long run. Real intentions to compromise and share and build anew were in desperately short supply, which meant that sooner rather than later all those high hopes for a harmonious future cushioned by oil wealth were bound to come to grief.

## THE PRICE OF FRIENDSHIP

The Yemens had been wed for a little over two months when they were swept up in first regional and then global developments that placed a terrible strain on their marriage.

On 2 August 1990, Saddam Hussein marched his army into Kuwait. An unprovoked invasion that would ignite the wrath of the western world – principally the United States, Britain, Saudi Arabia and the other Gulf States – it would result in the United Nations sanctioning an invasion of Iraq five months later. As the pressure to secure UN backing for a war dictated by the West's determination to secure its oil supplies mounted, Yemen's new relationship with Iraq was put to a terrible test.

President Salih neither applauded nor condoned Saddam's aggression against Kuwait, but Yemenis were disgusted by the way Saudi Arabia, the keeper of Islam's holy places, was impiously welcoming infidel American forces onto her soil in the build-up to invasion, and by the way Egypt – a fellow member of the ACC – was cravenly toeing the United States' line in exchange for some $14 billion of 'debt forgiveness'.[4]

Salih favoured an 'Arab solution' rather than an international United Nations solution to the crisis which, in the circumstances, amounted to taking Iraq's side. His position played very well at home. Yemenis stoned the Saudi and American embassies in Sanaa, marvelling at the way the latter's bullet-proof windows hurled the stones straight back at them. Like most Arabs, they were outraged by what they perceived to be American injustice and hypocrisy. Washington's apparent determination to crack down hard on Iraq for not doing the UN's bidding by withdrawing from Kuwait glaringly contradicted decades of blind eye turning to Israel's flouting of countless UN resolutions. Salih was between a rock and hard place, wondering if he might just get away with turning his back on Saddam in order to keep in with the world's only superpower, calculating that at the very least it would entail getting that superpower to back the appointment of a UN commissioner to monitor the treatment of West Bank Palestinians.

On 19 September the Saudis signalled their wrath at Yemen's refusal to condemn Saddam's invasion of Kuwait by hitting Yemen where it really hurt, in her pocket. Thanks to the end of the oil-fuelled boom, earnings from remittances sent back to Yemen from the various Gulf States had already plunged. Now the Saudis revoked the preferential terms on which Yemenis had been working in the Kingdom by telling some 800,000 of them that they had a month to liquidate their businesses, sell all their assets and clear off home. The Saudi revenge cost Yemen around $1.5 billion in remittances and unemployment leapt to 25 per cent.[5] Around half a million of the returnees, the poorest, found themselves sweltering in squalid refugee camps in Tihama. The lucky ones were given non-existent jobs with token salaries in a civil service that had been badly bloated since unification. By 1991 half the entire national budget was being consumed by the civil service wage bill.[6] Fifteen years on, I met one of these supernumerary civil servant refugees still squatting with his family in the crumbling ruins of Imam Yahya's old palace in Sanaa, without either electricity or running water.

If the Saudi vengeance was devastating, the American one – petty and vengeful – was just as damaging. It so happened that three months into the crisis it was Yemen's turn to take up one of the non-permanent seats on the UN's fifteen-man Security Council. Along with that of Cuba, Malaysia and Columbia, Yemen's support for UN resolution 678 sanctioning a US and British-led invasion of Iraq, was suddenly crucially important to the United States.

Accordingly, in late November 1990 Secretary of State James A. Baker III set off on a four-day arm-twisting tour of Sanaa, Bogota and finally Los Angeles airport, where he met his Malaysian counterpart. In his memoirs Baker vividly recalls the trouble he had convincing President Salih that America was not bluffing about its plan to invade Iraq. Although he clearly spelt out that continued payment of the US development aid package to Yemen, worth a useful $70 million a year, was dependent on Yemen's support for resolution 678, Salih was 'very unconcerned', merely observing that the entire crisis was 'like a summer storm' which would 'blow over'. An exasperated Baker warned him, 'The storm, if it comes, will be violent,' but Salih remained imperturbable. After politely serving Baker and his team a Thanksgiving dinner featuring mutton rather than turkey – Salih 'couldn't have been more hospitable', apparently – he unequivocally announced at a press conference that Yemen would not be supporting Resolution 678. Baker was thoroughly embarrassed, noting testily that although the Saudis had hinted he would be wasting his time in Yemen, Salih had given him 'no indication in private that he would reject my request quite so firmly in public'.[7]

Six days later, Yemen duly posted its 'no' vote, alongside that of Cuba. Within minutes an American diplomat was telling Yemen's ambassador to the UN, 'That was the most expensive "no" vote you ever cast', and just three days later all American aid to Yemen was stopped.[8] A gift to Salih from a grateful Saddam Hussein of a gold-plated AK-47 was probably little consolation.

## FAMILIARITY BREEDS CONTEMPT

Tempting as it is to cast united Yemen in the role of a newly married couple helplessly buffeted by outside forces too strong to withstand, it would be wrong to place all the blame for the souring of the union on the First Gulf War.

There are many reasons why divorce was on the cards as early as autumn 1992. Most of them are attributable to the fact that, for all his generous power-sharing offers, Salih and his highland Zaydis had retained tight control of the most important levers of power: finance and defence. In spite of repeated attempts by eastern-bloc advisers to reform it, the PDRY's treasury had remained as tightly run as it had been under British rule. Here was a perfect opportunity to overhaul the former YAR's corrupt and ad-hoc system by replacing it with southern best practice, but nothing of the sort happened because the crucial finance ministry was headed by a northerner. Similarly, led by a respected Hadhrami, the planning ministry might have taken a useful lead in decentralising the former YAR according to the PDRY's example, but it was hobbled by the overwhelming power of the finance ministry.

The main, far too simplistic, mechanism of the merger, the wholesale swapping of senior civil servants, failed. On both sides of the old border, local underlings – a deputy governor of a province, for example – retained real control while the imposed newcomer functioned as an idle figurehead, sidelined and mistrusted. The machinery of government soon seized up under the weighty pressure of mutual suspicion. Brian Whitaker, a journalist and author, has detailed how one side would be unwilling to compromise in a dispute without first testing the other side's willingness to give way on a second issue. The other side would then demand assurances of compromise on a third issue, and so on. This meant that disputes, instead of being tackled one at a time, became compounded and ever more intractable, until eventually the decision-making process became paralysed.[9]

The most obvious focus for this kind of trouble was the defence ministry. The southern minister of defence was shocked to discover how much military funding was being funnelled into subsidising the northern highland tribes, but his efforts to put a stop to the abuse inevitably brought him into direct confrontation with members of the president's own clan who occupied many of the most senior posts in the former YAR's army.

To add to the former south's woes – financial and administrative – a very promising brand new oil find in Hadhramaut in December 1990 was fuelling regret that al-Bidh had succumbed to Salih's bullying rush towards union. The opening of the Masila field meant that 40 per cent of Yemen's known oil reserves were now located in the territory of the former PDRY. Noisy complaints that greedy northerners were helping themselves to southerners' oil only exacerbated deepening divisions. The sad truth of the matter was that, united or not, Yemenis would never be as rich as their Saudi neighbours. Even with the new Masila field, its proven reserves amounted to a mere four billion barrels, compared with the Saudis' 261.5 billion barrels.[10]

Knowledge of this did nothing to help foster a spirit of generosity already strained by the drying up of remittances. Before unity, remittances of migrant workers earned in both the Gulf States and Saudi Arabia had accounted for at least 20 per cent of the income of both Yemens. After unity, the main – almost the only – source of income was oil, a business entirely in the hands of Salih and his people. In effect, unification had coincided with an important and unpopular shift in the balance of power from remittance-rich citizen and poor state, to poor citizen and oil-rich state. Between May 1990 and the spring of 1991 food prices quadrupled and unemployment climbed again, to 35 per cent. Flush with oil wealth himself, Salih was in a better position than ever to distribute largesse in the manner of the imams, to tie his people's prosperity and influence to their political biddability and loyalty to his person. Southerners deeply resented their exclusion from the networks of patronage that had been established in the YAR long before unity and were now giving northerners an unfair advantage over them.

Closer familiarity between the Yemens was breeding more and more contempt. On a trip to Aden in early 1992 furious, disenchanted crowds pelted President Salih's cavalcade with old plastic sandals, shouting, 'Go home Zaydis!'[11] A popular television comedy series, *The Tales of Dahbash*, which had been created by a group of actors from Taiz shortly before unification, had furnished southerners with a pejorative nickname for all northerners – *dahbashi*. Dahbash was a cheeky-chappy northerner, a lazy, bungling conman, a hopeless but lovable rogue, whose northern accent struck the southern ear as being as nasal and condescending in tone as President Salih's. In the former PDRY the word '*dahbash*' became shorthand for typically northerner behaviour, for anything that was dodgy or shoddy, from the chaotic way northerners navigated Aden's British-built roundabouts to the unjust and opaque manner in which Salih was running the country.

By that spring of 1992 north–south tensions had escalated as far as a string of assassination attempts, first against prominent southerners – Vice-President al-Bidh fled Sanaa to the safety of first Aden and then his native Hadhramaut – and then against northerners. None of the incidents was ever fully investigated or prosecuted. Al-Bidh made the holding of free and fair multi-party elections in four months' time, in April 1993, a condition of his return to Sanaa and government. An election, the first on the peninsula, was duly held. Ignoring signs that Yemen's commitment to transparency was not all it might be, the United States magnanimously forgave Salih's unhelpfulness in the lead-up to the Gulf War, and heartily congratulated him for holding the first democratic elections ever seen on the Arabian peninsula. A starry-eyed editorial in the *New York Times* titled 'A Real Arab Revolution' began:

> Something wonderful has happened in Yemen, a remote Muslim state on the southern flank of the Arabian Peninsula. About 80 per cent of the 2.7 million registered voters have elected 301 members of Parliament from among 3,545 candidates. Of 50 women who ran, two won. More than 40 parties took part in the election.[12]

The president's party, the General People's Congress (GPC), garnered 41 per cent of the vote but a new party, Islah (Reform), had gained a 21 per cent share by capturing much of the southern highland area that al-Bidh's YSP had hoped to win.[13] A loose grouping of religious conservatives (Muslim Brotherhood rather than jihadists), people who were not so radical they could have nothing to do with democracy, some highland tribal leaders and conservative-minded businessmen, Islah was led by the mighty Sheikh Abdullah al-Ahmar. The extent to which it was a creature of the regime was revealed five years later when Sheikh al-Ahmar admitted that even if Islah had won a landslide victory he still would not have sought to relieve Ali Abdullah Salih of the presidency.[14]

Al-Bidh, whose YSP had captured a mere 19 per cent of the vote, was bitterly disappointed and running out of options. Within four months of the elections he had retreated back to Aden. Not long afterwards he presented an eighteen-point ultimatum to Salih featuring, among other things, a last demand for financial decentralisation. If no action was taken, he warned, he and his fellow YSP ministers would resign from the government. Nothing changed. By October he was swearing he would never go to Sanaa again and the remainder of the year saw a steady slide towards civil war.

The ministry of culture ordered the Taiz actor who played the Dahbash to change his accent, and there were more angry accusations on both sides, and another spate of assassination attempts, and a scrambling to buy the loyalty of important tribes. The president could rely on the Hashid while the YSP briefly managed to secure some highland Bakil Confederation tribes' allegiance. An American satellite was registering alarming troop movements on both sides of the old border.

## WHO WEARS THE TROUSERS?

By the time Jordan brokered an eleventh-hour agreement to avert the conflict in February 1994, it was too late. Passions were too inflamed. Remembering how the Aden in 1986 had ended in a victory for the Moscow hard-liners, northerners baulked at the idea of being ruled by al-Bidh and his East German-trained and scarily efficient security service. Many southerners on the other hand, knew that al-Bidh had proved himself more of a Gorbachev than a Stalin while running the PDRY after 1986 and that the totalitarian police state was gone for good. They were convinced that President Salih and his Zaydi highland tribes planned to annex their land.

Conditions for conflict were excellent. The swapping of a few brigades from south to north and vice versa, instead of a real merger of the two armed forces, made it easy for local brigades to attack an isolated foreign brigade. Most such confrontations took place in the former YAR, the southern brigades therefore getting the worst of it. The old PDRY avenged itself by sending its army jets to bomb the northerners' two power stations, which left Sanaa and other towns with no electricity for weeks. Northern forces shelled the YSP's party headquarters in Sanaa for almost two hours and then seized the southerners' air base, while the south lobbed Scud missiles back at Sanaa. Radio Sanaa and Radio Aden traded insults; President Salih was 'Little Saddam' and Vice-President al-Bidh was 'Ali Salem al-Marxisti or Ali Salem al-Fascisti'. On 21 May al-Bidh formally announced the divorce, declaring the birth of another southern Yemeni state, the

Democratic Republic of Yemen, although he and his supporters were in control of no more than Aden and Mukalla at the time.

Al-Bidh might once have seriously fancied his chances of mounting a palace coup in Sanaa and then leading a Yemen-wide rebellion against the greed and corruption of the northern tribal elite that would result in the toppling of Salih.[15] He might have assumed that, with generous Saudi backing channelled through wealthy Hadhrami émigrés living in Saudi Arabia, he and his followers could prevail. The Saudis certainly expected the south to triumph. A senior Saudi official reportedly assured an American diplomat that the southern tribes would be bound to rise up in defence of Aden, 'You don't know the tribes like we do,' he told him.[16] An estimated billion dollars' worth of Saudi arms arrived in Aden. But none of it was to be, largely because President Salih made excellent use of the fact that al-Bidh was a Hadhrami.

The picture Salih painted of Saudis, Hadhramis (both in Saudi Arabia, as well as Hadhramaut) and al-Bidh all malevolently plotting together to destroy the noble ideal of a united Yemen was a powerful one, and guaranteed to unite all northern Yemenis and even many southerners behind him. Painting the separatists as godless Marxists also played its part. Leading northern clergy described the war as lawful, as a 'jihad in the name of God', and Sheikh Abdullah al-Ahmar piously endorsed their position by declaring that while the northern dead were bound for heaven, the southern separatists' were destined for hell. Having privately opposed unification back in 1990, Sheikh Abdullah had decided 'unity is part of Islam', which made those who opposed it 'infidels'.

Perhaps just as importantly, the US State Department set the priority of its alliance with Saudi Arabia to one side for a change and declared itself in favour of a united Yemen, simply because a reinforcement of the status quo seemed the best way to avoid destabilising the region and disrupting the flow of a useful three million barrels of oil a day through the Bab-al-Mandab, the lower opening of the Red Sea.

The superpower's support for Salih meant that no one – not Saudi Arabia nor any of the other GCC states – dared to recognise the breakaway Yemeni state that al-Bidh declared.

Six weeks later, after pounding Aden with artillery and howitzer fire, after subjecting its inhabitants to a siege that reminded many of those Sanaa had undergone in its history, northern tanks and APCs, under the command of an able PDRY general* who had fled north with Ali Nasir in 1986 and had an old score to settle, rolled into the city to be met by cries of 'Welcome!' A triumphant Sanaa Radio declared, 'Al-Bidh and his deviant gang wagered on their military machine. They have found themselves a scum drowning in the mud of treason at which all Yemenis spit!'[17] Al-Bidh and his closest supporters fled by boat from Aden to Oman. Those cries of 'Welcome' faded as soon as the invading forces were seen to include hundreds of Afghan War veterans and local religious extremists – forces which, like the tribes, Salih had been not only tolerating but encouraging as a useful counterweight to the Marxists. Bearded fanatics applied themselves to instituting sharia law by flogging people for drinking alcohol or talking to unrelated women, by ransacking Aden's recently reopened Anglican church and demolishing the city's famous Sira beer factory. The ancient port was then plundered by northerners claiming their war booty in the old time-honoured fashion: 'large garbage trucks given to Aden municipality by foreign donors were driven away northwards', even window-frames, bathroom fittings, door knobs and bed-sheets were taken'.[18]

The war cost united Yemen some 7,000 lives, as much as eight billion dollars[19] and any last hope of a happy marriage.

## TEN YEARS ON

In late May 2000 President Salih mobilised every resource of the state to mark the tenth anniversary of unification with the most lavish

* Major General Abd al-Rab Mansur al-Hadi, now vice-president of Yemen.

jamboree the country had ever seen. Sanaa's streets were cleaned and brightly lit, rubbish collected, doors painted, schoolchildren dragooned into synchronised displays of song and dance and a new model of tank unveiled for the obligatory military parade. All at an astronomical cost of approximately 200 million dollars.

The cost in negative publicity for Salih's regime was probably at least as astronomical because those entrusted with the job of ensuring the event's success felt obliged to crack the whip: the use of all pagers and mobiles was forbidden a week in advance; the number of extra checkpoints and road blocks meant that it was hard for people to travel to enjoy the holiday with their relatives in other parts of the country; school-leavers were informed that failure to participate in the parades would mean automatic failure in their exams; the sky over Sanaa was regularly torn by screaming fighter jets; the already meagre salaries of civil servants were halved in the month before in order to help pay for it all. Southerners, still smarting in the aftermath of the 1994 civil war, were left in little doubt that the union was a northern rather than joint success. The 1990 poster showing President Salih happily hoisting the new flag of Yemen with his Vice-President Ali Salim al-Bidh standing behind him had been reprinted for the grand occasion, but with al-Bidh air-brushed out.[20]

It had long been clear that the dream of national unity would not be the cure-all Yemenis craved, but Yemeni nationalism – the latest in a ruinous succession of previous 'isms' Yemenis had experimented with either under foreign tutelage or of their own volition – was failing too, thanks to the state's wild veering between bouts of action and repression such as the unity anniversary celebrations and long periods of inertia. President Salih's hope that the anniversary celebration's 'circuses' nationalism could begin to compensate people for their poverty and bleak futures was about to be dashed. The dramatic public exploits of a tiny minority who had no interest in the petty business of nation state-building having long before espoused another 'ism' – global jihadism – were about to thrust Salih's unity jamboree into the shade. Within five months of the celebrations, in October 2000, Yemeni members of al-Qaeda staged the movement's most audaciously dramatic attack to date by exploding a large hole in the side of the American warship, the USS *Cole*, while she was refuelling at Aden.

But if the attack on the USS *Cole* was al-Qaeda in Yemen's debut on the international stage, Yemen's modern jihadist roots had been struck at least twenty years earlier, in the soil of Afghanistan, in the youthful exploits of men like the country's best-known jihadist, Tariq al-Fadhli – whom, thanks to his cousin, Ahmad al-Fadhli, I first encountered at his house for lunch in December 2004.

# PART TWO

1 The old city of Sanaa, with President Salih's new mosque visible in the background

2 Aden's harbour, with a billboard poster of President Salih and the old Jewish cemetery in the foreground

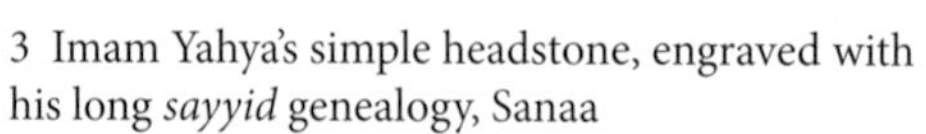

3 Imam Yahya's simple headstone, engraved with his long *sayyid* genealogy, Sanaa

4 Imam Ahmad, while on a visit to Rome in 1957

5 Sanaa's mobile history class, displaying images of Yasser Arafat and President Salih in his tribesman's costume

6 A statue of Queen Victoria, removed during the PDRY period but now back in the public garden at Steamer Point in Aden

7 Silent Valley, the half-filled last British cemetery in Aden

8 Queen Elizabeth II in Aden in 1954, knighting the Hadhrami *sayyid* businessman Abubakr al-Kaff

9 Wadi Doan, Hadhramaut, 'ancestral home' of Osama bin Laden

10 Wadi Doan's Indonesian baroque-style Buqshan Palace, the property of Abdullah Buqshan, a wealthy Saudi-Yemeni

11 Sheikh Tariq al-Fadhli (left), Afghan War veteran and now a leader of Yemen's southern secessionist movement, and his cousin Ahmad al-Fadhli

12 Leaders of Al-Qaeda in the Arabian Peninsula (AQAP) in a video released in early 2009, from left to right: Qasim al-Raymi, Said Ali al-Shihri, Nasir al-Wahayshi, Abu al-Harith

13 The last sultan of the Fadhli tribe, Nasir al-Fadhli, flanked by his policeman son Mustafa (left) and his nephew Ahmad al-Fadhli

14 Qat-time for the barrow boys in Sanaa's main *souk*

15 In the Marib desert, with oil-worker Ibrahim al-Harithi, friend and driver Walid, and Muhammad the Bedouin camel-breeder

16 President Ali Abdullah Salih arriving at a summit meeting in Qatar, June 2005

17 Sheikh Abdullah al-Ahmar, paramount sheikh of the Hashid tribal federation, eminence grise and kingmaker until his death in 2007

18 Tribesman, businessman and politician Hamid al-Ahmar with Islamist cleric Sheikh Abdul Majid al-Zindani at an Islah party conference in Sanaa, March 2009

19 Osama bin Laden's former bodyguard Nasir al-Bahri in conversation

20 Aref Othman in Aden, displaying a file of US-censored letters from his brother Othman Othman in Guantanamo Bay detention camp

CHAPTER FIVE

# FIRST GENERATION JIHAD

## AT HOME WITH THE AL-FADHLIS

'Welcome back, my dear! You are home!'

All Ahmad al-Fadhli knew when I called him from my hotel in Aden was that I was a friend of a friend, born there over forty years ago when it was still a British Crown Colony. But he had sounded as warm as if we had known each other for years so I happily accepted his kind invitation to travel a short way up the coast to spend a day with him at his banana farm.

He would send his driver and car to collect me, he said, but I must be sure to remember to bring my passport for presentation at checkpoints. 'All these security measures are an awful bore, aren't they? Ruddy bin Laden and ruddy War on Terror!' Ahmad chuckled, while I swiftly calculated that if that was his attitude he was obviously not on speaking terms with his cousin, Tariq al-Fadhli, an old friend of Osama bin Laden's. I felt a twinge of disappointment; much as I was looking forward to meeting Ahmad and seeing his farm, I had also been hoping for a chance to sound him out on the subjects of both jihadism in Yemen and Tariq's relations with bin Laden. Never mind, I reasoned, the al-Fadhli clan had doubtless cut their Tariq off just as most of the bin Ladens had disowned their Osama. I made a mental note not to embarrass Ahmad by so much as mentioning Tariq the next day.

While it was still cool, at around eight the following morning, I climbed aboard a Toyota Land Cruiser. Ahmad's driver, wearing the southern Yemeni tribesman's uniform of prettily striped *futa** and faded checked turban, politely produced one of his employer's cards to remove any anxiety I might have been feeling about being kidnapped and then we were on our way, easily clearing the checkpoint on the edge of town with a simple mention of the al-Fadhli name.

I found it hard to imagine a Yemeni banana farm. As far as my eye could see, there was no vegetation, just dust and stone on the one hand and a sandy beach and glittering Arabian Sea on the other. A light winter breeze was blowing a smoke of white sand from right to left, up the deserted shore, across the empty strip of asphalt we were speeding along, towards the baked and barren expanse reaching inland to a ridge of bare russet mountains. Shortly before we reached Zinjibar, the old Fadhli tribal capital, the view changed to more promisingly green plantations however, and soon we were hurtling off the road, along ever narrowing dusty tracks, past clusters of poor huts and ragged children, and a camel or two, and a brand new white mosque and on, plunging between rows of low banana trees straight to the middle of Ahmad's farm, to stop at last by a scruffy caravan. A few yards away, at a rusty folding table set under a single generously spreading eucalyptus tree, sat Ahmad. Bearded and beaming, he was dressed Saudi style in a long, pristine white *thowb* and red-and-white checked headcloth, with a mobile phone, a walking stick and a glass of Mecca's ZamZam water to hand.

'Marvellous stuff! Cures absolutely everything!' he exclaimed.

In a Queen's English hardly heard since the 1950s he chatted on charmingly. I discovered why he preferred to live in a caravan rather

---

* Yemeni sarong

than at either his Aden or Sanaa or even his Saudi residence. He was never happier than when on his ancestral tribal land, he told me, but he was clearly also very fond of reminiscing about a childhood spent as a member of the ruling family of the Fadhli tribe, under colonial British 'protection' until 1967 when he and his family had been chased off their beloved land by Marxist insurgents to a sad exile in Saudi Arabia.

In 1947, aged only six, he told me, he had been kitted out with a white cotton blazer complete with school badge, a khaki *futa*, shirt and turban, and sent to the colony's College for the Sons of Emirs and Chiefs. Despite its Spartan regime, it had failed to curb his Yemeni tribesman's rebellious streak and Aden's British masters had packed him off to Britain to a minor Gloucestershire public school, for a life of 'potatoes and frostbite and feeling hungry'. Ever the resourceful tribesman, Ahmad had set traps for rabbits and squirrels with the aid of a few horse hairs purloined from the school's stables and barbecued whatever he caught, until he was caught himself one day by worried firemen who had spotted a plume of smoke.

When his schoolboy derring-do stories ran out Ahmad spoke about his farm, explaining that he hoped banana-growing would keep his youngest son, Haidara, out of trouble and away from the Fadhli tribal calling to bear arms. 'You see, the trouble with us is that we like fighting much better than anything else,' he confided. 'Pay a Fadhli to build a house and it will be a slow business, pay him to fight and he's there with his gun in an instant!' We laughed together over how much trouble his ancestors had given Aden's British rulers in the mid-nineteenth century, about how one only had to consult the tribe's founding myth which featured an illegitimate Turkish baby washed up on the nearby shore in the sixteenth century to know that the Fadhlis had, in his words, 'always been bastards'. Then he suggested that if I was so interested in Fadhli tribal history I might like to meet his octogenarian Uncle Nasir, the Fadhlis' last sultan who, just like Ahmad, had been exiled in Saudi Arabia but had recently returned to live out his days among his own people. 'After that,' Ahmad suggested, patting his ample stomach, 'we might drop in on Nasir's son, my cousin Tariq, in time for a nice lunch. You've heard of him, have you? Well, he's the big sheikh here now – no one uses the title sultan any more – so he's got plenty of money from the government and a big new house, just there on that first roundabout into Zinjibar, you would have passed it. . .'

Evidently, my delicate scruples about not about embarrassing my host by mentioning Tariq were wasted, but what on earth was any friend of Osama bin Laden doing at large rather than safely behind bars, and being paid by the government in Sanaa to live with high status and in some luxury? It was baffling given President Ali Abdullah Salih's pledge to side with the West in President George W. Bush's global 'War on Terror'. Furthermore, why would Tariq al-Fadhli dream of inviting an infidel Englishwoman into his home for a 'nice lunch'?

I wondered if Ahmad could be all he seemed, if his nostalgia for his British schooldays was all an elaborate act designed to lull me into a false sense of security. After all, the al-Fadhlis had every reason to be nursing a special old grudge against the British who had built them up as local rulers of this land, called them sultans and flattered them with rich gifts and gun salutes for over a century before abandoning them to the Marxists. As I climbed back into Ahmad's car a terrifying thought crossed my mind: might the plan be to kidnap and deliver me to Tariq al-Fadhli for a video-recorded beheading?

Driving back through the farm and the tatty centre of Zinjibar and on north-east along the coast road, we turned inland, at a place called Shuqra – 'the first capital of the Fadhlis, where my ancestors used to plunder ships from and what have you,' Ahmad explained. It was Fadhli tribesmen, he proudly reminded me, who had given the British their perfect excuse to invade Aden back in 1839, by plundering the Indian *Duria Dawla* and parading her women passengers naked on the deck. Bouncing along a rough desert track, we seemed to be making for the distant shape of a tall edifice. Eventually we drew close enough for me to identify it as a mud brick fort, some four storeys high. Alone in its humble glory in that flat dun expanse, unshaded by any trees, with only a dusty chicken coop for company, it was hardly more appealing than Ahmad's caravan.

A wizened old man squatting in some rubble against a wall of the fort, with a dusty red car safety-belt circling his knees,* did not bother to register our arrival by looking up from the hubbly-bubbly pipe he was puffing on. Naturally assuming that we would find the venerable Fadhli patriarch lounging comfortably on cushions in the fort's cool interior, I took the old smoker for an ancient family retainer, until Ahmad presented him to me as 'Sultan Nasir of the Fadhlis'. Rising from his dusty corner, the man whom the British had honoured with gun salutes and stipends and rifles and even appointed justice minister of their still-born Federation of South Arabia, greeted me kindly and shepherded us into a reception room which was situated to one side of the main building. More like a car port than any reception room I had ever seen, dusty but comfortably open-ended to let a breeze tunnel through, it was furnished with low mattress seating scattered with bright silk cushions.

Between fretting and fiddling with a succession of malfunctioning pipes he had made himself, old Sultan Nasir made fascinating conversation. He and Ahmad squabbled amicably about how many times he had been married. Ahmad insisted it was forty-seven times. Nasir could not believe it, but knew he had only really loved his second wife, who had died half a century earlier. Neither he nor Ahmad could be bothered to calculate how many children he had fathered. What they could agree on was that since returning home from his Saudi exile in 1995 Nasir had been married five times, but only the last union, to a girl of eighteen by whom he had sired three children in the past six years, had been happy. 'The proof is in the pudding,' laughed Ahmad, pointing

* Known as a 'beyhan chair', any circular band of fabric slipped around the knees while sitting cross-legged to act as a comfortable support.

out that Nasir had treated this latest wife to a generator, a television and even a washing machine. I glimpsed her briefly inside the mud fort. Wearing a pair of fluorescent pink plastic sandals, a tomato-red silk dress with a solid gold belt and a lumpy brown henna face-mask, she was reclining in a darkened upstairs room with a low ceiling and packed-earth floor, watching television with her children, little more than a child herself, while her prized washing machine went about its noisy business, but without the help of piped water. Nasir clearly loved his young family. 'That Haroun!' he said, shaking his head and chuckling over his five-year-old son, 'he's always threatening to stone me if I refuse to give him money to buy more pet rabbits!' 'Have you changed your mind yet about sending them to school?' interjected Ahmad, who had confided to me in the car his growing anxiety that his youngest cousins would never learn to read and write, let alone understand computers or English. 'Pah!' was old Nasir's only reply.

Although educated to university level himself in British-ruled Sudan, Nasir was no fan of learning or, for that matter, much else about the modern world. Nor did he think much of Yemeni unification. Like so many southerners, he resented the new order as 'an occupation' by the northern tribal ascendancy in Sanaa. On the other hand, he did respect President Ali Abdullah Salih personally. Determined to eradicate any last trace of Marxism from the south by fostering a revival of the old tribal order, the president was paying Nasir an annual stipend equivalent to a government minister's salary and even dropped by to see him from time to time. Nasir had responded by astutely allying his family to the regime, marrying one of his daughters into Salih's northern highlander tribe, to the man generally reckoned to be the second power in the land, the military commander of the north-west district of the country which included Sanaa, Brigadier-General Ali Muhsin al-Ahmar. Nasir recounted how, shortly before the 2003 parliamentary elections, the president had dropped in to have a publicity shot taken of himself in friendly conversation with Nasir as he squatted there cross-legged in the dust as usual, puffing on his pipes. Plastered all over

Sanaa, the resulting campaign poster had soon been spotted by one of Nasir's grandsons, a student in the capital, who instantly recognised his grandfather but failed to notice that his *futa* had fallen open. It had been a friend who exclaimed, 'Who on earth is that old man with his balls on display?' Uncle and nephew roared with laughter at the memory.

Nasir's lack of self-importance and his remarkable good health, which he demonstrated by mock-challenging his stout nephew to a quick sprint, were impressive. Asked for the secret of his contented longevity, he slyly joked, 'I did not have very much sexual intercourse when I was younger – you see, I never had the permitted four wives, only ever one at a time.' A simple Muslim piety, frequent recourse to the well-thumbed paperback Koran he kept in the breast pocket of his shirt, seemed to be his mainstay. His ribald recreation of the Muslim holy book's version of the birth of Jesus – particularly his demonstration of the way Jesus had rocketed out of Mary's womb while she lay resting under a date tree – had us all laughing again, but the performance was cut short by the appearance of one of his seventeen sons, not Tariq the jihadist but a handsome and neatly dressed young captain in the local police. Young Mustafa al-Fadhli said he needed his father's advice: should he or should he not take a second wife? Both Nasir and Ahmad impatiently urged him to do no such thing. Wives were expensive and they did not always see eye to eye, they said. He should not follow the example set by his older brother Tariq, with whom, Ahmad reminded me, we would shortly be lunching.

Born three months before the British withdrew from Aden, Tariq had been a helpless babe in arms in 1967 when the Marxist NLF declared the Fadhli sultanate overthrown and its capital Zinjibar their new headquarters. Shaking their heads over the painful memory, Ahmad and Nasir recalled how, shocked by that British betrayal of the old treaties of friendship and both in London at the time, they had requested a meeting with Lord Shackleton* at the House of Lords and

* Edward Shackleton, the Labour peer and Minister without Portfolio tasked with the handover of Aden to the NLF in 1967.

been dismayed to hear that in his, as it turned out extraordinarily prescient, opinion, it would not be a couple of months but possibly as much as twenty-five years before they saw their home again. After hastily withdrawing a large sum of cash from his London and Zurich banks and spending a few months in Beirut, Nasir and his extended family had had little choice but to resettle in Saudi Arabia, living off the generous monthly stipends the Saudi royals paid to all the ousted former rulers of the Aden protectorates. 'Which, by the way, we are still being paid now we've moved back here,' Ahmad said, as we drove back up the dusty, rocky track towards the main road again.

Soon we were approaching a British-era roundabout on the far side of town. There, on its edge stood another fort-like structure, a still unfinished grey concrete three-storey edifice surrounded by a high wall: Tariq's new residence.*

## TARIQ AL-FADHLI

Appearing at the grand entrance to his fort to welcome us, surrounded by a handful of his eleven children, Tariq al-Fadhli's demeanour was as genially serene and modest as Osama bin Laden's. Although a decade or so younger and shorter than the world's most wanted man, he even looked like him but he was dressed in a manner that, with hindsight, perfectly reflected his allegiance to the new, united Yemen: his prettily patterned *futa* was complemented by a large and richly decorated *jambiyah*.

Smiling his welcome, he enquired kindly after a mutual friend, a former political officer and retired diplomat who had kindly arranged for Tariq to come to Britain in 1999 to study English and have some shrapnel removed from his nose. 'At that time I was not welcome in Arab countries like Jordan and Egypt,' he recalled, 'They didn't like

* Sultan Nasir al-Fadhli died in a Saudi hospital in November 2008, and was flown home for burial in a private plane, courtesy of the Saudi royal family.

*mujahideen* who'd fought in Afghanistan, but I had no trouble getting visas for Britain or the United States.' He told me that he had liked England very much, but not either the language school he attended or the family he was lodging with so he had not learned much English. My arrival was giving him a good idea, one that would never have occurred to his father: 'Perhaps you will stay here and teach English to me and my children?' he suggested, 'I can arrange an apartment and a car, and a driver for you.'

Leading us into a sitting room whose plush wall-to-wall carpet was spread with a square of plastic sheeting and covered with dishes of meats, fruits, salads, yoghurt, dates, great rounds of flat bread and mounds of saffron rice, he invited us to make ourselves comfortable. Although anxious to question him about both his past and his present, I observed the Arab custom of not speaking while eating and marvelled instead at the steady stream of servants moving in and out of the room bearing yet more dishes. On the alert for possible culture clashes, the infinitely courteous Ahmad made quite sure I was not offended when, according to Arab custom, Tariq finished his meal, got to his feet without a word and left the room.

We all reconvened to relax for the rest of the afternoon in a reception room quite unlike his father's breeze-block wind-tunnel. Elegantly hung with chandeliers and heavy velvet curtains, it was also richly carpeted and large enough to accommodate sixty or so on the green velvet cushions lining its walls. Tariq settled down with his mobile phone to hand. On a low table in front of him was another telephone, a copy of the Koran, a litre bottle of water, a packet of cigarettes and a generous bundle of freshly rinsed qat. While he rhythmically, steadily, plucked at his bundle of twigs, picking off the most tender green shoots of the shrub and popping them into his mouth, while his left cheek slowly swelled with the masticated residue, while he chewed and sucked on his cud and his gaze grew wider and brighter, he talked and talked and the reasons why he was not behind bars grew gradually clearer to me.

There are two stories about how Tariq became a jihadist. One, which I had heard from two sources before I met him, suggested that as a bored and disaffected teenager in Saudi Arabia, he had wrapped a car around a lamp post while out joy-riding one night and fled the country to join the anti-Soviet jihad in Afghanistan in order to escape a jail sentence. But the story he tells himself is different. According to Tariq his transformation into a jihadist started in 1985 when he was eighteen, with a desire to emulate an older brother who was studying in the United States but spending his college vacations piously fighting the Soviet infidel in Afghanistan. At his brother's suggestion Tariq began reading the seminal works of Sayyid Qutb,* listening to religious tapes, learning the Koran by heart and saving part of his Saudi army salary for the journey to Afghanistan.

Whatever the true catalyst for his espousal of jihad Tariq arrived in Peshawar, on the Pakistan side of the Afghan border in 1985, to find hundreds of other young Arab fighters, or 'Arab Afghans' as they were popularly known – Algerians, Egyptians, Libyans, Moroccans and Yemenis from both the north and south – all aflame with zeal for battling the godless Soviet Union, all inspired by pious tales of battlefield miracles, all looking for adventure, a higher purpose in life and perhaps martyrdom, most of them reliant on Saudi funding. 'I wanted to go to Paradise too!' Tariq said, but his disarmingly ironic grin suggested he had long ago mastered that youthful appetite.

Yemenis escaping poverty and unemployment at home and following their inborn bent for warfare in terrain as rugged and beautiful as much of their own were well represented among the Arab mujahideen in Peshawar. Close proximity to the Marxist PDRY meant that northerners were guaranteed to be at least as alert as the United States and Saudi Arabia to the moral and political evil represented by

* Today famous as the father of Islamic Radicalism, the Egyptian intellectual who first argued that rebellion against one's temporal ruler might be justified. Extremely popular among young Saudis outraged by the perceived hypocrisy of their worldly princes and Wahhabi clergy.

Soviet Communism. Most found that the road to adventure, religious righteousness and a steady income in Afghanistan was an easy one to take, especially when it carried with it two important blessings. First, they had been stirred into a fever of aggressive piety by some of their clergy who preached the puritanical Saudi Wahhabism that President al-Hamdi had begun encouraging in the mid-1970s as a means of combating the Marxism emanating from the PDRY, and of eliminating Zaydi elitism and securing Saudi funds for social welfare. Second, they had the support and encouragement of a powerful man, President Salih's distant cousin, Tariq al-Fadhli's future brother-in-law, Brigadier-General Ali Muhsin al-Ahmar, who was actively assisting Osama bin Laden's recruitment drive by funnelling jihad-minded youths his way. As far as the regime in Sanaa was concerned, it was only natural, only right and proper, that a portion of its unemployable youth would prefer to take themselves off to Afghanistan to cover themselves with glory doing what they did best, rather than slaving for the Saudis as domestic servants or labourers.

Tariq noticed that, although fewer in number, southerners were even more intensely committed to the anti-Soviet jihad than northerners. Usually they were political dissidents as well as religious zealots. Most zealous of all though were dispossessed exiles like Tariq himself, young men who had not set foot in their homeland since babyhood, if at all, but who dreamed of avenging the past and retrieving their birthright by taking the jihad on home to the Marxist PDRY just as soon as they were done in Afghanistan. These hybrid Saudi Yemenis, generally of southern Yemeni origins, were among bin Laden's keenest and most loyal followers. As bin Laden's former bodyguard, Nasir al-Bahri, put it to me, 'Bin Laden found a pool of young men who were second-generation exiles brought up by their parents on religion and jihad just ready and waiting. Many of their fathers had fought the British for independence and then the Marxist NLF in the 1960s, before accepting defeat and going into Saudi exile.' He went on to recall the closeness of the deracinated émigré community, how his father had worked for the bin Ladens and how, as a child in Jeddah, he had been hauled off to pay his respects to Tariq's father, Sultan Nasir al-Fadhli.

After a few months of military training in Pakistan, Tariq had ventured into Afghanistan, but only as far as Jaji where he had encountered a brigade of Arab fighters led by Osama bin Laden who had forged especially close friendships with southern Yemenis. Osama and Tariq had still more in common, of course; both of southern Yemeni origin, they had both been brought up in Saudi Arabia and experienced the quiet alienation of being forever on the fringes of Saudi society, of knowing that all the bin Laden wealth and all the al-Fadhli sultanate's prestige could not counteract what outsiders experienced as the haughty exclusiveness of the ruling Saudi Nejd elite. Tariq lingered three months at the camp and presumably discussed their shared dream of liberating the PDRY with bin Laden before penetrating on into central Afghanistan in search of a live battle front and action.

In May 1988, after nine years of ruinous warring against the mujahideen, Moscow acknowledged its expensive failure in Afghanistan and began a slow withdrawal. Convincing themselves that it was their divinely sanctioned intervention that had tipped the balance and defeated one of the world's superpowers, Afghan War veterans like al-Fadhli and bin Laden rejoiced in this sure proof that Allah was on their side. Bin Laden and his Egyptian physician ally, Ayman al-Zawahiri, began looking to the future and founded al-Qaeda, plotting to extend and export the jihad. Back in Saudi Arabia the following year, bin Laden tried to initiate the cleansing of the Arabian Peninsula of its infidels by suggesting to the head of the Saudi intelligence service, Prince Turki al-Saud, that the Kingdom give him and his Afghan War veteran followers a green light to rid the region of its single Marxist regime, the PDRY. He was shocked and angered by the prince's unequivocally negative response to the proposal. Meanwhile, busier fighting than politicking, Tariq soldiered on through the ensuing messy conflict between the Afghan mujahideen and the Afghan government left behind by the Soviets, acquitting himself sufficiently heroically at the Battle of Jalalabad in the spring of 1989 to secure his reputation as Yemen's bravest jihadist. At last, news of the demise of the PDRY and the sudden union of the two Yemens in May 1990 was his prompt to leave behind not only Afghanistan but his childhood home in Saudi Arabia and return to his ancestral home in south Yemen.

What he found there surprised and angered him. The godless Marxists he blamed for his family's humiliating exile and the pathetically impoverished condition of his homeland had not been comprehensively purged in the course of unification but were clearly still in power, controlling the local police and security services and maintaining their separate military establishment. Understandably, those Marxists were no more delighted to see Tariq than he was to see them. With ample justification, they feared that he had returned to Zinjibar to launch jihad against them and would wreak a horrible revenge before reinstating himself as the heir to the Fadhli sultanate and reviving the tribal order they had been struggling to eradicate for the past couple of decades. Tariq, almost undoubtedly with support and encouragement from Sanaa, courted confrontation with them by championing the revival of old tribal habits of gun-ownership and channelling funds collected from wealthy southern Yemenis living in Saudi Arabia into dispensing charity and building new mosques. Soon he had gathered enough support among Fadhli tribesmen who remembered his father Nasir's wise rule to be elected paramount sheikh of Abyan, and was crowned in the traditional Fadhli manner by having the fuse of a matchlock gun placed around his turban. He had also been joined by an army of up to 29,000[1] Afghan War veterans (most, but not all of them Yemenis) whom he gathered together into a loose but virulently anti-Marxist Islamist movement known as 'Islamic Jihad'.

Sanaa raised no objection, of course. The overriding urge to rid Yemen of any last vestige of the old Marxist order, added to a determination to fill the resulting ideological vacuum with a reinvigorated tribal order that would smooth the process of merging the two states into one, meant that President Salih was content to accommodate this small army of hardened jihadists when no one else in the region would have them. For Salih, ever the nimble dancer on the heads of snakes, it was a simple case of the enemy of my enemy (the Marxist leadership of the former PDRY) is my new best friend.

The 'Islamic Jihad' camps, including one in the al-Huttat mountains, near the town of Jaar, a short distance to the north of Zinjibar in Yaffa tribal land, were reportedly subsidised to the tune of $20 million by bin Laden, via Brigadier-General Ali Muhsin al-Ahmar,[2] and bin Laden himself reportedly travelled in and out of Yemen, meeting with his friend Tariq, preaching against the Marxists in mosques, dreaming of mustering a force of 10,000 pious al-Qaeda jihadists there in south Yemen 'who would be ready at a moment's notice to march to liberate the land of the two holy places [Saudi Arabia]'.[3] He even went so far as to offer hundreds of Saudis of Yemeni descent considerable sums of money to return to Yemen to 'live as good Muslims' and is believed to have held a six-hour-long meeting with Brigadier-General Ali Muhsin al-Ahmar, at Sanaa airport.[4] He seems to have been considering Yemen as a useful base for his global operations, and with good reason. Not only was it, in the words almost every news agency has used about Yemen since 9/11, his own 'ancestral homeland', and not only had Yemenis been greatly loved by Muhammad on account of their wisdom and faith, but the Arabic they spoke was closer to that of the Koran than any other dialect. There were more practical considerations: bin Laden had discovered in Afghanistan that, whatever their citizenship – Yemeni or Saudi – Yemenis made excellent recruits to his cause, proving hardier, braver and better fighters than many over-pampered Saudis. Yemeni jihadists were quick learners, energetic and young and commendably undemanding in the matter of equipment, food and accommodation, more than happy to subsist for months on a diet of stale bread mixed with water and a little sugar, for example. If they already had families, they were uncomplaining about being separated from them. As well as being particularly skilled at night-raiding, they were hard workers, excellent at building roads and tunnels and trenches.

By 1991 Tariq, with bin Laden's material backing and moral support, was openly engaged in violent jihad against the old PDRY's Marxist leadership. When a newly appointed Marxist local party secretary tried to call a halt to the return of land to pre-1967 owners like Tariq's own family, it was open season. Some of Tariq's Afghan Arab followers shot the official and tit-for-tat killings escalated. The Marxists got by far the worst of it, Tariq himself confirming their claim to have suffered 150 assassination attempts between 1990 and 1994. Tariq's activities, which could be construed as doing Sanaa's dirty work of terrorising the Marxists out of power, were instrumental in sending the country hurtling headlong towards the 1994 civil war. But the spiralling violence was all too easily dismissed as minor post-unification teething troubles and generally escaped the world's notice until late 1992, when two bombs exploded in Aden's luxury Movenpick and Goldmohur hotels, killing an Australian tourist and two Yemenis. The intended targets seemed to be not Marxists, for a change, but American soldiers briefly billeted at the hotels while in transit for tours of humanitarian aid duty in Somalia.

Tariq insisted to me that he did not instigate the bungled attacks, that indeed he had tried to prevent them because he believed that only Marxists – not the United States, which had kindly equipped the Afghan mujahideen with Stinger missiles and the like – were his real enemies. It is believed that bin Laden authorised what is now viewed as al-Qaeda's first attempted assault on US interests, but whether or not Tariq played a part in the incident, as the acknowledged leader of the Afghan War veterans he was blamed for it. Obligingly murdering Marxists was one thing, but planting bombs in hotels where Americans were staying quite another, as far as the regime in Sanaa was concerned, so Tariq fled inland, into the Maraqasha mountains that were part of Fadhli tribal land, to loyal tribesmen who performed their tribal duty to a fugitive by granting him their protection. There he withstood pressure to surrender to an entire brigade despatched to capture him, but at last agreed to face trial in Sanaa. In the northern capital, a fellow tribal leader, the powerful Sheikh Abdullah al-Ahmar of the Hashid Federation, accommodated Tariq at his home under a pleasant form of house arrest, while the trial was endlessly deferred. Whatever Tariq's involvement in the hotel bombings, the president clearly felt he owed him a debt of thanks for his unstinting campaign against the Marxists.

When Tariq returned to the south a couple of years later, during the civil war of 1994, it was as a man completely rehabilitated, as the proud commander of a Second Army Brigade composed of a mixture of Afghan War veterans and Fadhli tribesmen. As determined as President Salih, Brigadier-General Ali Muhsin al-Ahmar and Sheikh al-Ahmar* to see off the godless Marxists for good and all, he was delighted to be co-opted into the project of upholding Yemen's unity by ridding his homeland of them and helping to impose direct rule from Sanaa, thrilled to be taking Aden because it was something his Fadhli forebears had never managed to do while the British ruled it.

The civil war was regrettable and costly, and the veteran jihadists' revenge on the easy, beer-swilling ways of the Adenis chilling to witness, let alone experience, but some outsiders were impressed by the way President Salih seemed to be taming the Afghan War veterans by drawing them into mainstream Yemeni society. At a time when other Arab countries were closing their doors to home-coming Afghan War veterans, when Algeria, Jordan, Lebanon and Egypt were confronting their jihadists with violence and censorship that only inflamed the phenomenon and swelled their ranks with armies of recruits, a foreign eyewitness to Yemen's 1994 war and its aftermath was writing, 'Little Yemen may still serve as an important model of how Arab Islamists can cope with democratic principles and how tolerant they can be of secularists once in power.'[5] And Tariq al-Fadhli was the perfect poster-boy for this gently inclusive policy. The safe return of his family's land, a usefully generous stipend from Sanaa and a high military rank, a new

* The shared al-Ahmar name is a coincidence – the two men are not related.

Toyota Land Cruiser, membership of the president's ruling GPC party, a seat in the upper house of the Parliament and a blind eye turned to his maintenance of a twelve-man uniformed armed guard, seemed to cure him of all his jihadist fervour. The assumption in Sanaa was that with the Marxists brought to their knees and fleeing into exile at last, Tariq was just one of a majority of Afghan War veterans sensibly opting for an easy life.

At our first meeting in 2004 Tariq told me that although he greatly missed the freedom and excitement of jihad in Afghanistan – 'my wives won't let me go anywhere these days,' he joked – he had had no contact whatsoever with Osama bin Laden since 1995 and that he had never wanted anything to do with his old friend's attacks against the West. On the other hand he was no longer feeling nearly as closely allied to President Salih as he had been a decade earlier. The united Yemen he had fought to preserve in the civil war was proving such a terrible disappointment that he confessed he would love to see the British back in Aden – 'after lunch today, if possible!' When we met again three years later, his dissatisfaction with the status quo had intensified to judge by the gist of an old verse about snakes he recited for me: 'My allegiance is only to those who fill my hands with silver coins . . . We came to the voice of the Power, and we returned without any snakes even . . . And those who knew they already had their snakes clasped them closer . . .'

I gathered from this gnomic utterance that on top of his disgruntlement with the junior position of the old south in united Yemen, he was feeling the financial pinch – in short, that his annual stipend was no longer large enough to keep him on the side of 'the Power', that he was on the point of presenting himself as a snake's head the president would need to dance on. This revelation and the fact that he had turned his back on jihad just as soon as he had regained his family's land placed Tariq well within Yemeni tribal tradition. The imams, the Ottomans, the British, the Egyptians and the PDRY's Soviet backers had all had to recognise that what Yemeni tribesmen cared about most was money and land, not peace or religion or any ideology. Like the calming and extremely time-consuming Yemeni custom of chewing qat, these twin tribal priorities are sometimes cited as an important reason why the number of Yemenis actively engaged in jihad today is not a great deal larger than it is.

## THE ABU HAMZA CONNECTION

By the mid-2000s Tariq al-Fadhli was popularly viewed as the leader of Yemen's first generation of jihadists who, depending on one's point of view, had either grown up and opted for a peaceful life, or unforgivably sold out and betrayed the cause.

The country's second wave of jihadists were Afghan War veterans who did not follow Tariq's lead. They were men with little to gain or lose in the way of land or wealth, men who believed that having seen off the Soviet Satan in Afghanistan in 1988 and the Marxists in south Yemen in 1994, it was time to see off the West and any corrupt Muslim regimes too – in effect, to take on the world, as bin Laden was recommending. Some, like Nasir al-Bahri, for example, spent the 1990s fighting jihad wherever Muslims were under threat – in Bosnia, Somalia, Tajikistan, Chechnya – remaining close to bin Laden. Others parted company with him. In Yemen, many were led by an ex-Afghan Arab Yemeni known as Abu Hassan al-Mihdar, leader of the Aden-Abyan Islamic Army (AAIA), who had set up a training camp to the north-east of the Fadhli lands. The name of the movement had special resonance; a little-known *hadith* had prophesied that a mighty and victorious army of 12,000 faithful fighters for Allah would rise up out of the area comprising Aden and the territory of Abyan. To the extent that it thoroughly shared and publicly approved bin Laden's aims, the AAIA could be said to be 'al-Qaeda affiliated'.

One of the AAIA's priorities was to ensure that the Sanaa regime did not over-compensate for the costly mistake of not doing America's will in 1990 with regard to approving the invasion of Iraq by becoming too friendly with the United States. The western superpower was gravely offending Muslims everywhere at the time, not only by its solidly uncritical support for Israel but by its maintenance of a large military base in Saudi Arabia, the home of Islam's Holy Places. The AAIA would do its best to sabotage Salih's recent efforts to fill Yemen's empty coffers by granting the US's Persian fleet access to the shipping lanes in the Gulf of Aden and inviting her ships to refuel at Aden.

Simultaneous al-Qaeda attacks against US embassies in Kenya and Tanzania in early August 1998 should have served as a warning to the US navy to refuel elsewhere; it soon transpired that one of the bombers who survived the Kenyan attack had called a certain telephone number in Sanaa both before and after the operation. The number belonged to the head of al-Qaeda's Yemeni cell, yet another Afghan War veteran and friend of bin Laden's named Ahmad al-Hada.* No sooner had al-Hada received the calls from the al-Qaeda operative in Kenya than he had relayed the news to bin Laden in Afghanistan by a satellite telephone. Identification of that jihadist telephone exchange in Sanaa situated Yemen and Yemenis at the heart of the al-Qaeda enterprise for the first time. A biographer of al-Qaeda, Lawrence Wright, points out that the discovery enabled the FBI 'to map the links of the al-Qaeda network all across the globe'.[6]

Uninvolved in al-Qaeda's embassy bombings, the AAIA first drew world-wide attention to itself in December 1998 when it claimed responsibility for kidnapping sixteen westerners, most of them Britons, on an adventure holiday in Yemen. The AAIA was hoping to exchange its western hostages for six of its members whom the authorities had recently arrested for plotting to blow up the British consulate, a western hotel and the Anglican church in Aden. Tribal kidnappings of foreign tourists as a means of extracting funds from Sanaa – for a new well or school or road, jobs in the civil service, or a bigger stipend, or the release of prisoners – were one sure sign of how patchily the state institutions of the newly united Yemen were functioning, but they had

* Al-Hada's daughter was married to one of the future 9/11 hijackers.

also been an accepted modus operandi since at least the start of the 1990s. Confident of being treated as honoured guests and graciously entertained by their captors, growing numbers of tourists to Yemen had even begun to relish the idea of being kidnapped as a way of achieving an authentically Yemeni experience.

That all changed after December 1998. The AAIA men were not common or garden tribal kidnappers. Sanaa was belatedly waking up to the threat posed by the Afghan War veterans; a jihadist who had fought in both Afghanistan and Bosnia had recently murdered three Catholic nuns, two Indians and a Filipino who had been caring for elderly and handicapped Yemenis in Hodeidah. The kidnapping of the sixteen western tourists was not handled in the usual way. Instead of entering into negotiations with the kidnappers, Sanaa despatched a platoon of soldiers on a raid to rescue the hostages, but the operation did not go according to plan. In the ensuing skirmish four of the group were killed, three British and one Australian. Although the leader of the AAIA was swiftly arrested and executed, the group survived to be described by one US analyst in 2006 as 'one of the more resilient groups in the region'.[7] Yemen's fledgling tourist industry has still not recovered and Fadhli tribal land, much of the province of Abyan, is still considered especially jihad-friendly.

With three Britons among the dead, London was particularly interested in the bungled rescue and – like the US, after the African embassy bombings – gained from it a useful insight into the new anti-western ideology being propagated by Afghan War veterans. It soon emerged that a half-blinded, hook-handed Afghan War veteran who had spent some time in Yemen, an Egyptian preacher at north London's Finsbury Park mosque, had been closely involved in the faraway kidnapping. Abu Hamza al-Masri, as he was known, was not only in the habit of recruiting for the AAIA in London but had spoken to its leader on a satellite telephone he had bought for him and equipped with £500 of air-time both before and immediately after the kidnapping. More incriminating still, one of the six prisoners whose release the AAIA kidnappers had been demanding turned out to be Abu Hamza's stepson and another his son.* Abu Hamza was arrested and jailed under Britain's new anti-terrorism laws, but President Salih was soon requesting that he be extradited to Yemen for a string of other long-distance misdemeanours, including plotting to blow up a Yemeni and his donkey by having a bomb placed under the animal's saddle. However, Britain held onto him until 2004 when, armed with evidence that he had planned to set up a jihadists' training camp in Oregon, the US labelled him 'a terrorist facilitator with a global reach'[8] and demanded his extradition there instead. The request was granted in 2008, to come into force as soon as Hamza has finished his British prison sentence. Meanwhile he is reportedly still preaching jihad to his fellow Muslims via pipes connecting the cells in his Belmarsh prison.[9]

The tragic episode gave Britain an unpleasant taste of how difficult it was to do business with Yemen, to identify those with responsibility and sift the salient from the meaningless. What were Scotland Yard and the Foreign Office to make of a credible report from one of the kidnapped Yemeni drivers that the chief jihadist kidnapper had used the satellite telephone Abu Hamza had given him to make direct and personal contact with the second most powerful person in the land, old Sultan Nasir al-Fadhli's son-in-law and Tariq's brother-in-law, the promoter of jihad in Afghanistan, Brigadier-General Ali Muhsin al-Ahmar?

## WHOSE SIDE IS WHO ON?

The death of the four western tourists rattled and embarasssed the virtuoso dancer on snakes' heads, but it did not cause Salih to lose his footing. A few renegade Afghan War veterans with little but bloodshed,

* Abu Hamza's son, Mohamed Kemal Mostafa, served three years in an Aden prison before returning to Britain, where he worked for London Underground until 2006 when his foreign criminal record as a would-be terrorist was uncovered. In mid-2009, he and two brothers were convicted of stealing a million pounds' worth of luxury cars.

vengeance against the West and Paradise on their minds were far from being the liveliest or biggest snake he had to contend with in the late 1990s. In the space of six months, between June and December 1998, the guns and bombs of disgruntled tribesmen in the north-eastern oil-producing Marib region of central Yemen had blown nineteen holes in an oil pipeline Yemen was dependent on for 40 per cent of her revenue.[10]

Helping to explain why the jihadi threat was very far from the top of any Yemeni agenda was the fact that Yemen's security service, the Political Security Office (PSO), was itself a bastion of anti-western, tending towards pro-jihadist feeling, staffed as it was in large part by retired Afghan War veterans who had transferred their anti-Soviet feelings onto the West and Iraqi-trained army officers whose hostility towards the West had been fuelled by the humiliation of the first Gulf War. It was only to be expected that such people would at best play down or ignore, at worst aid and abet jihadist activities. So it came about that bin Laden's Egyptian second-in-command, Ayman al-Zawahiri, was permitted to come and hold meetings in a public hall in Sanaa, and that al-Qaeda's best counterfeiter was free to run classes in forging documents. Egyptian intelligence officers, determined to root out the jihadism that was threatening their tourist trade and Hosni Mubarak's regime, found their Yemeni counterparts extremely tricky to do business with: 'There were always problems,' one told the *Wall Street Journal*, because 'they [Yemenis] shared the same values of the people they were supposed to be arresting.'[11]

This was no exaggeration. An in-depth *Wall Street Journal* investigation revealed that early in 1998, before either the African embassy bombings or the AAIA's kidnapping of the western tourists of the same year, an Egyptian Afghan War veteran who had tired of jihad, or was desperately short of cash, visited the PSO headquarters in Sanaa to offer what any western intelligence agency and many Arab ones would have given millions of dollars and their right arms for: solid, detailed intelligence about the whereabouts, capacity and future plans of al-Qaeda and its affiliates. He divulged that Ayman al-Zawahiri was then in Yemen's southern highland city of Taiz, rather than in Afghanistan, and he offered to go and spy on the AAIA down in Abyan. But, instead of thanking him for his help and putting him to work, the PSO immediately contacted jihadist friends to warn them of a traitor in their midst. It was decided that the turncoat must be punished by swift deportation to Afghanistan where he would be murdered. Fortunately for him, he managed to escape to Egypt instead.

In 2000 – the year in which bin Laden sent Nasir al-Bahri to Ibb in Yemen's southern highlands to collect a new young bride and Yemeni members of his organisation tried but failed (because heavy explosives sunk the fibreglass boat they were being transported on) to blow up the USS *Sullivans* in Aden – Italian counter-terrorism agents had an astounding success. They tapped snatches of a bizarre telephone conversation between a Yemeni PSO officer (who was also a tribal sheikh and a businessman) and al-Qaeda's best forger in Sanaa.

Forger: How is the family?
PSO officer: What family? I spend all my time with the mujahedeen brothers?

. . .

Forger: Are you talking about a jihad operation?
PSO officer: Remember this well. In the future, listen to the news and remember well the words 'above your head'. Listen to the people who are bringing news.

. . .

PSO officer: This is a terrifying thing . . . It is a thing that will drive you mad. Whoever has come up with this program is mad as a maniac. He must be a mad man but he is a genius. He is fixed on this program. He will turn everyone to ice.
Forger: God is great and Muhammad is his prophet. They're sons of bitches.

. . .

PSO officer: The danger in airports.
Forger: Rain, rain.
PSO officer: Ah yes, there are really big clouds in the sky in international territory. In that state the fire is already lit and is just waiting for the wind.[12]

Understandably, the Italians decided these runic pronouncements were too vague to be immediately useful, but, fresh from his tenth anniversary of unification celebrations, Salih was about to be forced into a recognition of the fact that his Afghan War veterans were a clear and present danger. Mid-morning on 12 October 2000, a little fibre-glass motorboat loaded with 500lb of explosives drew alongside a gigantic billion-dollar American warship that was refuelling in Aden harbour and blasted a 32 by 36-foot-wide hole in its side, killing seventeen American sailors.

As a David versus Goliath *coup de théâtre* the attack on the USS *Cole* made spectacularly good propaganda, better even than the Afghan War veterans' much-boasted defeat of the Soviet Union. New converts flocked to bin Laden's global jihad, especially Yemenis, who took a natural awed pride in seeing their obscure and impoverished homeland capture the world's headlines for the first time since the British pull-out from Aden almost forty years earlier. The former deputy chief of bin Laden's bodyguards, Nasir al-Bahri, insisted to London's *al-Quds al-Arabi* four years later that al-Qaeda was an overwhelmingly Yemeni organisation:

> It can be said that the majority of al-Qaeda members are Yemenis. This is a fact no one can deny. The leader of al-Qaeda is of Yemeni origin. His bodyguards are Yemenis. The trainers in the camps are Yemenis. The commanders at the fronts are Yemenis. All the operations that were directed against the United States

> were coordinated with Yemeni members. Yemenis are spread all over al-Qaeda[13] –

He was overstating the case, but it is fair to say that Yemenis were furnishing the movement with most of its muscle and much of its popular support at this time. Al-Bahri did confirm to me that Yemenis and Saudis outnumbered all other nationalities in the movement in that pre-9/11 period. In terms of authority and influence within the organisation, however, they were outdone by the Egyptians who tended to be older and to have more and longer experience of clandestine political activity. Tensions among bin Laden's followers normally involved Eygptians and Yemenis. According to al-Bahri, Yemenis nicknamed the Egyptians 'pharoahs' on account of their patronising, haughty manner and boasted about how during the civil war in Yemen in the 1960s they had cut off 40,000 Egyptian noses and how happy they would be to cut off the rest them now in Afghanistan. The Egyptians meanwhile resented the Yemenis' vigour but lack of intellectual rigour, nicknaming them 'dervishes'. At this stage, each operational section of al-Qaeda seems to have been headed by an experienced Egyptian, assisted by a Yemeni deputy. 'Before 9/11 changed everything,' al-Bahri told me, 'it looked as if bin Laden was slowly easing the Egyptians out and replacing them with Yemenis everywhere.'

Whatever the Americans' strong suspicions, al-Qaeda's responsibility for the attack on the USS *Cole* was impossible to prove immediately. President Salih seemed more reluctant than anyone else to recognise the fact that a home-grown terrorist problem looked set to ruin Yemen's tentative rapprochement with the US and spoil Aden's slowly reviving reputation as a safe refuelling port. In a telephone conversation with Secretary of State Madeleine Albright Salih blustered that the attack on the *Cole* seemed to have been an accident, 'not a deliberate act'.[14] Within a couple of days an FBI team of sixty, led by John O'Neill, a man who had no doubt whatsoever that al-Qaeda was behind the incident, arrived in Aden to investigate, but President Salih was still in denial, wildly surmising to a *Newsweek* reporter that Israel might have been responsible.[15] One senior Yemeni official, perhaps recalling the devious manner in which Britain had taken possession of Aden in 1839, even opined to Egypt's *Al-Ahram al-Arabi* that the United States had blown up its own warship, as a pretext to capture Aden.[16]

In spite of some hindrance from Yemeni officials who naturally resented the sudden invasion of US policemen, with their bullying hurry and flash talk of technological miracles like DNA, despite almost as much resistance from Barbara Bodine, the American ambassador to Sanaa, who resented clumsy New York policemen ruining the US's delicately nurtured new relations with Yemen, it took the FBI team just a month to establish al-Qaeda's responsibility for the attack. They managed to link one of its masterminds – a Saudi-Yemeni named Walid Mohammad bin Attash but known as 'Khalid', an Afghan War veteran who had lost a part of one leg in Afghanistan and wore a metal prosthesis – to bin Laden.

Much later it would transpire that yet another Afghan War veteran and Saudi-born Yemeni named Abdel Rahim al-Nashiri, who had been working on the plans for a year and a half, training the local team and calibrating the bomb to inflict maximum damage, had escaped north, to the southern highland city of Taiz after the attack and received high-level protection from arrest there. In early 2002 al-Nashiri was seen out and about in Sanaa with the deputy director of the PSO,[17] and went on to plan an attack against a French oil tanker, the *Limburg*, near the Hadhramaut port of Mukalla in October that year.[18] It also transpired that prior to the attack on the *Cole*, al-Nashiri had been provided by no less a person than Yemen's interior minister with an invaluable laissez-passer saying, 'All security forces are instructed to co-operate with him and facilitate his mission.'[19] In addition, the FBI managed to extract a useful confession from another conspirator, in spite of the fact that he was protected by the PSO colonel who had demonstratively kissed him on both cheeks before the interview began.[20] Later still it was discovered that 'Khalid' and Ramzi bin al-Shibh,* a former Sanaa bank clerk with a German passport who later planned the 9/11 hijackings, had discussed the USS *Cole* operation at an al-Qaeda summit meeting in Kuala Lumpur a few months earlier.

By the end of 2000, when President Bill Clinton was preparing to vacate the White House, the average American knew more about Yemen than he or she had ever wanted to and President Ali Abdullah Salih had accepted two glaringly obvious truths: first, that his country was home to members of a global jihadist movement with access to enough funding and know-how to wreak serious damage on Yemeni as well as western interests, and second, that his PSO was unfit for the purpose of combating the nuisance.

However, unlike the new American president, George W. Bush, Salih was neither temperamentally inclined nor sufficiently powerful to confront the jihadists head on by declaring all-out war on them. Dancing on the heads of snakes rather than setting out to destroy the reptiles had always been more his style. Knowledge of the climate of opinion inside his PSO but also chats over qat with jihadist sympathisers like Brigadier-General Ali Muhsin al-Ahmar and the cleric Sheikh Abdul Majid al-Zindani, for example, would also have discouraged him from taking direct action. And then he had to consider the tribes whose custom it was to offer shelter to outlaws and whose cold appetite for cash he knew well. Furthermore, the jihadists' David-like determination to take on a Goliath West whose soldiers had been trampling the Muslim Holy Land since the First Gulf War, whose planes were still enforcing a no-fly zone over Iraq and whose dollars were still bankrolling Israel's occupation of Palestinian land, played far too well with far too many Yemenis at all levels of society for him even to contemplate a wholesale military crackdown. Anyway, how could one begin to police the contents of peoples' minds and hearts?

* Ramzi bin al-Shibh is the highest-value Yemeni prisoner at Guantanamo, charged with planning the 9/11 attacks.

In order to avoid Yemen becoming an international pariah again as it had been on the eve of the first Gulf War, in order to remove any risk of invasion by the US and instead access a few million dollars' worth of military equipment and surveillance technology, Salih had to convince America's new Republican president that he was willing and able to slay the jihadism snake, although that had never been and could never be his modus operandi. In effect, President George W. Bush was one more snake-head he was having to learn to dance on.

## CHAPTER SIX

# A TRIBAL DISORDER?

### INTO THE DESERT

Like most Yemeni offices, it was mysteriously, worryingly bare of papers and computers and empty of staff, but I had no choice except to hope and trust. Whatever this enterprise was, its boss, Mohammed Salih Muhsin, represented my best chance of visiting Yemen's central Marib desert, home to oil fields and famously restive tribes, and haven of fugitive jihadists. To my great relief, he arrived at precisely the time he had promised he would, with a fashionable mobile phone in one hand, some prayer beads in the other and no qat cud swelling his cheek.

The absence of that cud was an important clue, but there were others to alert me to the fact that I was meeting no ordinary Yemeni. Bearded, beatifically smiling but avoiding both my eye and the physical contact of a handshake, Muhsin was the Muslim equivalent of a born-again Christian. He was a person who believed he was practising his faith in a manner resembling as closely as possible that of the Prophet and his companions; technically speaking therefore he was a

Salafist. But there were at least two varieties of Salafist. If I was lucky he was not the al-Qaeda jihadist sort like Osama bin Laden but the more common and moderate variety. I surprised myself hoping he confined himself to restricting his womenfolk's freedom while waging harmless spiritual jihad against himself and refraining from politics rather than believing it his bounden Muslim duty to wage lethal violent jihad against the West and all her Muslim allies. On the simple grounds that he seemed to bear me no obvious grudge, I decided I was safe.

After graciously reiterating his willingness to be of assistance, he divulged a few facts. As the owner of a company involved in transporting supplies to Marib's oil fields, he was indeed in a position to procure me the requisite *tasrih* permit from the interior ministry without which I could not travel in a region renowned for its instability and frequent kidnappings. Better still, he could pass me off as a guest of one of the oil companies and, best of all, he would arrange for his nephew Ibrahim to show me around. When I enquired about payment for all these kind and valuable services, he smiled and raised a languid hand. I understood that we would not debase our new friendship with squalid money talk until I returned to Sanaa, satisfied.

Two days later, my taciturn northern highlander tribesman driver Walid and I drove east out of Sanaa in the direction of Marib with twenty photocopies of the requisite *tasrih* safely stowed in his Land Cruiser's glove compartment, one for every checkpoint we were likely to encounter. While we idled in the capital's chaotic rush-hour traffic, tut-tutting about the primary-school-age children dodging dangerously between the lines of cars to hawk their boxes of tissues, bottles of water and newspapers, Walid observed that although he bore no personal grudge against our friend Mohammed Salih Muhsin, he himself had no time for Salafism of any kind. A Salafist neighbour of his had paid for his puritanical zeal with his life when another neighbour had hurled a great lump of cement at him, he told me with quiet satisfaction, before adding that he had expressly forbidden his teenage son to loiter around the mosque after Friday prayers when such notions were easily picked up.

Taking advantage of Walid's rare talkativeness, I moved our conversation on to another 'ism'– tribalism. Although handsomely dressed from head to toe as a tribesman, Walid surprised me by declaring that he had about as little patience with tribalism as he did with Salafism. When I questioned him about his own highland Khawlani tribe, through whose land a part of our route to Marib lay, he insisted that it meant nothing to him, that there was no point in visiting his village because there was nothing to see, that he had no contact with his sheikh, a businessman who spent most of his time in Sanaa. A few months spent working as a driver for the team of Americans investigating al-Qaeda's attack on the USS *Cole* had – thanks be to God! – left him rich enough to build his large family of seven daughters and only son a home in Sanaa, where the power of the tribe was greatly reduced, he explained. Thank God he could think and act for himself, without the help of any sheikh. 'What are sheikhs good for?' he demanded of me, one hand on the steering wheel and the other resting lightly on the hilt of his *jambiyah*, before embarking on a long tale aimed at proving to me that only greedy sheikhs profited from lethal tribal feuds.

In about 1980 a member of Walid's northern highland tribe who lived about a mile from his village, a young man recently returned, wealthy and self-confident, from working in Saudi Arabia, took a fancy to a shepherdess from a neighbouring tribe who lived five miles away. Soon the pair – he with a group of his young men friends, she with a group of her girlfriends – were regularly meeting up to picnic in the mountains, greatly enjoying themselves out of sight of their elders. Inevitably, a male of the shepherdess's tribe got wind of these delightful goings on but decided that the whole business was altogether too dishonouring, too shameful – *ayb* (shame, dishonour, disgrace) is a key tribal word – to tackle head on. But tribal custom law, *urf*, dictated that some form of revenge had to be taken. Hostilities were duly opened by way of a minor provocation; a sheep belonging to the shepherdess's tribe was slaughtered and Walid's kinsman blamed for killing it. Unfortunately, even this expedient escalated alarmingly into a land dispute, the most serious of all kinds of dispute, in which the sheikhs of both tribes became involved, at great expense to both communities. Every year for a decade, Walid told me, the two tribes would go to war for two or three days. He himself had fought in two of those mini campaigns. 'We used to climb into the mountains at night, about a hundred of us, wearing camouflage, and just bang away at anything that moved. For all I know the dispute's still unresolved,' he said, 'and the sheikhs still profiting by mediating, although I do know for a fact that the man involved is dead and the shepherdess long married.'

Yemen would be much better off without her tribes, he told me, before changing the subject to gloomily forecast that we would be lucky to clear the first checkpoint on the edge of town without acquiring the tiresome encumbrance of an armed police escort, and he was right. After an hour or so idling at the checkpoint, we learned we would be sharing such an escort with a group of elderly Taiwanese tourists who were headed to Marib too, to view the meagre vestiges of an engineering wonder of the ancient world, the eighth-century BC Marib Dam. As soon as a blue and white Toyota pick-up complete with a posse of police and a mounted heavy machine gun appeared, we were all on our way again. Under a clear blue winter sky, only our strange caravan and the odd stray donkey moved. In that craggily lunar landscape coloured a uniformly Martian russet, nothing grew. It seemed to me that a hardiness honed by a determination to survive in this, the land their forefathers had inhabited, coupled with an imperative drive to avail themselves of the resources to be found in the kinder southern highlands and Tihama coast, were the keys to the Zaydi highlanders' centuries-old supremacy in this corner of south Arabia.

The descent from the mountains to the Marib desert was sudden enough to set my ears popping. We were both hungry and Walid almost visibly twitching for his daily qat by the time we arrived in the town of Marib, the province's capital. The place where we had arranged to meet Mohammed Salih Muhsin's young nephew, Ibrahim, was not so much a restaurant as a canteen – a large, strip-lit room with white bathroom-tiled walls and ceiling fans where serving boys who looked no more than ten hurled burning hot flat-breads and battered tin plates of bean stew onto Formica-top tables that were littered with newspaper and pestered by flies. Men, only men, gestured angrily at them, barking their orders above the already deafening background roar of the furnace oven.

A personable young man with a gentle smile – emphatically not a stony-faced northern highlander like Walid – dressed in a dazzling white *thowb*, embroidered belt and *jambiyah*, Ibrahim lowered his gaze like his uncle and proffered only his wrist on greeting me, but the English he had learned at a college in southern India was good and his demeanour towards me otherwise relaxed and perfectly friendly. Although in full-time employment with America's fourth-largest oil company, Oxy, which had taken a large bloc straddling the old border between the two Yemens, he confirmed he was free to assist me because he had just completed a run of night shifts so, while Walid drove off in search of the town's qat market, we drank glasses of sweet black tea and tried to converse.

'I'm wondering how people around here feel at the prospect of the oil running out – by 2017 or so, isn't it?' I shouted above the deafening roar of the oven. The question was a stupid one. It was hard to imagine how much poorer, rougher and simpler the locals' lives could be than they already were. The smells and the dust alone in that place would immediately have informed a blind, deaf and dumb person that the dream of oil wealth on a Saudi scale had never been and now would never be realised.

'No one's worried about that,' Ibrahim answered. 'They're thinking about the present. People say they wish no one had ever started pumping the stuff – far better that it stay underground than that it be exploited and the proceeds end up in the wrong pockets.' We spoke about where the oil money had gone, about Hadda, the Beverley Hills of Sanaa, about the gigantic new mosque President Salih had spent the past decade funding and building at a reported cost of $115 million but a suspected cost of $1.5 billion, and about the further billions being spent on Russian MiG fighters. Returning to the matter in hand, he suggested we visit a Bedouin friend of his who had worked as a foreman for the first American oil company to venture into Yemen in 1981, Hunt Oil Inc. from Texas. But, he explained, on our way out of town we would have to stop by the shop where he had left his AK47. 'They made a rule about six months ago; we're not allowed to carry our guns into the capital town of any province any more. So now we have a choice; either we can risk leaving them at a checkpoint or we can pay a shopkeeper to look after them.'

I wondered why he had not economised on both time and money by leaving it at home. As far as I knew, the more educated and urbanised Yemeni male was usually content to travel without a weapon but, equally, sure to own at least one. A member of the northern highland Abu Luhum tribe, an employee of the ministry of education, had recently informed me that any man who carried a gun advertised the fact that he was primitive, before admitting that he himself had five guns, one of them with telescopic night sights, which he had arranged neatly, in order of size, along his bedroom wall. Ibrahim told me that he had been given his first gun at the age of fifteen.There were plenty of tales of the lower floors of rural sheikhs' residences serving as mini-arsenals, stocked with not only rifles and ammunition but with rocket-propelled grenades, and even heavier weapons. There was no way of ascertaining the truth, but it was often said that there were three times as many guns as people in Yemen.

An insatiable appetite for firearms among tribesmen, first and foremost as a mark of both virility and wealth on a par with the *jambiyah*, dates back at least as far as the arrival of the British in Aden. Reinforced by both the British and the Ottoman habit of buying the tribes' loyalty with gifts of weapons, the appetite continued to rage in the post-colonial era. Although ranged on opposite sides of the Cold War divide, both the YAR and the PDRY had been ravenously hungry for Soviet armaments with which to threaten each other. An attempt to clamp down on the thriving arms trade, to close Yemen's handful of large arms bazaars and conduct a buy-back programme funded by America since 9/11, has not succeeded in stifling the old appetite. The domestic trade has become more furtive in Sanaa, for example, but it has continued and acquired an international dimension. As early as 2003, a United Nations report cited Yemen as the chief supplier of weapons to the more unstable areas of East Africa – Somalia, for example.[1] Many of the weapons and explosives used in regional al-Qaeda attacks have been traced back to Yemen; the missiles used to fire at the Israeli plane leaving Mombasa in late 2002 were acquired from Yemen via Somalia, and firearms used in the early 2005 attack on the American consulate in Jeddah were discovered to have Yemen defence-ministry markings.

Ibrahim patiently explained that, unfortunately, we were obliged to take his weapon with us if we were travelling out into the desert. No foreigner – certainly not an American or British person – was permitted to leave town without an armed escort. I was surprised but pleased to discover that somehow, in this case, he qualified as my armed escort. As soon as Walid returned, with an unusually large bouquet of quality qat twigs wrapped in pink cellophane, we set off past the town's gun market, a parade of about twenty tatty wooden booths where firearms that had cost only $150 five years earlier were now retailing for around $750 owing to a recent crackdown on arms smuggling across the long and hardly demarcated Empty Quarter border with Saudi Arabia. After retrieving Ibrahim's gun, we headed out of town on a good new asphalt road. Soon, our way lay over sand so we stopped to deflate the Land Cruiser tyres before making for the distant speck of a Bedouin camp.

Ibrahim's Bedouin friend received us graciously in a large central tent spread with carpets and scattered with bolsters. A dozen or so children – the youngest of eighteen, by two wives – scampered about with thermoses of tea for us, while our host remembered his American friends from Hunt Oil Inc. – David, Dick and Bill and Ron, the Englishman – and how satisfied he had been with their treatment of him and his payment, and how all that had changed as early as 1985. In the year before Vice-President George H. Bush had obliged his Texan friend and sponsor, Ray L. Hunt, by travelling all the way to Sanaa and on, east into the Marib desert to open Yemen's first oil field, 'more powerful people – people from Sanaa' had begun 'arranging jobs for their family and friends', which had angered the region's tribes. He went on to explain that things got worse, that foreign companies soon found they could only get permission to work in Yemen if they had the protection of one of the big sheikhs in Sanaa, who might have nothing to do with any of the local tribes.

'He's right,' interjected Ibrahim. 'Oxy, for example, is protected by Sadeq al-Ahmar, one of Sheikh Abdullah al-Ahmar's sons. . .'

'Those big sheikhs take a big percentage for themselves as a kind of commission for acting as the local agent,' Mohammed continued, 'which means they behave as if they have the right to rent out the land to the oil companies when, of course, it doesn't belong to them at all. The only benefit any of us locals see from our oil is the light we get from the oil flares!'

Kidnappings of both foreigners and Yemenis and attacks on pipelines and oil company personnel by heavily armed tribesmen intent on extracting from the government what they see as at least their just deserts – a clinic, a school, a well, jobs, a road or legal redress – have long been drawing unwelcome attention to the fact that the writ of the state does not often extend here. Both before and after 9/11, Yemen's al-Qaeda jihadists were less of a headache and a threat to the state than tribal disturbances in those desert wastes of Marib-Shabwa, in what is effectively – given that oil accounts for more than 70 per cent of the country's revenues – an important engine room of Yemen's economy.

## TRIBES VERSUS STATE

From a military outpost, high on a hill overlooking the mile-and-a-half-wide Wadi Harib that once marked the frontier between the YAR and the PDRY, a soldier was keeping a close watch over the Jannah-Hunt works which are all that remain of the pioneering Hunt Oil Inc. venture in Yemen. His tiny distant *futa*-clad figure, waving a gun in our direction, was enough to dissuade me from taking more photographs.

Instead, we glided on across the ocean of sand towards what Ibrahim called the 'Ukrainian camp', a gated settlement of mobile homes occupied by a Ukrainian firm named Vikoil that had been subcontracted by a British oil firm named Burren to carry out a preliminary seismic survey. While Walid purchased a little pink plastic bag of qat from a pair of salesmen in a black Fiat Panda who told him they made their living by journeying out to the oil fields every day with fresh supplies of the staple stimulant, I went inside the compound to speak to a Burren employee who had appeared at the door of one of the Portacabins. Over a cup of instant coffee, while a group of sullen-looking Yemeni workers sat chatting in a circle outside, I learned that Burren had mistakenly hired the cheapest rather than the most experienced team of seismic surveyors. Corner-cutting newcomers in a competitive field led by the Chinese and the French, the Ukrainians had not troubled to take local conditions into consideration. They had not held meetings with the tribes, let alone offered them tangible benefits, and so soon landed not just themselves but the soldiers deployed by the state to protect them, as well as local tribesmen, in very serious trouble.

Tensions over insufficient job opportunities with the Ukrainians added to the tribesmen's resentment at the interloping military's monopoly on protecting the foreigners had escalated alarmingly in November 2007. Early one morning, a few Ukrainians and a military escort sallied out of the camp to survey an oil line, only to find their path blocked by armed men of the Balharith tribe. Even as the sheikh and colonel parleyed, a tribesman sharpshooter stationed some distance away shot out the colonel's eye. That at least was the story the Ukrainians told about an incident that had rapidly developed into a pitched battle costing the lives of ten soldiers and six tribesmen. But Ibrahim, a member of the Balharith tribe himself, knew a different version. According to him, the blinded colonel had been asking for trouble having opened hostilities a few days earlier by kicking over the wheelchair of a disabled tribesman who had arrived at the camp with his son to ask if the Ukrainians could find work for his bulldozer. Both my British informant and Ibrahim agreed, however, that six weeks later the government had calmed the situation sufficiently to allow the Ukrainians to return to the camp, mainly by addressing the tribesmen's demands for work and distributing large sums of money. Ibrahim had heard that three million riyals of compensation had been received by the family of every dead tribesman – 'of course, the tribe only accepted that tiny sum because they'd already had their revenge by killing ten soldiers,' he added.

Whatever the precise truth of the tale, it amply illustrated one of Yemen's most serious shortcomings as a state capable of making a useful contribution to any 'War on Terror', to say nothing of providing an attractively secure environment for foreign investment. For the past half century, since the demise of the imamate and the proclamation of the republic in 1962, none of Yemen's leaders had faced up to the fact that tribal custom law – *urf*, in Arabic – which governed the lives of a sizeable and well-armed sector of Yemen's population, competed and sometimes clashed with Yemen's badly malfunctioning legal system. The mismatch and ambiguities frequently led to violence and bloodshed.

After thirty years in power, there could be no doubting Salih's gift for balancing forces, for dividing and ruling, for co-opting, charming, reconciling, bribing and so on, but wherever I went in Yemen I was treated to tales of violent confrontations between the state and the tribes. Just as in Ottoman times, some sheikhs are still known to wildly exceed their authority by ruling their territories as petty autocrats. A few miles from the bustling southern highland city of Ibb, the cruel tyranny of a sheikh who was also a member of the upper house of Yemen's parliament and one of Yemen's best poets, was making lurid headlines in early 2008. Accounts of Mohammed Ahmed al-Mansour's arbitrary confiscations of houses and livestock and extortionate taxes paled into insignificance beside tales of medieval tortures that members of his community had suffered in his private prison, at the hands of his personal militia. One victim complained he had been chained up, doused in cold water, denied any bedding or food and drink, terrorised by a snake and forced to eat a raw rabbit. Another had had his fingernails pulled out.[2]

But the tribes were certainly not always to blame. Tariq al-Fadhli had told me that his fortress home on the roundabout had been suddenly attacked by government forces in May 2004, all the glass in his windows shattered by their shooting and two of his private guards and a woman of his household injured before he discovered he was being punished for mediating in the generally accepted sheikhly manner in the case of a locally disputed water-pump. Only by putting in a direct call to President Salih had he managed to halt the assault. In due course and in accordance with tribal custom, he had been compensated for his injuries with five rifles.

As a Yemeni tribesman, albeit one who had spent much of his life in Saudi Arabia and Afghanistan, Tariq would have been familiar with the carefully calibrated system of compensation that often took the form of a certain number of guns or a slaughtered bull, but not all Yemenis and certainly not a prominent Adeni like the elderly proprietor of Aden's *Al-Ayyam* newspaper, Hisham Basharaheel, would either know or respect such customs.

In March 2008 I was invited to a qat chew at Basharaheel's Sanaa residence. An impressive multi-storey edifice shielded from the bustle of the noisy street behind high walls and a stout metal gate, it was surprisingly unfurnished inside, very poorly lit and teeming with armed men wearing bandoliers of bullets. I soon discovered why it looked and felt like a fortress under siege. My host had been on the point of selling up and moving back home to Aden when his ownership of the land on which the house was built was disputed by a family who aggressively daubed their counter-claim on his exterior wall. Undaunted, convinced all his paperwork was in order, Basharaheel had gone on looking for a buyer for his property and left his son and an armed guard in charge of defending it. But the rival claimants had not backed off and, one evening, in an exchange of gunfire outside the gate, one of them – a teenage boy – had been killed. Basharaheel's guard was already languishing in jail, charged with firing the fatal shot, but the dead boy's tribe was claiming that Basharaheel's son, sniping from an upstairs window, had been responsible and must be punished instead of the guard, with immediate incarceration and even execution. Old Basharaheeel had hurriedly fortified his home with more armed guards. He told me that neither he nor any of his family – certainly not his son – had left the place for weeks.

Leaving this embattled qat chew I had gone straight to a meeting with one of the president's advisers, an American-educated businessman named Faris al-Sanabani who happened to be in a position to brief me further on the saga. A tribesman himself, Faris explained that the tribal code of honour required Basharaheel to make an immediate and proper show of remorse for the boy's death by offering at least twenty rifles to his family in compensation. Although he cared little for tribal customs, Basharaheel had duly set about collecting the twenty rifles, but to no avail. The offering had not proved acceptable, which meant there could be no compromise, which meant that no less a person than the president himself had been forced to intervene. Al-Sanabani informed me that Salih had spent all that afternoon parleying with the elders of the dead boy's tribe, charming them with his detailed knowledge of and respect for their tribal genealogy, gently trying to persuade them to withdraw their demand – however correct from the tribal point of view – that Basharaheel's son be imprisoned.

On that occasion the president sided with the non-tribesman Basharaheel for the simple reason that he did not want the old man and his son being hailed as persecuted martyrs of the growing secessionist movement in the south of the country, which the family's newspaper was supporting. On another famous occasion he came down on the side of tribal law. Just before the outbreak of the war against the south in 1994, one of Salih's closest allies, a powerful northern highland sheikh, admitted that he had taken it upon himself to arrange the assassination of a deputy prime minister, Hassan Makki, to punish him for being too ready to compromise with the southern Marxists. After the war, the sheikh was permitted to make full and final amends for the assassination attempt that had killed Makki's driver and two bodyguards by simply slaughtering a bull outside Makki's house.[3]

Far from discouraging tribalism and promoting the rule of secular law, President Salih has generally encouraged the old ways, not just in the former YAR but in the former PDRY since 1990. Tariq al-Fadhli's smooth transition from jihadist to establishment sheikh was a good illustration. In the president's view tribes are a *sine qua non* for Yemen. His reply to a question put to him by *Al-Majallah* newspaper back in October 1986 about how far Yemen had moved away from the tribal system towards a modern state was as follows: 'The state is part of the tribes and the Yemeni people are an ensemble of tribes. Our urban and rural areas all consist of tribes. All the official and popular state institutions are made up of the *qaba'il* [tribes/tribespeople].'[4]

To overlook the fact that large sections of Yemen's population – people of the Tihama and Hadhramaut and even the southern highland towns of Taiz and Ibb, let alone Adenis and Sanaanis – would not describe themselves as tribespeople suggests a wilful ignorance of his own people. It seems possible that the question confused him; perhaps, to his way of thinking, tribal and state systems could not be compared in the first place, the tribes being a natural phenomenon and the state systems man-made ones. Which was better? A tree or a house? A mountain or an aeroplane? The world view behind Salih's refusal to regard tribalism as a man-made political system like any other resurfaced in a statement made by the paramount sheikh of the Hashid

Federation, Sheikh Abdullah al-Ahmar, in May 2000. 'The *qabilah* [tribe] is the foundation of our Arab society and to deny the *qabilah* is to deny our authenticity and our ancestors. It is the foundation and it is natural. And God says, "We have created for you nations and tribes so that they would know each other." So why do we approve of one part of the verse and try to omit the second part, and why do we say this nation and that nation but not this tribe and that tribe? God clearly says, "we created you nations and tribes".'[5]

There was still no acknowledgement of the manner in which tribalism could inhibit the development of state institutions and compromise national security. Evidence piled on evidence – the killing of soldiers by tribesmen defending their ancestral land, the jeopardising of the work of foreign companies involved in oil extraction, the freelancing vigilantism of the tribes and examples of them sheltering wanted jihadists according to the rules of tribal code of hospitality or for simple mercenary gain – had yet to drive home that lesson. Sarah Phillips, an acute Australian observer of Yemen's political scene, has defined the relationship between the Yemeni state and the tribes as 'often contradictory, with each at times increasing and at times diminishing the other's power, but both reinforcing traits in the other that provide considerable obstacles to state-building'.[6] Unregulated, ad hoc, highly personalised and utterly opaque would be other ways of describing the manner in which the competing authorities of the state and tribes are constantly being challenged, tested and renegotiated. The steps of the president's dance on the heads of his snakes are never routine and the dance never ends. The state as embodied by Salih and the tribes as represented by their sheikhs are willing partners in this endless dance. It suits them both well because it is what they both know best.

## REVENGE OF THE PREDATOR

I wondered if the tribal law governing the sheltering of an outlaw with no questions asked for at least three days meant that even an educated young tribesman like Ibrahim, a person employed by a western company, would feel bound by tribal custom to shelter a person branded 'a terrorist' by Yemen's western allies – bin Laden, for example?

'What do you think of Osama bin Laden, Ibrahim?' I asked him as we bounced on south across the sand into the former PDRY, in the direction of his family home where we were to spend the night.

'Do you want the truth?' he said, eagerly leaning forward from the back seat.

'Yes, of course,' I replied.

'Osama bin Laden's a hero, I think,' said Ibrahim, cautiously adding that he was sure the need for global jihad would evaporate if only America could bring itself to be more even-handed in the treatment of the Israel–Palestine question.

'Do you thnk there's any chance that he's hiding in Yemen?' I asked, and received an answer that confirmed my belief that, if history was anything to go by, Yemeni tribesmen's overriding interests were money and land, not any ideology about a restored Caliphate.

'No,' said Ibrahim, 'with that big a bounty on his head? Someone would definitely betray him! He wouldn't risk coming here!'

'If bin Laden called for Yemenis to go and fight jihad in Iraq, would you go?' I asked him.

'If he asked me to go and kill American or Israeli soldiers, of course, I would love to go, but I wouldn't go and kill civilians.'

Ibrahim's lucrative employment with Oxy and the cluster of excited and happy faces that greeted him when we arrived at his home a few minutes later amply accounted for his failure to beat a path to the jihad in Iraq. As head of the family since his father had died, he was clearly the happy object of at least a dozen women's deep devotion. His mother, his sisters, his teenage nieces who were happily learning to read at the age of fifteen, his startlingly beautiful but illiterate wife and his one-year-old baby daughter all doted on him. Three small nephews copied every gesture he made.

Early the next morning Walid piloted the Land Cruiser slowly around the low sand dunes on the outskirts of the Ibrahim's village, allowing us plenty of time for a good look at a school built with foreign aid but standing empty for lack of any teachers, and then at a circle of men in their pale shirts, patterned *futa*s and faded head-cloths sitting cross-legged in a small patch of shade next to a Toyota pick-up. I thought they must be having their breakfast.

'Breakfast? No. They're men from my Balharith tribe,' said Ibrahim. 'They're holding a strategy meeting. It's nothing so special, just that one of those guys owns some land on the coast, on the road between Aden and Abyan. He has paperwork proving his ownership and authorisation from the president, but the officials down there have decided to seize it. About a week ago soldiers removed the posts marking the plot and arrested the man he had employed to guard it. So those guys are planning to cut the road near here, to stop the flow of traffic to and from the oil fields.'

'Will it work, do you think?'

Ibrahim shrugged. 'Maybe, probably – because the state hates anything to disrupt the oil business. That's why the tribes around here are powerful. We've got some kind of chance of getting justice!' Proud of his tribe, he was surprised and pleased when I recalled that the suspected leader of al-Qaeda in Yemen in the period immediately before and after 9/11 had been a fellow Balharith, yet another Afghan War veteran named Qaid Sinan al-Harithi.

In the immediate aftermath of 9/11, when, on account of its lawlessness, Yemen was regarded as the likeliest refuge for jihadists fleeing the western onslaught on Afghanistan, President Salih had warded off a rumoured American invasion by speedily deporting whole planeloads of foreign Afghan War veterans. Anxious not to repeat the costly mistake of siding with Saddam Hussein in 1990, he had also hurried off to Washington to reassure President George W. Bush that he was on his side in the new global 'War on Terror', but Bush had given him to understand that he would have to prove it, that actions would have to speak louder than words. When Salih offered to help lower the international temperature by mediating a reconciliation between Baghdad and Washington, chattily quoting an old Arab proverb to Bush about taking care not to put a cat in a cage because it might turn into a lion, Bush retorted that the Iraqi cat had rabies which could only be cured by cutting off its head.[7] He then upped the pressure by demanding he demonstrate his new commitment to tackling jihadism by arresting a pair of al-Qaeda men suspected of playing leading roles in the attack on the USS *Cole* the previous year. The more important of the two had been Ibrahim's fellow tribesman, Qaid Sinan al-Harithi.

Within a month of his return from Washington, in December 2001, with pledges of millions of dollars, bugging equipment, helicopters, guns and bullet-proof vests as well as a hundred special-forces trainers, Salih duly went to work. Al-Harithi and four other alleged jihadists were tracked down to the Marib desert, to a village called al-Hosun where, outlawed by his own Balharith tribe, he and his companions were being sheltered by members of the powerful Abidah tribe. The president then despatched his son Ahmad at the head of a few hundred freshly American-trained special forces, with helicopters, artillery and tanks, to Marib to winkle them out. For two days the military followed the letter of the tribal law, parleying with local leaders, patiently working to convince them to flout the tribal custom that required them to shelter a fugitive, no questions asked. But either the pressure exerted by the din of helicopters overhead, or the shock of a jet suddenly breaking the sound barrier, seems to have destroyed all confidence and trust, and caused negotiations to break down and fighting to break out. After a three-hour battle that left eighteen dead and twenty-five wounded, the Abidah tribesmen gloried in a victory over the state: only five of them were dead, only seven had been wounded and their troublesome Balharith guest and his friends had made a safe getaway.[8]

The state did subsequently manage to arrest ten Marib sheikhs who were soon released, but, using an old tactic regularly resorted to by the imams, their sons kept hostage in their place. Three months later four of these boys explained to the *Daily Telegraph* that they were locked up because their fathers were still refusing to sign a pledge to 'fight terrorism and hand over al-Qa'eda suspects on an American list'.[9] Taken aback by Salih's unaccustomed determination to exercise some control over the region, and perhaps mollified by a raise in their stipends, twenty sheikhs did eventually agree to co-operate and soon the Marib-Shabwa oil region was bristling with checkpoints and crawling with military and informants in the pay of the Americans as well as Yemen's PSO.

Washington's initial delight at seeing President Salih go into action against al-Qaeda was tempered by disappointment at the failure of the operation and a fresh determination that if Yemen lacked sufficient skill, then the US itself would get the job done. The rumoured invasion of Iraq and signs that the Bush administration might once again be eyeing Yemen as the 'next Afghanistan', as next in line for invasion, meant that Yemeni sentiment against the US was running high, but Salih found himself having to agree to the US directly intervening in Yemen. On the understanding that no word of the embarrassing surrender of sovereignty ever leaked out, he gave the CIA permission to carry out an Israeli-style targeted assassination of the man who had escaped capture a year earlier, Ibrahim's outlawed kinsman, Qaid Sinan al-Harithi.

Intercepted mobile-phone conversations had convinced both the CIA and Edmund Hull, America's ambassador in Sanaa, that the Marib desert was still the right place to focus the hunt for Yemen's leading jihadists. An energetic Arabic-speaker with a counter-terrorism background, Hull had quickly got the measure of Yemen and its tribes and figured out the most efficient way of doing business in the country. He regularly travelled the road between Sanaa and Marib, with a full armed escort, sometimes wearing a Texan stetson, to spend hours chewing qat and crossing the palms of local sheikhs in exchange for useful intelligence. But none of those arduous excursions bore much useful fruit until late 2002, very shortly after Qaid Sinan al-Harithi was reported to have pulled off another propaganda coup for al-Qaeda by badly damaging a French oil tanker named the *Limburg* a few miles off the Hadhramaut coast.

On the afternoon of Sunday, 3 November, one of Hull's local spies watched the thickly bearded al-Harithi and five others climb into a black Toyota Land Cruiser and then phoned through the car details to CIA headquarters at Langley, Virginia. Final telephone permission for immediate action was then swiftly received from Salih, who was enjoying a holiday cruise in the waters off Aden. With a Predator drone launched from Djibouti 'loitering' noiselessly some 15,000 feet above Marib, equipped with a video camera fitted with a 900mm zoom lens that could read car licence plates, the job of locking onto and tracking the car was managed by means of al-Harithi's mobile phone signal and a global positioning system. Soon CIA operatives 7,000 miles away in Virginia had a real-time, close-up image of the Land Cruiser on their computer screens, and were watching it wind its way down a twisting mountain road towards a main road before it veered off into the desert along a sand track. Within a second of one of those operatives pressing a button, a five-foot-long AG-114 Hellfire missile fixed to the undercarriage of the Predator fired off, locked onto the Land Cruiser and blew it to pieces. The vehicle and all six of its occupants were instantly incinerated. Only Qaid Sinan al-Harithi was subsequently identifiable, by a mark on his leg.

'Did you know that he had a bad leg because, when bin Laden was living in Sudan, he was one of his bodyguards, and got hurt once while shielding him from bullets?' Ibrahim asked me.

Sanaa had hastened to put out its agreed cover story: some of Yemen's most wanted criminals had been hell-bent on sabotage and murder, headed for the oil fields, for pipelines and foreign workers, with a carload of weapons and a particularly dangerous cylinder of propane gas, when their car had simply exploded. The incident might have ended there, with most Yemenis feeling relieved that God in his wisdom had rid the country of some worthless hooligans, and with the CIA taking a quiet professional pride in a strike so surgically precise it had expunged the bad memory of two previous blunders by Predators in Afghanistan. Everything might have been fine if Deputy Secretary of Defense Paul Wolfowitz had not spoken out of turn. In an interview with CNN two days after the event, he revealed precisely what both Sanaa and the CIA had been so anxious to conceal: the US's sole responsibility for a 'very successful tactical operation'.[10] Wolfowitz may have calculated that such a thrilling victory in the 'War on Terror', occurring only a day before the mid-term elections, was simply too good a publicity opportunity to pass up, but the admission backfired badly.

The strike had been a relatively clean one – for a start, no wedding party had been accidentally incinerated – but there was an international outcry at Washington's double standards; on the one hand the Bush administration was reluctantly condemning Israel's targeted assassinations of Hamas leaders in the Gaza Strip, while on the other plotting precisely the same actions in other countries it was not even at war with. There were moral qualms about the dawning of a new era of assassination by remote control and about such 'extra-judicial executions' constituting a serious violation of international human rights law. The revelation that one of al-Harithi's five companions had been an American national of Yemeni origin made many Americans wonder how the US could justify summarily executing its own citizens in that way. But the reaction in the western media and parliaments was nothing compared to the repercussions of the affair in Yemen. Security concerns raised by a rash of anti-US demonstrations all over the country led to the hasty evacuation and temporary closure of the US embassy in Sanaa. The president was known to be both furious and alarmed. A high-ranking member of the ruling political party, Brigadier-General Yahya al-Muttawakil, seemed to be speaking for Salih when he complained to a *Christian Science Monitor* reporter at an afternoon qat chew a few days after the event: 'This is why it is so difficult to make deals with the United States,' he began, 'This is why we are reluctant to work closely with them. They don't consider the internal circumstances in Yemen.'[11] Over a year was to pass before

Salih could risk a formal admission that he had authorised the strike. He had braved not only the displeasure of friends in the region, notably Saddam Hussein's Iraq, but also the wrath of the large bin Laden-loving section of Yemen society in order to support the War on Terror, and this was all the thanks he got.

Not surprisingly, the dazzling Predator technology has not been employed since in Yemen.* For the two years that remained of his posting Ambassador Hull did what he could to remove the impression he had given to Yemenis who recalled the last years of the British in Aden that he was behaving like a colonial High Commissioner. Between 2001 and 2004 American aid to Yemen far eclipsed Europe's total aid contribution to the country. Although most of the money was spent on the military equipment which President Salih insisted he needed to secure his grip on the country sufficiently to do battle with al-Qaeda, some was spent on displays of 'soft power'. Targeted for assassination himself in revenge for the killing of Qaid Sinan al-Harithi, Hull was nevertheless to be seen out and about in Marib during his last summer in Yemen, laying the foundation stone of a $3 million Yemen Civilisation Museum that the US was helping to fund, handing over medical equipment for a new hospital (complete with a plaque indicating that it was the gift of the American people) and donating $40,000 to twenty-six local farmers for improvements in irrigation methods.[12]

I asked Walid and Ibrahim if, since we happened to be in the neighbourhood, they would mind going in search of the location of the famous Hellfire missile attack because I remembered passing by the place on my first visit to Yemen, in the winter of the same year Ambassador Hull left Yemen, 2004. The two-year-old incident had still been fresh in locals' minds, I recalled. The Yemeni manager of Marib's five-star hotel, the Bilqis Marib, had told me that Ambassador Hull had

* Predator raids against Pakistan's lawless, al-Qaeda and Taliban-ridden western tribal areas have been operating from air bases in Pakistan, and in Iraq. Drones are now only used in Yemen for surveillance purposes.

been a guest of the hotel on the very day of the strike and had received a call from Sanaa informing him of the mission's success. I had learned that instead of hurrying back to Sanaa, the doughty diplomat had continued his tour around the ancient sites – the ancient dam and the Queen of Sheba's temples – just as if nothing had happened. Our convoy of Land Cruisers with its armed police escort had set out east from Marib, guided by a local Bedouin in a battered old pick-up, along the same desert track used by the doomed al-Harithi and his five companions. When we stopped to allow the drivers to let more air out of their tyres at just the spot where the missile had struck, members of our police escort pointed out shards of broken windscreen still lying in the sand. One of them knew that Ambassador Hull had stayed at the Bilqis Marib the night before, but insisted that Qaid Sinan al-Harithi had been there too. Another swore that the smell of roasting flesh had wafted to a distance of three kilometres on that fateful Sunday afternoon, but none of them had had a good word to say about one of al-Qaeda's favourite martyrs. In their view he had been just a 'known trouble-maker', an outlaw from his own tribe, a feckless Afghan War veteran who had eked out a living by smuggling weapons across the Saudi border. They insisted that two years before his incineration by a Hellfire missile, he and his stash of weapons for sale had caused a shoot-out in Marib's gun market.

There was no hint of reverence in the way they spoke about their dead countryman, no sense that he and his luckless companions had achieved any glory as well as fame. Instead, they sounded sceptical that such a scruffy ne'er do well as old al-Harithi had had it in him to lead al-Qaeda in Yemen, bemused by his capacity to bring down on himself the wrath of the world's only superpower in the shape of one of the most advanced weapons systems ever seen.

## 9/11 – A SAUDI/YEMENI AFFAIR?

The deserts and oil fields of the Marib-Shabwa area continue to welcome fugitive jihadists. Seven years after the despatching of Qaid

Sinan al-Harithi by Hellfire missile, in February 2009, President Salih was visiting the region for the umpteenth time to complain to the local sheikhs that they were seeing 'the terrorists' in their villages but doing nothing to stop them. He had to admit that, for all the armed forces at his disposal, he was powerless to root them out without the tribes' co-operation.[13]

Salih knew as well as the tribes did that this had nothing whatsoever to do with them buying into the jihadists' brand of Islam, given that the tribes considered themselves and their customs more strong and ancient than Islam of any sort and had never allowed religion to get in the way of their own material interests. But he also knew that there would be no co-operation as long as sheltering jihadists made financial sense, as long as they could pay more, or at least as much as, he could pay in stipends and other benefits. And so he had paid them well. A close adviser to Salih admitted to the *Yemen Times* that 'paying the tribal leaders to co-operate was cheaper than any other way' of spoiling the region's reputation as a haven for jihadists.[14] It was also, of course, the tried and tested way that had worked for centuries, as the imams, the Ottomans, the British and most recently the Egyptians had all discovered to their immense cost. But by early 2009 the president and the tribes were both aware that the country's oil revenues were shrinking and with them, Salih's leverage. By the end of June, the grip of the state on the region was so dangerously loose that government forces were skirmishing with al-Qaeda jihadists, the latter killing up to three soldiers, and taking another seven hostages before creating an Internet video entitled 'The Battle of Marib'– described by Gregory Johnsen, the leading US authority on Yemeni jihadism as 'by far the most technologically impressive piece of propaganda I have seen it produce to date'.[15] The video warns Yemeni soldiers to keep out of the Marib and Abidah tribal regions in future.

Al-Qaeda can be confident that in the desert, oil-producing, tribal region of central Yemen it has found, if not a consistently and actively supportive working enviroment, then at least a non-judgemental one whose twin priorities – rejecting the writ of the state in their areas and financial gain – perfectly suits their purpose. But another aspect of Yemen's tribal society, its disregard for artificial national borders and identities, has also contributed to the spread of jihadism. Bin Laden's own impatience with national borders was made plain in the mid-1990s when he toyed with the notion of doing away with both the Kingdom of Saudi Arabia and the Republic of Yemen and replacing them with two more Islamically, as well as tribally, convincing entities: a Greater Hijaz* and a Greater Yemen, which would form the core of a reconstituted Muslim caliphate and carve up the rest of the Arabian Peninsula between them.[16] An examination of the backgrounds of the men bin Laden chose to carry out the prestigious 9/11 attacks on New York and Washington, however, is probably the best illustration of the debt al-Qaeda owes to supranational Yemeni tribalism.

Given that impoverished Yemenis were far less likely than wealthy Saudis to be granted the US visas that were a *sine qua non* of the operation, the fact that the majority of the 9/11 hijackers were Saudi rather than Yemeni passport holders is not in the least surprising. While all but four of the total of nineteen hijackers were Saudi citizens, five out of the remaining fifteen Saudi 'muscle' turned out to hail from just one of Saudi Arabia's thirteen provinces, Asir, a Yemeni possession during the fourteenth century and again during the coffee-enriched Qasim era of the seventeenth to eighteenth century.

In Asir, which is as mountainous and verdant as much of neighbouring north-west Yemen across the border, 'you feel you are in Yemen'.[17] In Asir, according to the journalist and author John Bradley, 'it is not unusual to see women driving pick-up trucks, although Wahhabi custom elsewhere [in Saudi Arabia] means that women are officially banned from driving. Locals, moreover, point the television aerials on their roofs toward Yemen, so they pick up Yemeni TV. In the

* Hijaz is a coastal emirate of Saudi Arabia, home to the Muslim Holy Places of Mecca and Medina as well as Jeddah.

mountains they wear *jambiyas*.'[18] And Bradley continues, 'Immediately it [becomes] obvious how different the people of the Asir region are in both character and style to those in the rest of Saudi Arabia.'[19]

A typically Yemeni pride in tribal belonging is far stronger in this comparatively undeveloped and impoverished south-western corner of the country than in the Kingdom's central provinces. Just as startling is the fact that a further four of the fifteen 'muscle hijackers' hailed from the tiny southern Saudi emirate of al-Bahah, also once a Yemeni possession. All four belonged to the large and famous al-Ghamdi tribe whose members had long been covering themselves in jihadist glory. Bradley notes that the Afghan cave in which the plot for 9/11 was hatched was known as the al-Ghamdi house and that the al-Ghamdis' superior fighting spirit had received a special mention in a poem bin Laden composed. Leaving aside the four non-Saudi pilots therefore, 'muscle' hijackers with links to Yemen via their regional backgrounds accounted for well over half the total – nine out of the fifteen.

It has been suggested that al-Qaeda's earliest attacks, those conducted in the mid- to late 1990s, in Yemen and East Africa and Saudi Arabia, all originated from the mountainous border region of south-west Saudi Arabia and north-west Yemen. The rubber dinghy used to attack the USS *Cole* was imported from the border area; the plot for the Kenya and Tanzania embassy bombings was probably hatched there; the attacks in Saudi Arabia were executed with weapons smuggled over that border.[20] But it was 9/11 and the investigation into the hijackers' backgrounds that first attracted real attention to the region and, eight years later, it was back in the news. In early 2009, Saudi security men hunting al-Qaeda in southern Asir discovered a remote cave high in the chain of Sarwat mountains straddling the Saudi–Yemeni border. It overlooked the home village of a prominent Saudi jihadist and was stocked with guns, video cameras, spare batteries, military uniforms and food.[21]

The uneasy and frequently renegotiated balance of power between the heavily armed state and the not only heavily armed but also internationally dispersed tribes supports President Salih's assertion that ruling Yemen is like dancing on snakes' heads. Along with his none too solid grip on power and the limitations imposed by the other urgent threats Yemen is facing, it goes a long way towards accounting for the unorthodox – some would say distinctly half-hearted – way in which he has tackled the job of fighting the jihadists. Non-confrontational, highly personalised, inconsistent and far from transparent, Yemen's approach to fighting the 'War on Terror' has raised first some tentative hopes among his western allies, then a great many eyebrows and finally, very serious doubts.

## THE YEMENI WAY

Within a year of 9/11 President Salih had managed to persuade just one of thirty senior Yemeni clerics and judges that Yemen would not be acting as President Bush's poodle if hundreds of the country's hurriedly jailed jihadists were subjected to a spell of Koranic re-education. A rehabilitation programme for jihadists was duly set up under the supervision of the single obliging Hamoud al-Hitar, who counted the fact that the Koran contained 124 verses about treating non-Muslims kindly and only one that advocated going to war with them the sharpest weapon in his arsenal.

Soon Judge al-Hitar was jetting off to London and Cairo to share his 'best practice' with foreign security services and granting long interviews to western news media. Although initially sceptical, even neighbouring Saudi Arabia warmed to Yemen's constructive solution to their shared problem and began channelling unlimited resources into a far more comprehensive rehabilitation programme for Saudi jihadists, which often included follow-up care in the shape of payment of wedding dowries, cars and furnished accommodation. Without adequate funding, however, the Yemeni version was showing clear signs of failing by December 2005, when the good judge, having re-educated and released 364 young men, suspended his sessions. Any self-respecting jihadist had long ago worked out that a chat with al-Hitar and a show of repentance was enough to guarantee him a 'get out of jail free' card.

Nasir al-Bahri, who had spent a year in jail in Sanaa before renouncing jihad and accepting government help to become a taxi-driver in Sanaa, explained, 'We all respect Judge Hamoud al-Hitar but he does not have any influence on radical youths. Militants view [Judge] al-Hitar as a safety belt they use to get out from behind bars, but what is in their minds does not change.'[22] Al-Bahri went on to divulge that members of the second-generation Yemeni jihadists, men like himself, had not been so much swayed by the judge's arguments as seduced by the advantageous deal on offer: release from prison and a little money to get started in life, in return for not staging attacks in Yemen, and guarantees of good behaviour by their families and tribal leaders.

If some of those who were freed in this way slipped back into their old jihadist ways, others who stayed in jail because they were considered too high up on Washington's most-wanted list to be released did not remain there long. At around dawn one morning in April 2003, ten al-Qaeda suspects, most of them charged with involvement in the attack on the USS *Cole*, escaped from a prison in Aden through a hole they later claimed they had managed to make in a bathroom wall. Some of these escapees were recaptured, only to escape again from another prison in Sanaa in February 2006, in a batch of twenty-three that included six Saudi Yemenis. On that occasion the story was that for two months the prisoners had patiently employed a sharpened spoon tied to a broomstick as a spade, and three cooking pots lashed together as a scoop, to tunnel 143 feet, straight to the ideally secluded women's washroom of a nearby mosque, where they lingered long enough to say the dawn prayer together before tasting freedom. Within little more than a year six of them were dead, another eleven had either been recaptured or had surrendered, but six were still at large.

Both prisons involved in these great escapes happened to be run by the PSO. On both occasions this fact, as well as the large numbers of escapees involved and the implausibility of their stories, led observers to conclude that, still riddled with Afghan War veterans and Iraq-trained military who had been freshly enraged by the western coalition's invasion of Iraq in the spring of 2003, the PSO had aided and abetted the escapes. One of the most persistent and cynical conspiracy theories frequently aired at qat chews in Sanaa was that, if not the president himself, then certainly Brigadier-General Ali Muhsin al-Ahmar, the PSO and leading jihadists were all in cosy cahoots. It was in the interests of the government, those theorists said, to promote and facilitate a certain measure of jihadist mayhem because America was sure to respond by stumping up more financial support and military hardware, which in turn would help Salih to consolidate his power. As one Sanaa lawyer succinctly put it, 'They [the Salih regime] frighten the USA with these guys and they frighten these guys with the USA.'[23] More credence was given to such conspiracy theories in late 2008 when a wanted jihadist who had taken refuge with one of the Marib tribes told a Yemeni reporter that he was 'ready to prove the reality that some [jihadist] attacks were planned in co-ordination and agreement with Political Security [PSO]'.[24]

Yemen's western allies have never been able to relax in the knowledge that Salih and his PSO, let alone the Yemeni man-in-the-street, view the jihadist threat with as much urgent singlemindedness as they do. Nor, given what American analysts frequently refer to as the president's 'revolving door'[25] policy, have they ever been able to gain an accurate idea of the number of leading jihadists behind bars at any given time. What was anyone to make of a report that the father of a man sentenced to ten years in jail for the bombing of the French tanker, the *Limburg*, in 2002 denied his son had spent a single day in jail, and revealed that the president had telephoned the boy on the day of his trial to beg him to play along with the charade by dressing up as a prisoner?[26] A bewildering game of hide and seek seems to have gone on in the case of

Khaled Abdul al-Nabi, a leader of the Aden-Abyan Islamic Army (AAIA). In 2003 Sanaa informed Washington that al-Nabi had been killed in a shoot-out, but in 2004 he was revealed to be still at large and, a year later, he had rejoined mainstream society as a farmer. In 2006 he was reported to be busy training jihadists for mercenary work fighting an anti-government rebellion in the north-west of the country. Finally, in August 2008, came the bewildering news that he had been captured after an exhaustive five-year manhunt.[27]

The astonishing leniency with which Jamal al-Badawi, one of the masterminds of the attack on the USS *Cole*, was treated after his escape from prison, first in 2003 and then again in 2006, galvanised a furious Washington into hitting President Salih where it hurt. It was simple enough to withhold Yemen's share of the Millennium Challenge fund, a grant of $20.6 million in October 2007, on the grounds that the country had not reached the required standards of good governance. Washington's patience had also been sorely tried by Sanaa's refusal to extradite, or even safely imprison, Jaber Elbaneh, a Yemeni-American jihadist with a $5 million bounty on his head since 2002. After training at an al-Qaeda camp in Afghanistan, Elbaneh had established an al-Qaeda cell in Lackawanna, NY before returning to Yemen to launch attacks on American oil industry employees in Marib. He was also one of the twenty-three escapees from the Sanaa jail in 2006. When at last he handed himself in to the authorities, shortly after the cancellation of the Millennium Challenge grant, it was in a manner guaranteed to try Washington's patience beyond endurance. Accompanied by four personal guards, Elbaneh strode into a Sanaa courtroom one morning to announce that he was a free man because he had placed himself under the president's personal protection. 'It's a very traditional thing in Yemen,' one of the president's advisers later explained to the *Washington Post*, 'You surrender yourself to a high-ranking official. His surrender was accepted on the basis that he would cooperate.'[28]

Salih was continuing to bank on jihadists behaving in as mercenary a fashion as Yemeni tribesmen had always done, as Tariq al-Fadhli had. He failed to factor the movement's fanatical integrity and the aggravating impact of a litany of errors by the West – the chaotic aftermath of the invasion of Iraq, the prisoner abuse at Abu Ghraib and Guantanamo Bay, and the execution of Saddam Hussein, to name only a few – into this equation. He failed to recognise the fact that he was dancing on the most determinedly poisonous snakes he had yet encountered. It took the slaughter of seven elderly Spanish tourists and their Yemeni drivers at the Queen of Sheba's temple to the sun in the desert near Marib in July 2007 to make him see that after three years of some success in combating jihadism the unorthodox Yemeni way – by damp-down rather than clamp-down – it was time for a change of tactics, time to try and wield as big a stick as neighbouring Saudi Arabia had been doing since 2003.

## CHAPTER SEVEN

# KEEPING UP WITH THE SAUDIS

### THE VALLEY OF THE KINGS

Since my first visit to Hadhramaut in 2004, a cluster of buildings with a magnificent view down into the Wadi Doan had appeared on the edge of the high plateau where nothing moved but the odd Toyota pick-up, speeding up-country with a load of fresh qat under a flapping tarpaulin. It turned out to be a brand new luxury holiday resort and closer inspection revealed matching studio cottages with iron-studded Hadhrami front doors, traditional wooden shutters with keyhole cut-outs, and even en suite western bathrooms. Two thousand feet below its airy terrace was another clear sign that the globalised age was prising open even this remote corner of southern Arabia from which Osama bin Laden's father had left for Saudi Arabia in 1930 and where the doughty Freya Stark contracted a near fatal attack of the measles a few years later. A thin new ribbon of asphalt road snaked its way along the wadi floor, more or less neatly linking dozens of small towns and villages clinging to the wadi's almost vertical walls.

The Wadi Doan was changing fast, but, gazing across the half kilometre width of the wadi floor to its opposite wall and imagining its 130-mile length, it was still easy to understand how Hadhramis had come by their belief that once upon a very ancient and prehistorical time a tribe of giants named the Ad had walked and worked the land, but ended up displeasing Allah by presuming to create a heaven and so been swept away in a punishing flood, leaving only imprints as gigantic as this wadi on the landscape. It was even easier to imagine how, fabulously enriched by the tolls charged on camels loaded with precious frankincense* bound for the Mediterranean and Europe, the Wadi Doan had been on one of the Roman world's superhighways. Those glory days are very long gone. In the intervening millennium-and-a-half its inhabitants have usually had to seek their fortunes elsewhere. Sailing away east to India and Indonesia in the eighteenth and nineteenth centuries, they returned to build homes that reminded them of their exile. Many of the Wadi Doan's mud high-rises are painted luminously faded orange, turquoise, violet, pink, peppermint green and primrose yellow, and adorned with flower motifs. Others, not so colourful but more grandiose than anything else in Yemen, are the property of men who, like Osama bin Laden's father, migrated to the new Kingdom of Saudi Arabia after 1930 to ride the wave of the oil boom.

Near the village of Sif, set lonely and unlikely as a space ship on a patch of stony ground, is a mansion built in the same neo-classical style and to almost the same scale as London's Buckingham Palace. Rarely occupied and tightly shuttered, it belongs to a member of the al-Amoudi family now resident in Saudi Arabia. Of mixed Hadhrami and Ethiopian parentage, Muhammad Hussein al-Amoudi is a Saudi citizen who, after amassing a Saudi fortune in property and construction, progressed to oil

* Frankincense, also known as olimbanum, was used in worship by both pagans and monotheists for millennia. It is the resin of the hardy *Boswellia sacra* tree which thrives in south Arabia.

interests in Sweden and Morocco and emerged as Ethiopia's largest investor and yet still, to judge by his palace in the Wadi Doan, remained true to his Hadhrami roots.

More striking even than al-Amoudi's is a multi-storey edifice painted a glorious patchwork of bright colours, a family mansion known as the Buqshan Palace, two floors of which were converted for use as a hotel in 2006. Thanks to their long service as one of the sturdiest pillars of the Hadhrami community in Jeddah, the Buqshans are the leading royal family in this Valley of the Kings. A close friend of the Saudi royals in the mid-twentieth century, Ahmad Said Buqshan acted as chief sponsor and guarantor of all Hadhramis seeking work and the necessary residence permits. His first question to a countryman who arrived in the Kingdom was always 'Where are you from in Hadhramaut?' and 'Who is your father and your father's father?' before he checked their accent for Hadhrami authenticity by asking them to pronounce the Arabic word for flour. His son Abdullah has ensured that the family name is as famous in Hadhramaut today as al-Kaff was in Tarim between the world wars, as synonymous with the Wadi Doan in particular as the name Ford is with Dearborn, Michigan. The saying '*andak Buqshan*' is Hadhrami Arabic for 'as rich as Croesus', but no grand factory complex attaches to it, no product. Abdullah Buqshan, who recently funded the restoration of the psychedelic palace hotel, the building of the new road, new schools and clinics in the wadi as well as the brand new tourist resort overlooking it, consolidated his father's wealth with lucrative dealerships for Bridgestone tyres and Komatsu bulldozers, perfume and jewellery. His own modern residence in the wadi, a large complex of buildings next door to the psychedelic palace hotel, boasts a large swimming pool.

After bin Laden, the best-known Hadhrami name in Saudi Arabia is bin Mahfouz. The patriarch of the clan, Salim Ahmad bin Mahfouz, also hailed from the Wadi Doan and reportedly pawned his precious *jambiyah* to raise the cost of his passage to Jeddah by dhow in the 1930s. Starting out as a humble money-changer, he was making his mark and a gigantic personal fortune by the 1950s, having convinced

King Abdul Aziz that the new country urgently needed its own bank, the National Commercial Bank.

The eldest of his three sons, Khaled, proceeded to inherit the biggest bank in the Middle East, but he was not as lucky as his father. While he was never convicted of any wrongdoing, his purchase in the 1980s, of a 20 per cent stake in an institution notorious for arms trafficking and money laundering for criminals and terrorists, the Bank of Credit and Commerce International (BCCI) inevitably sullied the family name. A charitable foundation named Muwaffaq (Blessed Relief), which he established in 1992, landed him in more hot water. Long before the declaration of President Bush's 'War on Terror', US intelligence officials were suspecting Muffawaq of funnelling donations to al-Qaeda. Once again, nothing was proved. Khaled loudly asserted his opposition to jihadism, and any journalist or author who alleged a shared ideology and close links between the Hadhrami Saudi banker bin Mahfouz and the Hadhrami Saudi global terrorist bin Laden was immediately sued and always lost. An often repeated report that the two families were related by marriage, that one of bin Mahfouz's sisters was one of bin Laden's wives, has been similarly denied and retracted. Nevertheless, Khaled's son Abdulrahman wasted little time in visiting the US consul in Jeddah after 9/11 to assure him that the bin Mahfouzes were with, rather than against, the US in the new 'War on Terror'.[1]

The al-Amoudis, the bin Ladens, Buqshans and bin Mahfouzes have all tried to pull their weight for Yemen since unification in 1990, especially in the formerly Marxist south of which Hadhramaut was a part. If Buqshan is most visible in the Wadi Doan itself, his name emblazoned on smart signposts detailing his charitable giving, bin Mahfouz's oil company Nimr expended half a billion dollars on a bloc in the Shabwa area before withdrawing from the sector in 2003. Both Buqshan and bin Mahfouz have been involved in the long-delayed and murky project to redevelop the port of Aden. Al-Amoudi has also contracted to build two large hotels in Sanaa, and the bin Ladens have built the new road leading from the Hadhramaut port of Mukalla west, almost as far as Aden.

That the Wadi Doan should have generated such an especially entrepreneurial streak in a Hadhramaut known for its entrepreneurs is surprising given that it produces nothing itself except some thirty-five tons a year of the best and most expensive honey in the world, sold on the comb in large, round tins.* Mentioned in the Koran, honey of any kind is prized all over the Muslim world, but the Doan variety is famed for its medicinal and aphrodisiac powers and particularly loved in Saudi Arabia and the Gulf States where a kilo of the product of the *apis mellifera yemenitica* can fetch $150. Back in the mid-1930s the first British political officer in the Hadhramaut, Harold Ingrams, tried to promote the honey's export to Britain by sending a sample tin to the Colonial Office for testing but it failed to excite any interest. 'It is probable that such dextro-rotatory honey would be regarded with suspicion, whilst its unattractive flavour and odour would be further obstacles to its sale',[2] was the expert negative response. Undaunted, the following year, one of the Hadhramaut sultans marked the coronation of King George VI with a gift of a hundred tins of the exotic elixir, some of which found its way to Buckingham Palace, Downing Street and two London hospitals.

Hadhramaut honey has had a bizarre walk-on part to play in the 'War on Terror' since 9/11. Shortly after the attacks, American intelligence officials divulged that they had been keeping a close watch on the Middle East's luxury honey trade for the past two years, suspicious that because the product's 'smell and consistency' made it 'too messy' for customs officers to want to handle, it was proving a useful medium in which to smuggle cash, drugs and weapons.[3] Along with thirty-seven other Middle Eastern enterprises suspected of involvement with bin Laden's cause, two Yemeni honey shops, one in Sanaa and another in Taiz – the latter humbly listed its address as 'by the shrine, next to the gas station, Jamal Street, Taiz' – had their assets frozen. In the end, no

* Devastating floods in October 2008 killed a number of beekeepers and destroyed some 37,000 beehives in the Wadi Doan (*Yemen Times*, 17–19 November 2008).

firm link to al-Qaeda was established, but honey merchants all over Yemen enjoyed mocking the allegations. A better-established link between Osama bin Laden and honey seems to be that according to his fourth wife – a Yemeni from the southern highlands region whom he married in 2000 – he eats a lot of it.[4] It is also known that his Hadhrami paternal grandfather, Awad bin Laden, scraped a precarious living from beekeeping in the Wadi Doan in the early decades of the twentieth century.[5]

At the southernmost end of the Wadi Doan, far from al-Amoudi's Buckingham Palace and well to the south of the Buqshan Palace, at the spot where the wadi's high walls narrow into a claustrophobically shaded cul de sac, is al-Ribat, the bin Laden family's home village. By the mid-1930s, when the painstaking Harold Ingrams reported that it contained 800 fighting men with 100 rifles between them,[6] the poor beekeeper Awad's illiterate eldest son, Muhammad bin Laden, had already left it, first for a docker's job in Mukalla and then to Ethiopia and finally to what was about to become the Kingdom of Saudi Arabia.

Possessor of an abundance of Hadhrami virtues, adventurous and self-reliant as any al-Kaff, Muhammad bin Laden was an astute businessman and as gifted a builder and engineer as the men who had built the first road out of the Wadi Hadhramaut in the 1930s, Tarim's hundreds of mosques and the soaring mud skyscrapers of Shibam. He was also hard-working and reliable, so he was soon employed as a bricklayer for the jointly owned Saudi–American oil company, Aramco, where he earned the respect of his American employers and began to take on projects himself before setting up on his own, to profit by the building boom. He then caught the eye of the Saudi minister of finance, who recommended him to the obese King Abdul Aziz, who entrusted him with the delicate task of constructing a ramp up the side of his palace to enable him to drive straight into his second-floor bedroom. Once close to and appreciated by the royal family, especially by its relatively liberal al-Faisal branch, he was made. By 1950 he was renovating and expanding the Prophet's Mosque in

Medina. Saudi Arabia urgently needed roads, so he built most of them. Even his death, in a plane crash over the southern province of Asir in 1968 did not inhibit his company's rise; in the 1980s the Bin Laden Group was entrusted with the most prestigious, and still ongoing, public work of all – the renovation of Mecca's Grand Mosque.

But bin Laden Snr built himself a comparatively modest mansion in al-Ribat, so the bin Ladens are more practically remembered there in a road and school of the same name and a project to bring running water to the village. I arrived there one mid-afternoon at qat time, to wander through the tight cluster of houses, feeling like an intruder watched by unseen eyes, marvelling at the tangible prosperity of such a remote place, guessing it was entirely dependent on remittances earned in Saudi Arabia and the Gulf. Two of its inhabitants – a man with the fiery stare of a habitual qat chewer and a rifle slung over his shoulder, and his young son – passed me without a glance or a nod, let alone a greeting. Like the rest of the Hadhramaut interior, al-Ribat holds itself aloof from the outside world.

While Hadhrami men are quiet and guardedly polite in their dealings with strangers, the women of the wadis signal their reserve by adopting not just the full black rig of their Saudi sisters but also black gloves and socks and very tall, pointed straw hats that are said to keep their heads cool when herding their goats in the palm groves or working in the fields. Just over a hundred years ago a doughty first British visitor to the Wadi Doan, Mabel Bent, found them far more colourfully dressed, in blue embroidered dresses which were short in front and long at the back and showed off 'their yellow-painted legs above the knee', but noted a similar wariness; when she tried to establish contact 'they fled precipitously like a flock of sheep before a collie dog'.[7] In more recent times, they have been known to throw stones at tourists who stop to photograph them. A year before 9/11, when a small army of FBI agents was hard at work unravelling the story behind the attack on the USS *Cole*, already suspecting bin Laden's involvement and learning that two of the bombers had had Hadhrami accents, some of them visited the Wadi Doan but learned nothing. In the aftermath of 9/11, when Hadhramaut seemed an obvious place to search for its world famous son, a small army of foreign reporters beat a path to al-Ribat. If they were lucky they discovered that, just like anywhere else in Yemen or the wider Muslim world, there was plenty of admiration for the West's most wanted terrorist. Usually, the then rough track along the wadi to bin Laden's home village was barred by security officials and the locals tight-lipped.

Al-Qaeda's astonishing attacks on those towering symbols of American power and wealth struck a special imaginative chord in the land of the mud-brick skyscraper, where the light is usually as dazzlingly clear as it was on that September morning in New York. Bin Laden's attack on the American superpower and the billionaire migrants of the Wadi Doan are compelling modern proofs that high, bright dreams of worldly power and wealth still can and do come true for Hadhramis. A large magazine photo-montage I spotted on the wall of a teahouse in a village near al-Amoudi's palace seemed to me to proclaim this fervent faith. Comprising a background of high snow-topped mountains, a middle ground of Manhattan skyscrapers looking uncannily like the famous 500-year-old mud skyscrapers of nearby Shibam, and a foreground resembling the sandy floor of a wadi, graced by a shiny red Toyota Land Cruiser and dotted with palm trees, it spoke volumes. On closer inspection, I noted that someone had embellished the bizarrely glamorous scene with a biro scribble of two tiny aeroplanes, making straight for the Manhattan mid-ground.

## BAD NEIGHBOURS

Hadhramaut reveals how large Saudi Arabia looms in the affairs of Yemen. Not only have tens of thousands of the traditionally adventurous and entrepreneurial Hadhramis chosen to migrate to the Kingdom to seek their fortunes while maintaining a strong connection to their homeland but, until very recently, one could be forgiven for thinking this vast and mostly desert eastern half of Yemen was a part of Saudi Arabia. Until the turn of this millennium no one had succeeded in demarcating an Empty Quarter border between them.

A Treaty of Jeddah set that to rights at last, in June 2000. By its terms Yemen formally accepted Saudi Arabia's right to rule over various southern provinces that had briefly belonged to the Yemen of the imams (Asir, Najran, Jizan), and Saudi Arabia implicitly abandoned any ambition to expand, by way of a corridor, straight down through the Hadhramaut to the Arabian Sea. The Kingdom's oil exports, basic food imports and other trade would have to continue to use the Iranian-controlled Straits of Hormuz, or the currently Somali pirate-ridden Bab al-Mandab strait at the bottom of the Red Sea. That Saudi dream of gaining a corridor via Hadhramaut to the open ocean was widely suspected of being the real issue at stake in the 1994 civil war, the main reason why, forgetting its old fear and loathing of the PDRY's Marxists, Saudi Arabia had swiftly funnelled a billion dollars' worth of support to al-Bidh's secession movement.

If the Jeddah Treaty scuppered that scheme, the Saudis could console themselves with the hope that the proper demarcation of their 1,800 kilometre-long southern border would end the Kingdom's creeping contamination by Yemeni arms, qat and drug smugglers, economic migrants, child traffickers and Africans gravitating towards the richest country on the peninsula in search of work. But simple demarcation was not enough, they discovered and, by September 2003, Yemen was loudly protesting a Saudi initiative to erect a physical barrier consisting of an $8.5 billion concrete-filled pipeline raised three metres above the ground and embellished with an electronic surveillance system.Yemen angrily reminded her neighbour that the Jeddah Treaty had clearly stipulated a neutral thirteen-kilometre zone on either side of the border to allow for tribal to-ing and fro-ing and livestock grazing. With only seventy-five kilometres of wall in place, construction was halted. Both sides did then agree to set up watch-towers and regular patrols, but the problem was still unresolved.

By late 2008, Saudi Arabia's efficient hounding and rounding up of its jihadists since 9/11 had sent many fleeing straight across the border into Yemen where they seemed to be injecting a new vigour into Yemen's al-Qaeda cell, and Yemeni drug-smugglers had never had it so good. Furthermore, Yemeni sheikhs whose tribal lands straddled the border were exacerbating the situation. In March 2009, for example, an army of tribesmen near the western end of the border closed one of the busiest crossings to all Saudi vehicles; they were demanding the right to work in Saudi Arabia according to the preferential terms of an agreement signed between their sheikh's grandfather and the first Saudi king.[8] Small wonder that the bulk of Saudi Arabia's armed forces have long been concentrated in the south of the country, within striking distance of the Yemeni border, or that by mid-2009 the Saudis were identifying Yemen as their most pressing internal security threat[9] and allocating approximately $2.5 billion to the erection of a border system involving radar, surveillance cameras and hi-tech communications as well as physical barriers.[10]

I was a long way from that border, in the Hadhramaut port of Mukalla, at the time of the *Eid al-Adha* holidays in December 2007, when I felt closest to Saudi Arabia and the other oil-rich Gulf States. Mukalla has fared much better than Marib from its oil wealth. Its shops and banks and currency exchanges, busy late into the night, were teeming with prosperous-looking young men dressed in jeans, T-shirts, trainers and baseball caps, rather than in *futa*s and head cloths. Many were oil workers from the nearby Masila field, currently by far the most productive in Yemen. Others were migrant workers from Saudi Arabia and the Gulf States, back home for the holidays. Mukalla is now a lively seaside resort with an elegant corniche and some large luxury hotels, popular with wealthy Sanaanis. In addition to its oil wealth, a new law providing for the restitution of land to its former owners fuelled an extraordinary property boom in the town after unification. The unsettled time that followed – the first Gulf War in which Yemen's perceived siding with Saddam Hussein against the West and Saudi Arabia led to the Kingdom expelling some 800,000 Yemenis – had given Saudi Hadhramis another strong incentive to own a patch of their own homeland. Thousands had got busy buying plots of land they had never even seen and erecting buildings they hoped never to have to inhabit, clinching the deals by fax and telephone. Between 1990 and 1994 the town had tripled in size.[11]

The pace of growth slowed dramatically after 1994. Because the leader of the secessionist south, Ali Salim al-Bidh, was a Hadhrami, the punishment meted out to the region in the form of a heavy northern military presence was more onerous than that experienced elsewhere in the south. Used to a measure of self-government and proud of its separate traditions, Hadhramaut was suddenly on a far tighter leash. The Hadhrami charged with housing and land distribution around Mukalla, for example, was pressurized by the region's new northern highlander governor to parcel out plots to northerners from the army and security services, and was fired after only two months when he failed to comply. Resentment towards the northern conquerors mounted when it became known that local land was being brazenly requisitioned for use in settling northern highlander feuds.[12] Another important reason why, to Sanaa's way of thinking, Hadhramaut had to be closely watched and shielded from undue Saudi influence was because it was home to the richest oil field in the country, which was also placed firmly under northern control. As military commander of Hadhramaut, one of President Salih's uncles was well placed to assume the responsibility – or rather, commandeer the contract – for providing security for the foreign oil companies, a move which deeply antagonised Hadhramis who had been performing the task perfectly adequately before the war.[13]

Much of northern Yemenis' distrust of Hadhramis and their close links with their diaspora in Saudi Arabia is attributable to the conviction that the Kingdom remains as powerfully involved in Yemen's affairs, as implacably hostile to their Republican regime in Sanaa, as it was during the 1960s. There is also an irrational but powerful feeling of injustice. Why should Allah have poured out his blessings on a group of primitive Bedouin with no rich and ancient history and no special mention in the Koran to boast of? Why should everything have come up roses for Saudi Arabia and the other Gulf states and everything have turned to ashes for Yemen? How was it that in spite of their human-rights record and disdain for democracy, Saudi Arabia was still respected and considered in the affairs of the western world while poor Yemen was ignored and despised? For Yemenis it was a clear case of bad luck and the world's double standards, a fine illustration of the proverb, 'if a rich man ate a snake, they would say it was because of his wisdom; if a poor man ate it, they would say it was because of his stupidity'.

Hundreds of thousands of Yemeni migrant workers in Saudi Arabia before 1990 swallowed their tribesmen's pride – it was *ayb*, shameful, for a tribesman to toil with his hands – and slaved for the Saudis as household servants or building-site labourers. Now, with the visa regime much tighter and plenty of cheaper non-Arab migrant labour to be had from Bangladesh and the Philippines, from people who can be relied on to steer clear of jihadism and go home when the work runs out, Yemeni guest workers are not as welcome in any of the Gulf Cooperation Council (GCC) countries as they were in the 1970s and '80s. In fact, the six GCC states – Saudi Arabia, Bahrain, United Arab Emirates, Qatar, Kuwait and Oman – feel about as keen to include Yemen in their economic zone as many Europeans feel about welcoming Turkey into the European Union. They foresee their labour markets being inundated by Yemenis who earn an average of $900 a year to their $35,000,[14] by people who – according to the crude popular stereotype – live for qat and guns and jihad. Only Saudi Arabia, increasingly alarmed by the spectre of Yemen collapsing into chaos, is said to be torn between wanting to keep Yemen cordoned off behind the latest thing in electronic border barriers and well away from the GCC, and recognising that the best way to defuse the Yemeni ticking time-bomb would be to open its borders and labour market to allow young Yemenis a means of earning a living.[15]

Yemenis deeply resent the fact that their wealthy neighbours are not helping to alleviate their poverty in a decent and constructive fashion by employing enough of them or by investing in Yemeni industry, while still feeling entitled to throw their weight around. 'The Saudis treat Yemen as their back yard,' one Sanaani political analyst complained to me, claiming that it suited Saudi Arabia to maintain Yemen at a debilitating level of poverty and instability rather than to assist its sustainable development. He reminded me how, ever since the time of Imam Yahya with whom relations had been cool thanks to the disputed ownership of Asir, Najran and Jizan, the Saudis had undermined Yemen's sovereignty and eroded the integrity of its tribal order by paying thousands of Yemeni sheikhs generous annual stipends. 'We have 9,000 sheikhs in Yemen, and about 6,000 of them have been receiving money, Saudi riyals in cash, from the Special Office which is headed by one of the crown princes, with no banks, no records involved,' he told me. 'The late Sheikh Abdullah al-Ahmar of the Hashid Federation, for example, was receiving 3.5 million dollars a month,' he continued. 'Although Yemenis hate Saudis, the Saudis know how to spread their influence by their wealth – they have corrupted everything in Yemen.'

While I could understand why the Saudis might be subsidising independence-minded southerners in the vague hope of one day being rewarded with a pipeline through Hadhramaut, I could not see what they gained by pouring millions of riyals into the bottomless pit of Yemen's northern highland tribes. 'Maybe the Saudis are paying off the tribes now,' my informant reasoned, 'in the hope that one day, when the south is ready to secede from the north again, they'll be able to pay them to stay home instead of fighting for President Salih and unity, and then – finally – the Saudis will have their oil pipeline through Hadhramaut and they'll be able to ignore the Jeddah Treaty.'

As far as the West was concerned however, Saudi Arabia's most baneful influence on Yemen was not this murky meddling but the spread of its Sunni Wahhabi Islam since al-Hamdi opened the door to it back in the mid-1970s, desperate for funding for education and a counterweight to the south's Marxism. By 1994 a devout Zaydi politician was publicly lamenting its deplorable effects on Yemen: 'Wahhabism is a child of [Saudi] imperialism and its spearhead in our country. Both are one and the same thing. How do we stand up to an enemy we don't see? We are seeing imperialism in our country in its Islamic guise. In reality, we are fighting something which is more dangerous than imperialism.'[16] He was right. The spread of Wahhabism toYemen would not matter so much if not for the fact that – put very simply – global jihadism of the al-Qaeda kind is Saudi Wahhabism reinforced and made more intolerant by Salafism and finally rationalised into violence by fury at the West's unjust handling of the Palestine question and disgust at the hypocritical manner in which the Kingdom's Wahhabi religious establishment has tolerated the impious excesses of the royal family and the trampling of Islam's Holy Places by infidel army boots since the first Gulf War.*

The relationship between global jihadism and Saudi Wahhabism has been uncomfortably clear since 9/11, but with implications that look far more serious for Yemen than for Saudi Arabia. It is yet another sad case of 'If a rich man ate a snake, they would say it was because of his wisdom; if a poor man ate it, they would say it was because of his stupidity'; Wahhabism might not have done wealthy Saudi Arabia much good but it could prove catastrophic for poor Yemen. Unlike its rich neighbour, Yemen cannot afford to neutralise its spreading jihadist threat with lavishly funded re-education programmes and an inexhaustible supply of houses, new cars and wives. If Yemen is fast breeding jihadists, it is not because radical Islam has a special appeal for Yemenis, or because violence and intolerance are in their blood, but in large part because jihadist groups can afford to pay adherents who have no other means of earning a living.

* All US troops in Saudi Arabia were withdrawn after thirteen years, in 2003.

## WHAT KIND OF ISLAM?

In the middle of Tarim, a famous old town in the Wadi Hadhramaut, is an open-air eatery purveying stringy chicken and rice at dented tin tables spread with striped plastic sheeting. A plague of starving kittens and qat-sellers hugging bundles of qat the size of sleeping toddlers, wrapped in damp towels for freshness, only add to the place's charm. Popular with the trickle of western tourists who still risk travelling the road east from Marib across the desert to see the town's hundreds of mosques and now derelict mansions built by generations of cosmopolitan and entrepreneurial Hadhrami *sayyid*s, I noted on my second visit in late 2007 that it was also attracting groups of young men who were neither tourists nor Yemenis, nor even Arabs to judge by their clothes and the language they spoke.

Dressed in *futa*s and plastic sandals but also long jacket-style cotton shirts with mandarin collars and pill-box hats, they turned out to be Indonesians who had journeyed all the way from Jakarta to Hadhramaut to immerse themselves in the language and meaning of the Koran. One of them told me that the local *madrassah* they were attending – the Dar al-Mustafa – had become famous among Muslims the world over since its opening in 1993, after the demise of the godless PDRY. Recalling not only Hadhramis' centuries-old habit of sailing away to seek their fortunes and preach Islam in south-east Asia, I also recalled al-Qaeda's links with jihadist movements in that region, with Indonesia's Jemaah Islamiyah, for example. Hadhramaut's remoteness from any power centre and yet openness to the outside world seemed to render it ideally suited to hosting an international terrorist network and there was no denying the fact that the locations of some of al-Qaeda's goriest triumphs – the explosion of Saudi Arabia's Khobar Towers in 1996, the East African embassy bombings in 1998, the attack on the USS *Cole* in 2000, the bombing of the Bali nightclub in October 2002 – perfectly mirrored the nineteenth and early twentieth century reach of the Hadhrami diaspora. That was surely more than coincidental, as was the fact that the three leaders of Indonesia's Jemaah Islamiyah were all Afghan War veterans of Hadhrami descent.* In short, it seemed to me thoroughly likely that if those Indonesian youths were the sort of Muslims I suspected they were then Hadhramaut, occasionally pinpointed by the media as bin Laden's 'ancestral homeland', might be even more accurately described as al-Qaeda Central, its true and natural hidden heart.

But the longer I spent happily chatting to them, the harder it was to imagine that those friendly youths had come to sleepy, dusty Tarim to nourish their minds and hearts on hatred for people like me and dreams of martyrdom. Nevertheless, I told myself, appearances in Yemen could be more than usually deceptive, so I went in search of their Dar al-Mustafa madrassah on the rapidly expanding eastern outskirts of town. A large, two-storey complex of buildings, it had a fine green dome, a high white minaret and a conspicuously self-respecting air about it. A doorman swiftly summoned a British Muslim of Pakistani origin, a former graphic design student from Manchester named Zafran, to attend to me.

Impressively serene and courteous, Zafran revealed that he had come to Tarim in search of the biggest question of all: what are we doing here on Earth? With this goal in mind and before embarking on a three-year course in the traditional Islamic sciences of Jurisprudence, Arabic Grammar, Theology, Hadith (the sayings of the Prophet) and Sciences of the Heart, he had spent eighteen months learning Arabic. Tactfully anticipating my big question, he explained that the college was Sufi in its teachings and therefore had nothing to do with Salafism, whether of moderate or the jihadist variety. Under the supervision of its revered dean, a Hadhrami *sayyid* of venerable lineage named *Habib* Omar al-Hafiz, the Dar al-Mustafa was not engaged in training suicide bombers but missionaries, men who would return to their Muslim homelands with Islam's real message of love and peace in their hearts.

* Abu Bakar Bashir, Abdullah Sungkar and Jafar Umar Thalib.

'We don't have to show the world what Islam is any more,' Zafran declared. 'We have to show people what *true* Islam is.' Clearly, the Dar al-Mustafa's richly cosmopolitan mix of students and graduates represented no threat whatsoever to either Yemeni or world peace. I subsequently discovered that President Salih had not only turned a blind eye to its reverence for Sufi learning and *sayyid* lineage – the latter an elitist affront to a Republican of his tribal origins – but even conferred his blessing on its peaceful work by honouring it with a visit or two.

On the whole, however, Salih's record in combating the spread of jihadism in the vital but delicate area of religious education has greatly disappointed Washington. Although a reasonably good start was made in January 2002 when the PSO rounded up and deported some six hundred suspicious foreigners studying in madrassas, the momentum soon stalled. A declaration of intent that schools of all levels teach a moderate form of Islam from a standardised curriculum was not implemented and nor was a new scheme for closer supervision of Yemen's 72,000 mosques. A 2004 survey conducted by the ministry of religious endowment revealed that the vast majority of imams were still unlicensed to preach and that as few as one in twelve mosques were supervised.[17] By 2005 the prime minister was having to admit to a gathering of education officials that an estimated 330,000 Yemeni children in some 4,000 unlicensed 'underground' religious schools were still being nourished on violent hatred of the West and Jews, on doctrines that would 'bring a disaster to Yemen and this generation'.[18] Three years later, one in five of those schools was still escaping scrutiny.[19]

In Washington's view the picture was bleaker still in the more immediately relevant area of higher education. Two of the Wahhabi world's most revered and influential Salafists – Sheikh Moqbel al-Wadei and Sheikh Abd al-Majid al-Zindani – were Yemenis. Just as Osama bin Laden would do, Sheikh Moqbel al-Wadei had broken away from the Saudi religious establishment in the late 1970s, puritanically objecting to its symbiotic relationship with the Saudi royals. Back in Yemen he felt freer to propagate his message of hatred for Christians and Jews and warn his disciples not to sully themselves by participating in the democracy that President Salih started building after 1990. By the time he died, in July 2001, al-Wadei had established a network of six madrassahs with thousands of students between them, all over Yemen. The first and largest, Dar al-Hadith, was located near Yemen's north-western border with Saudi Arabia, at Dammaj, and was exciting the attention of western intelligence agencies before 9/11. It was known that many of its graduates were imbibing a hatred for the West there before graduating to the liveliest battle-fronts of the Islam versus West confrontation – Afghanistan, Bosnia, Tajikistan, Algeria, Chechnya.[20] John Walker Lindh, the 'American Taliban' arrested in Afghanistan in 2001, had studied at Dammaj. However, al-Wadei's personal antipathy towards Osama bin Laden and disapproval of his global jihad as well as his complete lack of interest in politics seem to have secured the president's protection of his schools.

By far the better known of Yemen's two great Saudi-trained Salafists is the flaming red-bearded octogenarian Sheikh Abdul Majid al-Zindani. A pharmacist by training who has devoted his life to proving that science and Islam were compatible by identifying Koranic references to such phenomena as black holes and photosynthesis, al-Zindani also claims that students of his al-Iman University in Sanaa had proved that the coccyx – the origin of all human life, according to the Koran – is indestructible, and that God has helped him to the discovery of a herbal cure for HIV/AIDS – 'Eajaz-3'.[21]

A household name in Yemen long before he opened his university, al-Zindani began his august career in Yemen in the mid-1970s when the popular President al-Hamdi welcomed him home from Saudi Arabia, appointed him the country's chief religious authority and gave him a free hand to promote Saudi Wahhabism as a prophylactic against the PDRY's Marxism. By the early 1980s al-Zindani – always a fervent enemy of Marxism – was in Saudi Arabia, acting as an important link in the chain of people engaged in steering both Yemeni and Saudi youths towards the anti-Soviet jihad in Afghanistan. The early 1990s found him back in Yemen, however, helpfully championing the cause of the north against the infidel Marxist south and mediating between Salih and the Afghan War veterans. Salih appreciated having him on his side, helping to uphold Yemen's unity, but he was a loose cannon. In the aftermath of 9/11 al-Zindani preached that President Bush had conspired with Jews to attack his own World Trade Center. No wiser a year later, he appeared on Egyptian television waving an AK-47 around while describing Bush as the infidel governor of Muslim lands.[22]

The 'War on Terror' was already in its third year by the time the US Treasury Department and the United Nations felt they had gathered enough evidence to rebrand this Yemeni national treasure a 'Specially Designated Global Terrorist'. According to their information al-Zindani had fundraised and bought arms for al-Qaeda and acted as one of the movement's spiritual mentors and even, it emerged later, had a hand in selecting the attackers of the USS *Cole*.[23] For his part, al-Zindani admitted to having met bin Laden in Jeddah in the early 1980s and to collaborating with him to ensure a steady supply of Saudi Arabian and Yemeni jihadists to Afghanistan in accordance with US foreign policy at the time, but he has refused to either own or disown any subsequent or current contact with the world's most wanted terrorist. Annoyed by rumours that al-Zindani's Al-Iman University was packed with jihadists and bristling with weapons, Salih characteristically refrained from directly confronting al-Zindani head-on by sending in the troops. Instead, he informed al-Zindani that, since he had decided to honour the establishment with his presence at its annual graduation ceremony that year, his bodyguards would naturally be conducting a routine but thorough search of the whole campus. Unsurprisingly, nothing was found and Salih went on to score points with his people in early 2006 by boldly vouching for the colourful cleric on television, insisting that he was 'a rational, balanced and moderate man', that he knew him well and could 'guarantee his character'.[24]

Confident of support from both Salih and elements of the Saudi religious establishment, al-Zindani noisily lambasted Washington for trying 'to dry up the springs of Islam' instead of just tackling terrorism[25] and for blackening his name as it had blackened Saddam Hussein's by alleging he was hiding weapons of mass destruction. But he settled back into his role as a loyal supporter of Salih, confining his political activities to taking a rigidly conservative line on matters involving the curtailment of women's freedoms. In early 2008, for example, he was gathering 2,000 Salafists and powerful conservative tribesmen at his university for a conference aimed at inaugurating a 'Commission for the Propagation of Vice and Virtue' – a religious police force like Saudi Arabia's feared al-Mutawaah. In the spring of 2009, when Yemen's parliament voted in favour of setting a legal minimum age at which girls can be married (of seventeen), al-Zindani issued a fatwa against any age restriction.

Funded by various Gulf State and Saudi Arabian donors but resembling a hurriedly erected refugee camp or an army barracks, al-Zindani's university occupies a large hill on the scruffily unfashionable northern edge of Sanaa. Alongside its neat rows of Nissen-style huts, it boasts a mosque that looks like a windowless out-of-town superstore. On the day I drove around it in the friendly company of a minder picked up at the gated entrance, I saw only one student, an African. The only two journalists, both Yemenis, to have been granted permission to research feature articles about the place discovered that the foreign students who made up a tiny fraction of the student body – roughly 150 out of 4,650 in 2007 – tended to be more inclined towards jihadism than the vast majority of their Yemeni counterparts.[26]

## THIRD-GENERATION JIHAD

The suspicious escape of the twenty-three jihadists from the PSO jail in Sanaa in February 2006 and the wholesale slaughter of seven Spanish tourists and their Yemeni drivers in Marib in July 2007, followed by the killing of two elderly Belgian women tourists and their Yemeni driver by four gunmen hiding behind a pick-up truck in

Hadhramaut's Wadi Doan in Janaury 2008, marked the end of the period in which Salih's skill at dancing on the heads of a second generation of jihadists by bribing them had kept Yemen free from attack.

Bin Laden's former bodyguard Nasir al-Bahri suggested a main reason for the change. 'This is not Sheikh Osama Bin Laden's strategy at all,' he told the *Gulf News*. Identifiying a third generation of jihadists who looked to the ruthless Jordanian Abu Musab al-Zarqawi, the leader of al-Qaeda in Iraq since 2006, for guidance and inspiration, he explained: 'This is the Iraq generation. They are young people who went there for jihad. They are inexperienced, misguided and wrongly mobilised.'[27]

A tacit aspect of the truce the regime had made with some first- and second-generation jihadists had had a direct bearing on Iraq; if Yemeni jihadists would refrain from attacking Yemeni interests, then the state would put no obstacles in the way of them fighting jihad elsewhere. Sheikh al-Zindani, for example, encouraged Yemeni youths to go and fight in Iraq. Al-Hikma Association, a charity linked to one of Yemen's political parties, reportedly helped recruit and transport fighters for the great cause.[28] Yemenia flights from Sanaa transported dozens of jihadists to Damascus; an Iraqi exile on one flight overheard a forty-strong contingent openly discussing their plans.[29] The president's powerful kinsman, Brigadier-General Ali Muhsin al-Ahmar, reportedly handled the Yemeni jihadist traffic to Iraq after March 2003 as efficiently as he had the traffic between Yemen and Afghanistan in the 1980s. An estimated 2,000[30] Yemenis made up the third largest contingent of foreign fighters in Iraq – the largest after the Saudis and Libyans.[31]

The America-led invasion of Iraq presented all the Muslim world with such a powerfully strong argument for jihad that even my prosperous tribesman oil-worker friend, young Ibrahim, had longed to be off there battling American forces. Ahmad al-Fadhli had told me about a young Saudi cousin of his who had made his way to Iraq via Yemen and Syria and only began to doubt his commitment to the cause when he was invited to become a suicide bomber. A treasure trove of documents captured by US forces on the Syrian border in 2007 included lists of foreign jihadists, complete with details of how they had reached Iraq, from where and with how much money. Most of the Yemenis hailed from Sanaa, but one of the lists described a twenty-three-year-old Hadhrami named Salim Umar Said Ba-Wazir* who, like so many of his Hadhrami forebears, had travelled from Yemen by way of the Far East, via Malaysia. After supplying his home telephone number in case his family needed to be informed of his death, he had poignantly added in brackets, 'do not inform the women'. Most of these jihadists had listed their occupations simply as 'martyr', 'fighter' or 'suicide bomber',[32] and had donated hundreds, in Ba-Wazir's case 1,500, dollars to the cause. After Abu Musab al-Zarqawi's death by American targeted assassination in June 2006, some began making their way home again. Russian spies hunting for the men who had killed four Russian diplomats in Baghdad, tracked one of them down to Aden where he and another Iraq veteran were in the process of forming a 'Brigade of Martyr Abu Musab al-Zarqawi' to fund-raise and recruit more jihadists.

This third generation were not amenable to golden handshakes and deals as Tariq al-Fadhli and Nasir al-Bahri had been. They were committed to the violent destruction of anyone and anything that ranged itself on the side of the West: President Salih, some Spanish tourists, some Belgian tourists, a foreign-owned oil facility, Yemeni police and security officers. All were now fair game. Judging by a plethora of statements on their websites, jihadist groups were proliferating so fast and energetically that it was impossible to know where one ended and another began, which one was in alliance with which, or which was affiliated to al-Qaeda proper and how closely, or whether Osama bin Laden exercised any control at all any longer. If it was the case that Yemenis featured prominently in what Jason Burke calls the 'al-Qaeda hard core'[33] that had monopolised the jihadist scene

* Typically, Hadhrami family names begin with 'ba'.

between 1996 and 2001, they were at least as well represented in this more diffuse and fragmented phase of the generation of jihadists who had won their spurs in Iraq between 2003 and al-Zarqawi's demise in mid-2006.

Al-Qaeda in Yemen (AQY) was the name of the organisation led by Qaid Sinan al-Harithi, who was killed by an American Predator in the Marib in 2002. Down but – while there was jihad to be waged in Iraq – not entirely out, AQY had received a new lease of life in 2006 thanks to the jailbreak of the twenty-three second-generation jihadists. By March 2008, its ranks boosted by veterans of the war in Iraq, it was thriving again, putting out a slick online magazine titled *Sada al-Malahim* ('Echo of Epics') which was very similar in both design and content to the more established Saudi *Sawt al-Jihad* [Voice of Jihad] but more geared to criticising Salih's regime and to trying to appeal to the tribes for support than its Saudi counterpart. A sample issue contained articles titled 'Seven Years of Crusader Wars', 'The Ruling on the Soldiers and Helpers of the Pharoah of Our Time', 'The Power is in Firing [Guns]', 'The Ruling on Escaping from the Tyrants Prison and its Persecution', 'Letter from the Daughter of a *Mujahid*' and 'Preventing and Treating Colds'.[34] Another group, calling itself the 'Unification Battalions', planned attacks on the British and Italian embassies and the French Cultural Centre in Sanaa in 2005. Yet another, the Yemeni Soldiers' Brigades (YSB), was first heard from after the attack on the Spanish tourists in 2007, and again in March 2008 when it misfired three mortars at the US embassy in Sanaa and succeeded only in injuring a dozen schoolgirls, to whom it then politely wished a speedy recovery. YSB also claimed to be part of a group named 'Qaeda al-Jihad', and went on to attack a foreigners' compound in Sanaa in April 2008. A month later it seemed to have joined forces with AQY in Yemen, but then to have fallen out over strategy, with YSB carrying out a number of little assaults on oil installations and police stations and AQY apparently preferring to conserve its energies for more dramatic, global headline-grabbing attacks. By

July 2008 yet another group – 'Yemeni Islamic Jihad' (YIJ), or perhaps 'Al-Tawheed Battalions of Yemeni Islamic Jihad' – appeared to have merged with YSB. An absurdly unprincipled organisation, the YIJ demanded $5 million of protection money from Saudi Arabia and the UAE to refrain from carrying out attacks.

Yemen's malfunctioning security and legal structures are acting as excellent recruiting sergeants for jihadism in its third phase. Privation and torture are a well-documented feature of jails run without supervision by Yemen's PSO and the National Security Bureau (NSB), a rival security structure founded in 2002, with American funding, after it had become clear that the PSO was riddled with jihadist sympathisers. The slaughter of the two Belgian women tourists and their driver in the Wadi Doan in January 2008 was justified as retaliation for the alleged death by torture of a fellow jihadist while in jail. Relatives of wanted jihadists were taken as hostages. The case of a well-known jihadist, an Arabic professor known as Abu Zubayr, was highlighted by international human-rights groups; in July 2007 his three younger brothers – Amir, Mouad and Mohammed al-Abbaba – were all arrested and placed in solitary confinement for two months. Almost two years later, they were still being held without trial and their brother was still at large.[35] If Yemen's jails were exacerbating the jihadist problem so was President Salih's sudden change of tack, the abandonment of conciliation tactics and his authorisation of a violent crackdown on dozens of suspected jihadists who were thrown into jail for years on end, without any hope of a fair trial.

The new campaign began in July 2008, after a suicide ramming of a police compound in Seiyun, only a few miles' drive from Tarim in the Wadi Hadhramaut itself, by a third-year medical student who had been raised in Saudi Arabia and longed to fight in Iraq. When his jihadist group carelessly posted a photo of the happy martyr on a website, the PSO wasted no time in using it to facilitate a bumper trawl of thirty jihadists in Hadhramaut, fifteen of whom reportedly confessed to planning operations in Yemen and Saudi Arabia. Fresh leads gleaned through their interrogation pointed to another nest of jihadists residing in Mukalla; stores of arms, military uniforms and women's clothing were found at a house in Hadhramaut's main port. From Mukalla, police followed the trail back inland, across the empty plateau, down into the Wadi Hadhramaut, to a house in Tarim where, after a two-hour gun battle that cost the lives of two policemen and five suspected jihadists (one of whom had escaped in the mass jailbreak of 2006), a search unearthed more arms, 'fifty large sacks loaded with gun powder and large amounts of TNT explosives'[36] as well as computers and paperwork relating to planned attacks.

Nevertheless, on 17 September that year, jihadists staged their most dramatically sophisticated operation since the attack on the USS *Cole* eight years earlier: an assault on the American Embassy in Sanaa. It was the third try at the target, the second attack in six months. At approximately nine in the morning, half a dozen suicide bombers – three of them wearing explosive vests and all dressed in military uniforms – managed to drive two police cars through the outer ring of the embassy compound's reinforced perimeter defences. No Americans, but nine Yemenis and an Indian – four civilians and six security guards – were killed in the blast. The loud-mouthed leadership of one jihadist group proudly claimed responsibility for the attack, but it transpired that the more impressively organised, funded and staffed AQY was its perpetrator.

By the year's end it was abundantly clear to both Salih and his western allies that, almost two decades on from the fateful influx of thousands of Afghan War veterans into the country, AQY was thriving again and Yemen once again serving as a refuge for jihadists from all over the Muslim world. The lists of those arrested in various police trawls showed that there were Syrian, Kuwaiti, and Saudi veterans of the war in Iraq as well as fugitives from countries where campaigns aimed at eradicating jihadism had been going on far longer and with greater efficiency than in Yemen. In the coming year, as American Predator attacks began an efficient culling of jihadists for whom Pakistan's ungoverned western tribal areas had been a sanctuary, there would be more and more reports of an escaping flow in the direction of Yemen.[37]

The country's jihad scene was changing, the confusion created by a profusion of groups gradually clearing as passions roused by scenes of carnage and prisoner abuse by US forces in Iraq grew calmer. A few months before the attack on the US embassy in Sanaa, in March 2008, AQY's on-line magazine had carried an article by a wanted Saudi jihadist who suggested that, since most members of al-Qaeda in Saudi Arabia were either dead or locked up, it would make sense for those left alive and free to join forces with AQY. They could all help each other out, he argued, by combining the 'life and the money of the Saudi mujahideen' with the 'land, life and experiences of the Yemeni brothers'[38] – a suggestion that was soon endorsed by bin Laden's right-hand man, Ayman al-Zawahiri. The formal merger, along with some personnel changes, was declared in a video recording accompanying the web-posting of the January 2009 edition of *Sada al-Malahim*.

The head of AQY, a second-generation Yemeni jihadist, one of the twenty-three escapees from jail in 2006 and bin Laden's former secretary, Nasir al-Wahayshi, assumed the leadership of the freshly amalgamated Al-Qaeda in the Arabian Peninsula (AQAP). Much to the embarrassment of the Saudis, Said Ali al-Shihri, a Saudi citizen of Yemeni tribal origin who had graduated from a Saudi re-education centre after six years at Guantanamo, was appointed his deputy. Within the month al-Wahayshi was calling for a jihad uprising of Yemen's tribes against a new invasion of 'the land of faith and wisdom' (the Prophet Mohammed's famous description of Yemen) by 'French, British and Western Crusaders', his own take on the joint action by navies from all over world to rid the Arabian Sea and Gulf of Aden of Somali pirates. He mentioned that training camps for jihadists destined for Palestine were being set up in Yemen and he reiterated that tourists, Yemenis guarding western embassies and, of course, representatives of any Muslim regime (including Yemen's) that was doing the West's bidding, were now all valid targets. In the opinion of one foreign analyst, the merger had injected 'gravitas' into a previously shambolic jihadist scene.[39]

In March 2009, AQAP claimed responsibility for two suicide attacks – the first, by a nineteen-year-old from Taiz, killed four South Korean tourists in the Hadhramaut town of the mud-skyscrapers, Shibam; the second, three days later, targeted a visiting delegation of South Korean diplomats and investigators en route for Sanaa airport, but harmed no one except its teenage attacker. The co-ordination and careful targeting of the attacks were unnerving; the mystery of why South Koreans had been selected as victims was cleared up when it was recalled that South Korea was lined up to be the brand new LNG plant's first customer a few months later.

Al-Qaeda in Saudi Arabia's strategy to beat a retreat back into Yemen, in order to be able to plan operations in the Kingdom from a safe base, was test-driven in August 2009 with a first bold plot to assassinate a member of the Saudi royal family. Prince Mohammed bin Nayef, chief of counter-terrorism in the Kingdom, had been contacted by a Saudi member of al-Qaeda who had fled to Yemen but claimed to have seen the error of his jihadist ways, and to be ready to turn over a new leaf and take advantage of Saudi Arabia's generous re-education facilities, just as another Saudi jihadist on the run in Yemen had recently done. The twenty-three-year-old Abdullah Hassan al-Asiri's approach was kindly welcomed, his attitude of repentance construed as entirely appropriate to the holy month of Ramadan. The prince graciously agreed not just to receive him at his own home in Jeddah, but to send his jet to collect him from Najran, close to the border. On arrival at the evening Ramadan gathering at the royal mansion, al-Asiri was presented to the prince. He informed him that several of his fellow jihadists in Yemen were also ready to turn themselves in, suggesting that the prince reassure one of them directly by speaking to him on al-Asiri's mobile phone. Clearly, that call was the agreed signal for detonation. A plastic bomb weighing between 100g and half a kilo that he had either inserted into his rectum or secreted in his underpants exploded and tore him to pieces but somehow failed to harm the prince. Bin Nayef declared that his close shave with death would not force him to review Saudi Arabia's forgivingly generous carrot and stick counter-terrorist strategy, the same strategy that Yemen had pioneered but had to abandon in 2005 for lack of adequate carrots. Yemen's foreign minister revealed that al-Asiri had travelled to Najran from Marib. By the autumn of 2009 Yemen was competing with the tribal border area between Pakistan and Afghanistan and Somalia for the title of 'The World's Most Welcoming Jihadist Sanctuary'.

The economic gulf separating Saudi Arabia and Yemen, which enabled the former to run a lavish and reasonably efficient re-education for its jihadist delinquents while the latter had had to abandon the effort, might have been the most salient difference between the countries and an important reason why jihadism was on the rise rather than waning in Yemen, but it was not the only one. Saudi Arabia was a functioning state, governed in its entirety to the satisfaction of a substantial portion of its population. Yemen, by contrast, was a chronically malfunctioning entity, patchily governed with the acquiescence and to the satisfaction of a rapidly shrinking percentage of its population, home to two domestic insurgencies as well as al-Qaeda by the end of 2009.

## CHAPTER EIGHT
# AL-QAEDA, PLUS TWO INSURGENCIES

### ON THE ROAD TO RADFAN

After a fine lunch in the air-conditioned sanctuary of the Aden Hotel, we were all behaving as if we were off on a jaunt to the seaside. But we were headed to Radfan, a sharp thorn in the side of the British in Aden back in the 1960s, a hotbed of the south's renewed bid for secession from Sanaa half a century later in the spring of 2008.

Squeezed tightly together on the back seat of the luxury Land Cruiser so that I could be decently segregated in the front passenger seat, my three male companions joked and laughed and ordered the driver to turn up the air-conditioning. One last fiddle with the controls, and we were off. Through the sleepy baked centre of Aden we sped in our refrigerator on wheels, its tinted windows protecting us from the blinding white sunlight and the dazzle off the Arabian Sea which was visible to our right in the gaps between apartment blocks and new government buildings hung with outsize portraits of President Salih. Round the English-made roundabouts we went on past Crater, the extinct volcano heart of Aden with its neat grid of

British-built streets where FLOSY and the NLF had slugged it out and Mad Mitch's Argyll & Sutherland Highlanders had bagpiped a temporary conquest, past the British-built blocks of Maalla where British servicemen had once lived.

At last I was feeling free to discard the black scarf I had been wearing in token Benazir Bhutto style for weeks in Sanaa. Traces of Aden's British and Marxist times gone by, when women had felt free to study, work and go out alone and unveiled, had been fading fast since the north tightened the union of the two Yemens following the war of 1994, but they were still not completely erased, and the sea views helped. Even northerners found it easier to breathe, to relax, here in Aden. Sanaa's *jeunesse dorée* with time on their hands and money to burn were in the habit of racing down in their Land Cruisers from their highland eagle's nest of a capital to let their hair (and themselves) down by drinking and clubbing and going to the beach. The acme of comfort in British times, the old Crescent Hotel, had weathered the immediate post-Marxist period as a brothel but was now scheduled for a makeover.

The owner of our Land Cruiser and so the de facto leader of our expedition was a military psychiatrist but also a wealthy émigré businessman whose Emirates passport seemed to be no obstacle to his continuing to act as a sheikh of his gigantic Yafai tribe by dispensing largesse and political advice and influence. Impressively attired in a striped business shirt with cufflinks, a *futa* worn like a bath-towel around his wide girth, flip-flops, gold-rimmed spectacles and a tribal head-cloth, Dr Mundai al-Affifi was instantly likeable. The initiator of the expedition was Ahmad bin Ferid, a serious young journalist and a scion of the former ruling family of the once restive Upper Aulaqi Sheikdom which bordered on Dr al-Affifi's Lower Yafai. Our third travelling companion, described to me by Dr al-Affifi as a 'prominent citizen of Aden', turned out to be the proprietor of Aden's oldest bookshop.

Safe in my bag was another *tasrih* to travel outside the city, obtained from a policeman who forbore from refusing my request on the grounds that I should have applied at least twenty-four hours in advance and instead smiled and said, 'If it is God's will I want you to visit Radfan because it's my home.' As he handed me the permit, he had added with an odd mixture of pride and regret, 'Of course, you know that we in Radfan started the revolution against you British imperialists back in the sixties?' In theory, a *tasrih* was all I needed, but if I was right in thinking that Salih regarded the southern secessionist movement as the most dangerous snake's head he had to dance on simply because he cherished the 1990 union of the two Yemens as the proudest and most concrete achievement of his thirty years in power, I thought I had better secure some extra insurance. A verbal laissez-passer from Yemen's minister for local administration, whom I encountered in the lobby of the Aden Hotel would do, I had decided. Rather to my surprise, the kindly official had not been able to think of any good reason why I should not visit Radfan. Saada, at the opposite end of the country, near the Saudi border, where an on–off war had been in progress since the summer of 2004, was completely out of bounds and, thanks to jihadist activity, Marib could not be visited without an armed police escort, and the situation in Hadhramaut changed from week to week for the same reason, but Radfan should be all right, he thought. Anyway, I was welcome to call him on his mobile if I had any problems.

So unworried was he by my plan, I almost doubted my calculation that southern secessionism was giving President Salih many more sleepless nights than third-generation jihadists or even another flare-up of the troubles in the north. Although completely unrelated to its southern counterpart, the so-called al-Huthi rebellion in Saada resembled the southern insurgency in two important respects. Both groups of rebels had identified the regime as their enemy and both disturbances had deep roots in the past. If the southern uprising harked back to British times, the al-Huthi one had reawakened animosities last aired in the Royalist versus Republican civil war of the 1960s. In both cases, Salih had tried to work his old magic with promises and gifts and flattery and dividing and ruling and compromise but it had failed, in very much the same way as it was also failing to bring the third-generation jihadists of AQAP to heel. Because the two unrelated insurgencies were snakes' heads he could not dance on he had resorted to the only other strategy he knew: force. If thousands of lives had already been lost in the north-west since the first outbreak of fighting in the north-west in 2004, the First Saada War as it was known, thirteen southern lives had been lost, four of them in Radfan, by the end of 2007 and the trouble showed every sign of escalating.

I soon discovered that all three of my cheerful companions as well as the managing editor of Aden's *Al-Ayyam* newspaper whom I had met that morning shared a passionate conviction that unless the outside world was swiftly apprised of the heavy-handed manner in which Salih was tackling southern discontent there would soon be another civil war. It was a while before I understood that they were working on the badly mistaken assumption that if I was sufficiently interested in Yemeni affairs to ignore the travel advice of my own government, then I must be engaged on an important clandestine mission for that government, and therefore ideally placed to convey their alarm to the West. Together, they had calculated that if I could only witness the tensions in Radfan with my own eyes, surely powerful men in London would listen to my account of the situation, sympathise with their plight, support their liberation struggle, and influence powerful men in Washington to do the same. I realised I was witnessing a perfect example of what the foremost historian of the British capture of Aden, Gordon Waterfield, identified as 'the eternal surge of Arab optimism', but anxious as I was to explore Aden's hinterland I did nothing to dispel their delusion.

It was still early afternoon when our car slid to a smooth halt at the first checkpoint on the edge of town and I produced my *tasrih* for perusal, and we waited, and waited, watching qat wads the size of golf balls swell in the cheeks of the soldiers, until suddenly the mood changed. Suddenly, they were yanking open the back door of the car, yelling at us to hand over our identity documents and mobile phones,

Harvard COOP
1400 Massachusetts Avenue
Cambridge, MA 02238
(617) 499-2000

HARVARD COOP 617-499-2000
thecoop.com

STORE:03000 REG:040 TRAN#:5779
CASHIER:STEVEN B

Yemen: Dancing on
*TRADE*
9780300117011 T
(1 @ 20.00) 20.00

Subtotal 20.00
T1 Sales Tax (06.250%) 1.25
**TOTAL 21.25**
**CASH 22.00**
**CASH CHANGE 0.75-**

1400 MASS AVE
CAMBRIDGE MA, 02138

V182.39 04/02/2011 01:10PM

CUSTOMER COPY

Harvard COOP
1400 Massachusetts Avenue
Cambridge, MA 02238
(617) 499-2000

HARVARD COOP 617-499-2000
thecoop.com

STORE:03000 REG:040 TRAN#:5779
CASHIER:STEVEN B

Yemen: Dancing on
*TRADE*
9780300117011 T
(1 @ 20.00) 20.00

| | |
|---|---|
| Subtotal | 20.00 |
| T1 Sales Tax (06.250%) | 1.25 |
| TOTAL | 21.25 |
| CASH | 22.00 |
| CASH CHANGE | 0.75 |

REFUNDS/EXCHANGES within 7 days
WITH RECEIPT
Vault Guides, Study Guides,
Test Prep & Gift Cards
are NOT returnable
OTHER RESTRICTIONS MAY APPLY

V182.39 04/02/2011 01:10PM

CUSTOMER COPY

pushing and shoving at my companions. Ahmad bin Ferid, the bookseller and I suffered in silence but Dr al-Affifi gave as good as he got, bellowing back, clasping his hands to the hilt of his *jambiyah* which was tightly lodged along with his mobile phone and Emirates passport in the rolled waistband of his *futa*, roaring at them: 'I'm the sheikh of the Yafai tribe! Get your hands OFF me! RESPECT ME!'

To my surprise, they backed away from him, disappearing with a haul of only three mobiles, some identity cards and my passport. Badly shaken by his manhandling, sweating into his elegant shirt, Dr al-Affifi pointed out that this was typical barbarian, thuggish northern Yemeni behaviour, that this was precisely why southerners' patience was running out, this was why there would soon be war. 'Now you've seen for yourself what's happening here! Let's see what will happen next!' He was anxiously ensuring that our stories would tally under interrogation when the soldiers returned, commanded my companions to squeeze up again and shoved a qat-chewing young cadet and his gun onto the back seat beside them. A Toyota pick-up loaded with a mounted gun and a posse of soldiers swerved to a halt in front of us. A few minutes later, still minus our documents and most of our mobile phones, we were ordered to follow it back to Aden. On the way Dr al-Affifi raged at the skinny youth. After confirming that the boy was a tribesman, he lectured him angrily about it being '*ayb*' – a shameful mark of dishonour according to the tribal code – to treat a sheikh and a foreigner in this fashion.

I was more disturbed by the loss of my passport than by the cadet's lack of tribal manners. I was also concerned for my companions' safety, recalling young Ahmad bin Ferid telling me that his articles on the subject of southern discontent had already landed him in serious trouble. Six months earlier plain-clothes security men had bundled him into a police car and repeatedly punched him in the stomach before dumping him in the stony wilderness far outside Aden, to make his way back as best he could. To press home his point, he had proceeded to show me pictures on his mobile phone of a bare bloodstained back with a *jambiyah* buried in it, up to the hilt. Claiming that a dispute over land ownership had pitted this luckless southerner against seven carloads of well-armed northerners, he told me that it had taken two doctors to hold the victim down and three attempts by a third to remove that weapon. The picture, along with one of a crowd of the victim's fellow tribesmen rallied in protest outside the hospital, had been reproduced in all its colourfully gory detail on the front page of that day's edition of his newspaper. While I had nothing to fear from the fall-out of our aborted expedition, its repercussions for my friends might be worse than serious, I realised, as we arrived back at almost exactly the point we had started out from, the police compound directly opposite the Aden Hotel.

A PSO officer in *futa* and flip-flops sauntered towards us, grinning. He had our passports and mobiles in his hands but no explanation. We were not about to be interrogated and my companions would not be tortured. In fact, we were free to leave, though not to Radfan, of course, and he was confiscating Dr al-Affifi's car. Deflated and overheated, Dr al-Affifi and I made for the cool of the lobby of the Aden Hotel. Flopping into one of its plush sofas, he tossed his headgear onto the seat beside him in a gesture of resignation that instantly demoted him from a mighty sheikh to a weary businessman. Within a few minutes, however, a surprising sequel to our mini drama was restoring him to his sheikhly dignity and offering me a rare view of Yemen's tribal inner workings. One after another he began fielding a flood of calls from Yafai tribesmen up country, from Sanaa, from members of the substantial Yafai diaspora in Abu Dhabi and Dubai, even from the United States. There was some excited discussion about mounting a protest at our treatment by rallying Yafai tribesmen to close the road through their territory to any army or police vehicle.

Small wonder those policemen had tried to confiscate Dr al-Affifi's mobile phone, I thought; he had an army at his instant command. Here was ample justification for President Salih's unorthodox style of ruling, for his custom of dancing rather than stamping on the heads of his snakes. What real choice did he have when a single word from a very wealthy émigré like Dr al-Affifi was all it would take for thousands of well-armed tribesmen to rise up and sever a main artery linking south to north, to effectively destroy Yemen's unity by creating a fact on the ground? Dr al-Affifi wisely refrained from saying that single word; he feared the loss of his Emirates citizenship if he was branded a serious trouble-maker in Yemen. 'No, no,' he was telling all his callers, 'no need for action, thank you – I just hope they return my car.'

A few days later a couple of state-owned newspapers printed articles about the incident, alleging that I was a British spy, intent on stirring up trouble in the south and reasserting British influence over the area, but I was safely back in London by the time I heard about them. Less than a month later, however, President Salih cracked down hard on southern separatism for the second time. If a few months earlier, in late 2007, an angry rash of demonstrations had been broken up by riot police with tear gas, live ammunition and thirteen deaths, there were now tanks on the streets and mass arrests of almost three hundred secessionists. The corpulent Adeni bookseller was among those rounded up in the middle of the night, but he was released after questioning.Young Ahmed bin Ferid was not so lucky. Along with the elderly leader of the movement, a Hadhrami from Mukalla named Hassan ba-Oom, whom I had also briefly encountered in the lobby of the Aden Hotel shortly before departing on our aborted expedition to Radfan, he was thrown into a Sanaa jail.*

## IRRECONCILABLE DIFFERENCES

Weather-beaten but fresh in a rose-pink shirt, no *jambiyah*, and a *futa* adorned with a striking pattern of blue flowers, Hassan ba Oom had not looked much like a conviction politician, but at the time of our

* Released after four months, Ahmad bin Ferid left Yemen to claim political asylum in Austria. Dr al-Affifi's car was returned after two days.

brief encounter at the Aden Hotel this former head of the Hadhramaut branch of the old PDRY's ruling Yemeni Socialist Party (YSP) had already earned himself arrest, a beating up and two months in jail for organising a peaceful separatist rally in Mukalla the previous autumn.

Ba-Oom's background was no more typical of members of what was becoming known as the Southern Mobility Movement than Dr al-Affifi's. Southern disaffection had first coalesced into the makings of an organisation with branches all over the south among army officers of former PDRY who had a special axe to grind. After their defeat by the north in 1994, thousands of southern military were among some 80,000 other southerners humiliatingly forced to take early retirement on inadequate pensions. Still mistrusted as Marxists by the YAR's military, they had found themselves unable to pull the right strings, tap into the right patronage networks or even grease the right palms, to earn themselves a decent living. Young southerners wanting to join the national army soon encountered the same obstacles, as did southerners seeking jobs in the oil industry. The protest movement, which first appeared under the cumbersome name of 'Retired Military Consultation Association' had been bitterly nicknamed the 'Stay-at-home-Party'. But back in late 2006 its reasonable demand for equal rights and a level playing field had been too modest and abstract to fire many imaginations. It had not begun to gather adherents and a momentum of demonstrations and rallies with arrests, injuries and deaths until 2007, until it had hardened its message into an outright demand for secession. Southerners of all kinds – not just the military, or old Marxists like ba-Oom who lost power by unity with the YAR, or intellectuals who fondly recalled the British era, or aspiring oil-workers – were agreed that while they had nothing left to lose, they had a little oil wealth and a lot of dignity and peace of mind to gain by trying to break free of Sanaa again.

Even ambitious and high-flying southerners who had secured themselves good government jobs in Sanaa after unification sympathised with the desperate frustration of those left behind and remained acutely aware of the gulf still separating northerners from southerners.

'One feels like an outsider here in Sanaa,' an Adeni government minister told me, 'but is it they who can't accept us or we who can't accept them?' Some believe that unification per se is not the problem, that the real trouble is Salih's northern tribal regime and the way in which it has been imposed on the south. In other words, it is the regime that needs changing, not the country that needs dividing. If that were generally agreed to be the right remedy, a good many northerners would rally to the cause too, but those calling for southern independence sincerely doubt that even a new president would solve the problem. They are people who believe that a century and a half of separate existence have rendered the two parts of Yemen simply too different in too many essential ways to be welded into one unit.

At the root of the problem lies the rule of law, or rather, lack of it. One southerner, a former government minister, explained to me that in the north's era of the imams and Ottomans, it was accepted that if someone wanted a malefactor arrested he had to pay for the service, but, equally, it was understood that if the malefactor wanted to escape imprisonment he would have to pay even more. Neither the British nor the Marxists countenanced such a modus operandi in the south, he told me. Another southerner who had prospered in Sanaa since unification, a member of parliament who feared the country would have to divide again, told me 'It's a difference of mentality – we didn't notice it immediately. We southerners were brought up to respect the system you work within, to believe that finances were sacred, that you only took what belonged to you and that if you were entitled to something you'd get it. Here in the north an entitlement has to be fought for, and you end up spending a lot of money.' Sultan Nasir al-Fadhli was old and wise enough to make a fair comparison between the British era and the present day: 'There are much better roads now, but in British times there was the rule of law; no one could be imprisoned for more than forty-eight hours without charge.'

The most solid fuel firing the anger engine of southern separatism was the less abstract, horribly tangled business of land ownership. Southerners with outraged tales of woe about the theft of their land

and property by a horde of greedy northern carpetbaggers since the civil war were two a penny. The managing editor of *Al-Ayyam* informed me that in the course of the past four years the northerner military commander in charge of the south had helped himself to an area of land 'nearly the size of Bahrain'. An Adeni judge I met told me how he had only managed to retrieve some land he had been robbed of by 'running from pillar to post' and bribing someone with 15,000 riyals – approximately £600. I recalled the circle of Balharithi tribesmen I had seen near Ibrahim's home one early morning, plotting revenge on behalf of a fellow tribesman whose land near Aden had been stolen. I also remembered my friend Ahmad al-Fadhli telling me that he had seized the opportunity presented at lunch one day with his uncle Nasir, his cousin Tariq and Tariq's brother-in-law, the powerful Brigadier-General Ali Muhsin al-Ahmar, to voice the common southern complaint: 'By all means buy our land if you [northerners]can afford it, but don't just take it!' he had told the Brigadier-General.

A few days after our checkpoint incident I learned that Dr al-Affifi's willingness to throw himself and, by extension, his mighty and well-armed Yafai tribe, the biggest of all the southern tribes, into the southern independence struggle had elevated him to the rank of a poisonous snake in the president's eyes. Summoned to Sanaa for a meeting with Salih, Dr al-Affifi had backed up his general point about the north's ill-treatment of the south by recounting the tale of the theft of his own real estate in Aden. Soon after unification, he told Salih, he had invested in twenty-two different plots of land in Aden and even opened a private hospital in the city's most salubrious Tawahi district. In the wake of the 1994 war, that hospital, complete with $200,000-worth of medical equipment, had been commandeered as a military barracks for a period of twenty years. To add insult to injury, nineteen of his twenty-two plots had been confiscated without explanation or right of appeal, let alone compensation.

Instead of instructing an underling to look into the matter, the president had summoned Brigadier-General Ali Muhsin al-Ahmar to make a frank appeal to Dr al-Affifi's baser nature thinly disguised as an invitation to serve his country: there must have been some mistake, so Dr al-Affifi must have his land back, and would he care for a plum posting as director of the army's medical services too? Or could he fancy being the governor of Abyan? 'No, thank you. I don't want or need a job,' Dr al-Affifi had replied, 'and my land and hospital are not my first concern. The most important thing is that you stop demonising all southern separatists as a bunch of Marxists and agents of foreign powers and allies of al-Qaeda, and take the trouble to talk to them.' The sending in of tanks and rounding-up of 300 rebels, including Hassan ba-Oom and young Ahmad bin Ferid, was ample proof that Salih had rejected his advice.

A source of particular humiliation and frustration for Adenis was the regime's failure to remedy the economic mess left behind by the baneful application of Marxist economic theory. They wanted Aden turned back into the money-spinning marine transport hub it had been in British times thanks to its excellent natural harbour and strategic location between East and West, near the foot of the Suez Canal. Some suspected that Salih's strategy was to punish the south for daring to rebel in 1994 by deliberately ensuring that its capital remained 'a village', but the cock-up theory seemed more credible. A shaming tale of corrupt and incompetent politicians (a Hadhrami government minister nicknamed 'Mr Ten Per Cent' was said to have purchased at least two London properties with a single backhander), added to al-Qaeda's attacks on the USS *Cole* in 2000 and the French oil-tanker, the *Limburg*, in 2002 sending the price of marine insurance sky-high, all seem to have contributed to the delay and failure. The upshot of almost twenty years of bad luck, bungling and rampant greed has been that in late 2008 Dubai Ports International, which already runs Dubai's South terminal as well as the ports of Jeddah and Djibouti on either side of the Red Sea, assumed the running of Aden too.* Expert outside

* Yemen's Aden Ports Company and Dubai Ports International (35 per cent) and Abdullah Buqshan (15 per cent) announced the creation of a 50/50 joint venture company in April 2009.

observers pointed to the obvious danger of a monopoly which would mean Aden remaining the 'Cinderella of the East' for decades to come.

President Salih has shown no remorse or understanding. His reply to a *New York Times* reporter's question about north–south tensions in July 2008 was rough and sarcastic: 'We built the infrastructure, including electrical projects, roads, universities, and we restored public properties which were confiscated during the rule of the Marxist party [Marxists' YSP]. And we see such an uproar now because we created comprehensive development in the south. This is because of our efforts in the south.'[1] A few months later a government analysis of economic activity in the Aden area revealed the dismal reality behind his angry bluster: more than three-quarters of all investment projects in the area between 1992 and 2007 had either failed to materialise or been seriously delayed. Fifty per cent of potential investors cited lack of land as a main obstacle; 49 per cent blamed a lack of co-ordination between government departments; 47 per cent mentioned abandoning their plans after suffering intimidation; legal problems ranging from constant changes to the law to delays in granting judgments were serious obstacles; 12 per cent had not been able to afford the bribes demanded.[2]

## THE SAADA WARS

President Salih's handling of what was known as the al-Huthi rebellion in the Saada governorate, up near the Saudi border, has only reinforced the impression that his considerable powers of mediation and persuasiveness were on the wane, that his dancing days were over.

Among Yemenis, the true causes of the unrest which began in 2004 remain as obscure as they did to the outside world which generally, but mistakenly, explains it as either a self-contained sectarian struggle between a minority of Yemeni Shiites and a majority of Yemeni Sunnis, or as a proxy war between Shiite Iran and Sunni Saudi Arabia over supremacy on the peninsula, in which the al-Huthis are raised to the rank of an organisation like Hezbollah, or finally, as a local jihadist movement guaranteed to ally itself with al-Qaeda. If all three of these accounts are certainly wide of the mark, the truth remains hard to discern. The manner in which I was able to build up a picture of conflict amply illustrates this opacity.

The first official I spoke to about the rebellion in 2007 was an adviser to the president who provided me with the regime's official version. A simple class conflict, he explained, the issue was a clear throwback to 1962 and the end of the imamate and its accompanying ascendancy of a few hundred *sayyid* families who claimed descent from the Prophet. It could also be characterised as a contest between modern Republican Zaydis, President Salih among them, who wore their Zaydism so lightly it was more or less Sunnism, and resentful die-hard Saada Zaydis intent on destroying the republic and restoring the imamate. In his view, the al-Huthi clan – a respected Zaydi theologian and his multiple sons – were just arrogant Zaydi *sayyid*s, elitist snobs, irritatingly proud of their guardianship of Zaydi Shiism in Saada, the ancient stronghold of the eighth-century first Zaydi imam, who had managed to gather a couple of thousand similarly superior *sayyid*s to launch a bid to declare Salih's rule illegitimate and unrighteous in the old Zaydi way. Born two years after revolution that had swept away both the imam and the *sayyid* ascendancy, my informant claimed that he had never even heard of *sayyid*s until the outbreak of the rebellion. 'Now I know much more. People from the old *sayyid* families tend to be very good-looking and very intelligent, but they also tend to be bitter about what they lost in the revolution. But actually, they haven't been so discriminated against. Some of them have found good jobs. Right now the ministers for sport and trade are both *sayyid*s.'

I heard other more or less plausible accountings for the virulence and intractability of the conflict. Apart from the belief that it was a proxy war between Iran and Saudi Arabia, there were reports that a number of Sunni Iraqi army officers, hurled out of their jobs and fleeing post-Saddam Iraq, had regrouped inside the Yemeni military after 2003 and were venting their spleen against Shiism by stoking the regime's ire against al-Huthis. There was a widespread belief that the al-Huthis were protesting against their region having been marginalized and starved of funds in a protracted punishment for its having acted as a bastion of support for Imam Badr's Royalist cause back in the 1960s. Once I was told that the conflict could be blamed on the demarcation of the nearby border with Saudi Arabia since 2000; people who used to make lucrative livings by smuggling goods and weapons to and fro across the frontier were simply kicking against new state controls. A Saada tribesman I encountered in a café near the American embassy in Sanaa one morning assured me that it was nothing much, that it all boiled down to a petty local dispute between two neighbouring sheikhs. The editor of a Yemeni newspaper could shed little useful light but claimed to be able to discern four different strands in the rebellion. In his view it comprised a few die-hard Zaydis, a few anti-western ideologists with political links to Iran, a good many more mercenary adventurers and many, many more tribesmen simply struggling to defend their families against the army's brutally heavy weaponry.[3]

Rather more useful clues as to the rebellion's real causes and character emerged from examining the Zaydi background of the conflict which is traceable back to the era of greater openness and freedom of expression and association that optimistically accompanied the unification of the two Yemens in 1990. Large religious summer schools preaching a Zaydi Islam that had not been promoted or openly aired since before the 1962 revolution were set up in Saada and surrounding predominantly Zaydi areas. These establishments drew their energy and popularity not just from a world-wide resurgence of religious faith as a means of self-definition that resulted from the end of the Cold War but also from a more urgent and growing determination to stand up to the alien Salafism and Wahhabism being imported into the area by migrant workers returning from stints in Saudi Arabia and by Saudi-trained and funded religious leaders like Sheikh Moqbel al-Wadei of the Dar al-Hadith centre, at Dammaj. Until his death in 2001 Sheikh al-Wadei raised local Zaydi hackles by preaching vehemently against any kind of Shiism, even one as close to Sunnism as Zaydism. Folllowers of this counter-active flowering of Zaydism became known as *Shabab al-Muomineem* [Believing Youth]. By the end of the decade they could boast twenty-four summer schools, with perhaps as many as 18,000 students in the Saada governorate alone, and forty-three more in other governorates.[4]

But the movement was splitting into moderates and extremists. The latter earned the nickname 'the al-Huthis' on account of their charismatic *sayyid* preacher leader, Hussein Badraddin al-Huthi, one of Yemen's first MPs and son of a prominent Zaydi theologian. The al-Huthis' bold chanting of 'Death to America and Israel!' during a televised Friday prayer session in Sanaa's main mosque in 2003, amounting to an alarmingly frank expression of criticism of Salih's decision to side with the United States in its 'War on Terror', was what triggered the countdown to conflict. While the president could be confident that they would not join forces with al-Qaeda given their visceral hatred of Salafism and Wahhabism, he had every reason to fear that a rising tide of fury against him for his having allied Yemen with a superpower that had recently outraged Muslims everywhere by invading Iraq might easily lead to his assassination by bomb or bullet, like his two immediate predecessors. When al-Huthi rebels scrawled anti-regime and anti-US graffiti on government buildings in Saada and began distributing literature attacking Salih for being an American stooge, he had hundreds of them arrested, but still the movement grew. Al-Huthi exhorted his followers to stop paying any taxes to Sanaa, to cut the main highway between Saada and the capital, to occupy government buildings in Saada and to take up positions in the mountains in preparation for a guerrilla war. Salih posted a bounty of $55,000 on Hussein Badraddin al-Huthi's head and ordered his troops in, under the regime's most notable Zaydi turned Salafist who happened to have the military command of the region, Brigadier-General Ali Muhsin al-Ahmar.

Against well-armed and highly motivated tribesmen who knew their land well, the troops' going was tough. Only after ten weeks of warring and three days of intensive skirmishing about the Maraan Mountains did the regular forces manage to kill the rebel leader. But first his octogenarian father and then one of his younger brothers, Abdul Malik al-Huthi, stepped into his shoes and, with the help of two more brothers, continued the struggle. The martyred Hussein has been honoured ever since in the movement's slogan which he generated two years before he died by commanding his followers to shout it: 'With God's will you shall find those who will make the shout with you in other places. Make this shout with me: "Death to America and Israel." '[5] In 2005 the Second Saada War broke out and the year after that, the third, and so on. For all the new roads and their tanks and fighter jets the government forces soon discovered that they were at about as much of a disadvantage as the Egyptians had been back in the 1960s. The region's jagged mountains and roomy caves – the same region the last Imam Badr and his Royalists roamed in the 1960s – have always favoured the rebels.

What had become absolutely clear by mid-2009, in spite of a ban on both domestic and foreign reporting of the conflict, was that in the course of five years, through six surges of fighting known as the six Saada wars, in which the regime's regular troops armed with fighter jets and tanks battled suspiciously well-trained and highly motivated tribesmen in some of Yemen's harshest and most mountainous terrain, an estimated 150,000 inhabitants of the region had been displaced and thousands of troops and non-combatants killed. Also absolutely clear was that the conflict was spreading well beyoned the Saada governorate, east to the governorates of Amran and al-Jawf towards Marib. In the words of one Yemeni political analyst, 'With every new round of confrontation, clashes increase in their intensity, scope and repercussions, and new grievances are provoked, thereby multiplying the points of conflict.'[6] If Yemen was Nasser's Vietnam, then Saada seemed to be shaping up into Salih's.

By early 2006 he was already reckoned to have some 20,000 troops engaged in quelling an uprising that had only attracted a tenth of that number in the beginning.[7] In the summer of 2007, Salih and Brigadier-General Ali Muhsin al-Ahmar had concluded that the conventionally equipped army was too clumsy a beast for the job. In order to fight thousands of tribesmen skilled in mountain guerrilla warfare they needed to hire thousands more similarly skilled tribesmen. A plan to create a 'popular army' of 27,000 mercenaries, the majority of them Hashid tribesmen, was mooted. The eldest son of Yemen's Hashid sheikh, Sadeq al-Ahmar, for example, obligingly despatched 1,000 tribesmen to Sanaa for some military training but was relieved when they proved surplus to requirements. Hashid tribesmen fighting the mainly Bakil tribesmen of the Saada area was a dangerous prospect; traditionally, Yemen's two largest and most powerful tribal federations avoid conflict with each other. But the Hashid Federation of tribes are divided in their attitude to the rebellion to judge by the variety of political stances adopted by the many influential sons of its late paramount sheikh, Sheikh Abdullah al-Ahmar. Other tribes with less to fear by getting mixed up in the argument, tribes whose lands were nowhere near Saada, were gleefully answering the lucrative call to arms and helping to ensure the escalation of the conflict.

Late in 2007 Ahmad al-Fadhli had introduced me to yet another of his cousins, not Tariq the jihadist but Tariq's younger brother, Walid the mercenary leader. Younger than Tariq and blessed with the almond-shaped eyes, slicked-back hair and smile of a matinee idol, Walid welcomed me to his fine mansion near Zinjibar with its crenellated gate posts, gravel drive, ornamental fountain and manicured lawn, before divulging that he had recently returned from leading 300 Fadhli tribesmen up north to fight the al-Huthis, and would surely be heading back there soon. 'Anyone with enough money to pay me can have as many of my fighters as he wants, to fight whoever he wants,' he boasted, when I ventured to question the wisdom and morality of Fadhlis battling tribesmen with whom they had no quarrel, on the side of a regime that Walid, as a southerner, probably disliked as much as any al-Huthi. He offered to take me with him on his next campaign, promised he could arrange the crucial *tasrih* for me, but the next time we met, in early 2008, the annual campaigning season had not yet begun.

The Fifth Saada war did not break out for another two months, in May 2008, after a mysterious bomb exploded in a Saada mosque. Fighting soon spread to other northern highland regions, to Amran and Hajja and to Bani Hushaish only twenty miles north-west of Sanaa, close enough for Sanaanis to hear the fighting. It was beginning to look as if the rebels might be capable of toppling the regime, but President Salih suddenly surprised everyone by choosing the thirtieth anniversary of his accession to power to unilaterally declare hostilities at an end. Perhaps his denunciation of the rebels as 'ignorant forces of darkness who have adopted deviant terrorist and racist ideas'[8] sounded hollow, even to him. Perhaps persistent rumours had reached him that his army was deliberately perpetuating the conflict for financial gain by selling arms to the rebels. Perhaps the news that his son Ahmad's Republican Guard and his kinsman Brigadier-General Ali Muhsin al-Ahmar's regular military had been using the conflict as a cover for their own bloody rivalry, fighting each other rather than the al-Huthis, had reached him. Alternatively, there were many who suspected Salih himself of orchestrating that lethal struggle for the succession.

## ON TWO FRONTS AT ONCE

The desperate voices of southerners clamouring to be released from union with Sanaa reached a crescendo in the spring of 2009 with the news that Tariq al-Fadhli had switched allegiances. In a clear break with his paymaster in Sanaa, he was openly championing independence for the south. Referring to a new state called not South Yemen but 'South Arabia', he was turning his back on his Yemeni identity and the ghost of the old PDRY to recall the stillborn 'Federation of South

Arabia' which the retreating British had tried to bring about, complete with its flag, its army and its national anthem. Addressing a mass of protestors waving old PDRY flags, at a mass rally in Zinjibar and in an interview with Aden's *al-Ayyam* he boldly declared that united Yemen, President Salih's proudest legacy, 'was born deformed, grew up disabled and now is thankfully buried'.[9]

I was not surprised to hear of his volte-face. If none of the Fadhlis I had met – not old Sultan Nasir, nor Ahmad, nor Tariq, nor Walid the mercenary – had actively denounced the union of the two Yemens, they had left me in little doubt of their dismay at its practical implementation. I vividly recalled Tariq's ominous recital at our last meeting: 'We came to the voice of the power, and we returned without any snakes even . . . And those who knew they already had their snakes clasped them closer.' Suddenly, with Tariq championing the cause, the Southern Mobility Movement seemed to be acquiring what it had sorely lacked for the three years of its existence: a leader of charisma and energy, to say nothing of a reputation for bravery. On the other hand, that same jihadist background as well as his alliance with Salih in the 1994 war and his willingness to take Salih's gold for the past fifteen years might count against him, not to mention complaints that he had sold a lot of tribal land to northerners. Ideally, the movement needed a leader without a jihadist, or a Marxist, or a Yemeni unionist, or an exile past, but with Yemen's last Marxist leader, the Hadhrami Ali Salim al-Bidh who had recently removed from an exile in Oman to another in Austria also offering himself for the position, the choice of candidates seemed uncommonly limited. At around the same time, my companion in trouble at the Aden checkpoint, Dr al-Affifi, excitedly called me from Saudi Arabia late one night to inform me that members of his own mighty Yafai tribe had been badgering him to step into the breach. Some were claiming that no single leader of the movement had emerged, not for lack of discipline or decently trustworthy candidates, but because of a reasonable fear that such a leader would be assassinated – mostly likely in a 'car accident' – the instant he made himself known.

Nevertheless, Tariq al-Fadhli was in the forefront of the liveliest secessionist activities over the summer. Within days of his turncoating there was violence in Radfan over the siting of a new military checkpoint, but the Fadhli capital of Zinjibar was bristling with soldiers and more checkpoints and Tariq under siege in his fortress home on the roundabout. A week later, with a death toll of eight, including security personnel, and eight southern newspapers, including *Al-Ayyam*, forced to stop printing, international human rights organisations were in full cry, but not so foreign governments. When the United States issued a boldly unequivocal statement of support for Yemeni unity and Saudi Arabia and the Emirates followed suit, it was clear that no matter how justified and aggravated the southerners' grievances, Yemen's integrity as a bulwark against the spread of jihadism came first in the minds of the outside world. The fear was that AQAP would hitch its star to the secessionists' wagon, adding its own weight to the centrifugal forces tearing Yemen apart, before stepping in to take charge.

Sure enough, the leader of AQAP, Nasir al-Wahayshi, issued an Internet declaration of support for the southern independence movement: 'Injustice, oppression and tyranny should not be practised in the name of unity,' it said, 'We in the al-Qaeda network support what you are doing; your rejection of oppression practised against you and others, your fight against the government and your defending yourself.'[10] But it cautioned southern separatists against making plans to set up either another Marxist state or a democracy with political parties because 'such parties give our *umma* nothing but disunity, subordination and submission to the enemies'. An Islamic state governed by sharia law was the answer to all the south's problems,[11] al-Wahayshi claimed.

However, there were no signs that common cause had been made or any alliance established between any of the three movements, a fact which might have reassured Yemen's western allies but was no comfort at all to President Salih. On 21 May 2009, the eve of the nineteenth anniversary of unification, Yemen's president issued a terrible warning couched in an apocalyptic vision of the country's near future. If people set the ball of national fragmentation rolling, catastrophe would surely ensue: 'You will be towns, sub-districts and statelets and there will be door to door fighting. No street will be safe and there will be no airplanes flying in the air or boats at sea coming to or leaving from Yemen.'[12]

Thanks to neighbouring Somalia, the words 'failed' and 'state' were already being linked in Yemen, but there was little agreement about how that failure would come about or how catastrophic it would be for most Yemenis, given the hardiness of tribal structures and the fact that especially the majority northern Yemenis had long been accustomed to relying on themselves rather than any state for their needs. For some time, both domestic and foreign observers of Yemen's political landscape had been agreeing that in order to stand a chance of preserving the country's integrity, Salih would have, in the words of one Sanaani political analyst, to 'accept a level of decentralisation he's not even contemplating at the moment'. Some thought eight different regional entities joined in a Yemeni federation would work, others that twenty-one would be more realistic.

But it might already be too late for such finely calibrated compromises. While north and south are two obvious entities, there remains a question over whether Hadhramaut would want to go it alone too. Southern secessionists optimistically insisted to me that Hadhramaut would not because it would have to employ an army of mercenaries to defend itself – 'Hadhramis make business, not war', I was told – but there remains the question of Saudi Arabia's interest in a corridor to the ocean. For Salih the stakes are far higher than they were in 1994. Most of the country's remaining oil reserves and a brand new $4 billion gas liquefaction plant, which he is too optimistically assuming he will be able to rely on for revenue when the oil runs out, are located in the south. There are some who argue that a four-way fragmentation of the state on the simple basis of economic viability is the most likely scenario: Sanaa, the northern highlands and northern Tihama with the port of Hodeidah would continue to be run by the Saudi-subsidised northern highlander tribes; Hadhramaut would be bankrolled by Saudi Hadhramis; the wealthy southern Yemeni diaspora in the Gulf States – people like my friend, Dr al-Affifi – would subsidise Aden and its hinterland; Yemen's only industrial giant, the Taiz-based Hayel Saeed conglomerate, powerful both as an employer and as a source of charity, would effectively underwrite the central southern highlands.

In the late summer of 2009 the sixth Saada war broke out. Sanaa's launch of the unambiguously named 'Operation Scorched Earth' began with the collapse of the year-old ceasefire Salih had announced and a rocketing of Abdul Malik al-Huthi's headquarters in Saada. At last the complicated and obscure conflict began registering on the Richter scale of international news, thanks to international aid agencies' warnings that the Saada situation was a humanitarian disaster in the making, as well as to counterterrorism agencies' opinings that Yemen's increasingly hospitable chaos was guaranteed to attract jihadists from all over the Middle East, Pakistan, Afghanistan and East Africa. By November the conflict had spilled over into Saudi Arabia with Saudi jets obliging Sanaa by bombing al-Huthi-held villages. Fears of the obscure domestic insurgency escalating into into a dangerous regional proxy war between Saudi Arabia and Iran looked increasingly justified. The regime in Sanaa irritated its counterpart in Tehran by renaming the capital's Iran Street after Neda Agha Soltan, the young girl student killed at a rally to protest against the outcome of Iran's June elections, while Iran retailiated by naming one its thoroughfares The Martyrs of Saada Street. Against the looming background fear of Iran's imminent acquisition of a nuclear weapon, the United States and all the GCC were at pains to reiterate their support for Yemen's integrity under Salih's rule, and overlooked his highly dubious presentation of both al-Huthi and southern insurgencies as additional fronts in the old 'War on Terror'.

Alarmed that Tariq al-Fadhli was emerging as the de facto leader of the Southern Mobility Movement, Sanaa was accusing him of inciting his Fadhlis to open fire on the motorcade of the chief of the PSO in the south. Tariq, heading the ministry of the interior's most wanted list, had been given two choices, either to surrender or to leave the country.

My attempt to visit Tariq in Zinjibar in October 2009, in the company of his cousin Ahmad's youngest son, the banana farmer Haidara al-Fadhli, ended in predictable failure. After the chief of Aden's tourist police deeply regretted that he could not take responsibility for issuing me with the *tasrih* I would need to pass any checkpoint, I found myself paying a second visit to the city's central security establishment opposite the Aden Hotel. There the polite northerner in charge kindly explained to me that even if I had been a friend of the Fadhlis for five years, even if Walid al-Fadhli the mercenary was preparing a lunch in my honour, even if Tariq al-Fadhli would obviously not dream of harming a hair on my head, he could not guarantee my safety. I quite understood; he would have had to provide me with an armed escort, while knowing perfectly well that such an entourage would be a red rag to the bull, if not of Tariq's Fadhli tribesmen followers, then of the area's assorted other jihadist groups who were also restive.

From Haidara, who was supporting Tariq (unlike his brother Walid the mercenary, who remained a supporter of the government) and who had seen Tariq the day before, I was able to ascertain that none of the family had been injured but that the third floor had been burnt out and that one of his four wives had needed smuggling out to Aden to have a baby. I learned that Tariq was frustrated at having his phone tapped and at not being able to move out of his fortress on the roundabout for weeks, but that the place was not under siege. Government forces were two kilometres away, so that visitors and supporters like Haidara were free to come and go. Clearly, if Tariq was topping Yemen's most wanted list, his capture was not sufficiently urgent to risk enflaming the southern insurgency by turning him into a martyr. 'If they really want me, they will have to come and kill me here in my house,' he had told Haidara.

Small wonder President Salih was more preoccupied with his two domestic insurgencies than with what al-Qaeda might be plotting next. Like the Yemeni man-in-the-street, he had good reasons to rank the jihadist threat to his country a distant third to the independence movement in the south and the al-Huthi rebellion in the north. It seemed to me that these two more urgent priorities also went a long way towards accounting for Yemenis' frequent dismissal of bin Laden and al-Qaeda as merely the inflated bogeyman of a western imagination that seems always to have needed an enemy of supernatural dimensions to test its mettle. When in Yemen I was often politely reminded that the Cold War-era West had created the 'terrorist problem' for itself back in the 1980s by choosing to fund and arm Afghan mujahideen in the belief that their radical Islam was a lesser evil than Soviet Communism. I had soon discovered that any mention of al-Qaeda to a Yemeni was more likely to elicit the quietly humorous observation that a small, poor town in the southern highlands bore the same name than any opinion or fact about bin Laden's global jihad. Long before western analysts like Jason Burke set about modifying the average westerner's view of al-Qaeda as a tightly controlled, efficient and hierarchical organisation, Yemenis were perceiving it rather as an emotion-led climate of political opinion that waxed and waned in response to a number of factors – anger and humiliation felt at the West's foreign policy in the region, the economic situation, an individual's treatment by state authorities, the energy generated by the charisma of a leading jihadist, and so on.

It seemed important to remember too that long before the Yemeni man-in-the-street worried about what might be happening in Zinjibar or Radfan or Saada or what AQAP might be plotting against oil pipelines and foreign tourists in Marib or Hadhramaut, he would be worrying about who and how much he would have to bribe to get his mother or wife into hospital or how he would manage to feed and house his extended family on a single salary, or even where the next meal was coming from.

Busy securing his own grip on power by the only two means he understood – 'dancing on snakes heads' or resorting to force – Salih had run the country and its minimal resources into the ground. During his thirty years in charge of the military tribal republic he inherited, he had not promoted the development of Yemen into a modern nation state which the majority of its people were content and proud to inhabit. The Prophet's reported high praise – 'Faith is Yemeni, wisdom is Yemeni' – had been twisted into a bitterly funny joke: 'Rumour has it the author of that *hadith* is still under investigation in Heaven for its fabrication.'

If a large number of Yemenis were beginning to wonder if the integrity of their modern state was worth preserving, if the risk of a power vacuum and even a jihadist takeover seemed worth taking, Salih was at least partly to blame.

# CHAPTER NINE
# CAN THE CENTRE HOLD?

## PAYING FOR POWER

'I look at this country, and I see a plane ready to take off!'

'In what direction?'

'I can see you don't believe me,' said Faris al-Sanabani, pausing for another forkful of steak, 'But we have everything in Yemen!'

The president's smart public relations supremo, who doubled up as a wealthy businessman with his own security company and English-language newspaper, knew at least as well as I did that Yemen had almost nothing, that its oil and water were running out, that jihadism was on the rise, that corruption was endemic, southern secessionism à la mode and, at the time, a fifth Saada war was in the offing. Equally, we were both aware that the rule of law was a distant dream, the population exploding, unemployment running at 40 per cent and the president spending billions Yemen could not spare on Russian fighter planes.

It was March 2008 and only the previous evening a western diplomat had told me that, at a recent gathering of his counterparts from other western embassies, all had agreed that Salih's removal from power was vital if Yemen was to avoid disintegration. But even with him gone, the diplomat had confided, not one of them had been able to suggest a plan to reverse the country's decline. 'Of course we'd start by raiding the president's foreign bank accounts for a few billion dollars, but that wouldn't stop the rot,' he had said.

There was clearly no question of Yemen being about to 'take off', although from where al-Sanabani and I were sitting, dining off steak and chips in a fashionable restaurant in Hadda, a southern suburb of Sanaa, it was hard to believe the outlook was all gloomy. We were surrounded by unveiled, wealthy women from the Gulf States and foreign businessmen; the lighting was low, the air-conditioning soothing, the service attentive. Looking around me in that oasis of luxury, I might almost have swallowed al-Sanabani's ludicrous line if I had never seen the dreary destitution of towns like Mocha or Marib, or the squalor of ancient Zabid, if I had not met women who had been married off at the age of nine, if I had not known that a city as vast as Taiz had no mains water supply for weeks on end, or that so much of rural Yemen remained without electricity or that around half the population could not read. I dreaded to think what the camps filled with people fleeing the on–off war in Saada were like, what out-of-bounds Saada itself looked like.

A mere twenty-minute drive from old Sanaa to wealthy Hadda is a journey from the third world to the first. Hadda's clean, quiet avenues were lined with glamorous eateries and the fortress palaces of the rich and influential concealed behind high blank walls and iron gates, and protected by armed guards. I had visited a few of them. A former prime minister's home boasted a basement library and a reception room the size of a hotel conference hall. While lunching at the palatial residence of a member of Yemen's upper chamber of parliament, I had learned that the second power in the land, Brigadier-General Ali Muhsin al-Ahmar, occupied a neighbouring mansion. Another gigantic marble-floored palace, the home of a former minister of transport, had a swimming pool and tennis court. The al-Ahmar clan's stronghold in the capital, a cluster of high-rises in Hadda, was located not far from the American and British embassies with their anti-al-Qaeda fortifications. Al-Sanabani himself was proud to have built his own brand new home in Hadda of stone quarried from a whole mountain he had purchased near Marib, rather than from cement, and to have employed a skilled craftsman to create traditional stained glass and alabaster windows for him. In the main, however, the wealthy of Hadda seemed to have looked to the architecture of Saudi Arabia and the Gulf States for inspiration, rather than to Yemen's famously decorative native style.

In old Sanaa it is much easier to believe oneself in the remote and mysterious heart of Arabia, in a place with a claim to being the longest continuously inhabited city on earth, founded by one of Noah's sons and visited by the Prophet's father and son-in-law. Residing in one of the hundreds of high-rise fortresses fashioned of stone and brick with decorative frostings of white plaster-work around stained-glass half-moon windows, with uneven floors and steeply winding central staircases wafted by burning incense, one experiences a style of Yemeni life far more compellingly attractive than anything on offer in Hadda. In Hadda there are no sturdy, prettily patterned minarets greeting God's new day with a crackle of amplified electronic feedback, before their muezzins' preparatory coughs give way to the shattering surround-sound of the call to prayer. The rich of Hadda are too distant from the old city to enjoy the full effect of those competing wails mounting to heaven like the cries of hundreds of prisoners in an overcrowded dungeon, ricocheting off the nearby mountains and then fading to a sporadic grumble as more workaday noises start up in the narrow alleyways: the roar of engines and the braying of donkeys, the banging on old wooden doors and shrieking from high windows, all the sounds and stinks of the souk.

Barring a few restaurants, Hadda after nightfall is silent and dark, while old Sanaa is at its most seductive, the coloured half-moon windows of its high-rise palaces aglow with jewel light. After ruminating the afternoon away in their above-ground-level niches, on rolled carpets or battered car seats, with their qat and their bottled water and their cigarettes, the merchants and carpenters and blacksmiths in the souk are back in business. Each dimly gas-lit niche and cupboard shop is like a window opened in an advent calendar and, in the low glow of hissing paraffin lamps, a row of crouching qat sellers resembles a group of priests engaged in some mysterious pagan rite. Men returning from the *hammam* with towels slung over their shoulders and a group of their elders lounging companionably on the steps of a mosque suggest the closest kind of community life, as does the fact that if one has visited old Sanaa more than once one is guaranteed to be recognised and greeted, as if one has never left. 'You are welcome' and 'I love you' shout the children in the only English they know. More than anywhere else in Yemen, old Sanaa has the power to persuade one that 9/11, Osama bin Laden and the global 'war on terror' are just sad, bad figments of the western imagination.

Our first-world Hadda surroundings and even the excellent steak were not improving al-Sanabani's spirits. He began railing against Yemen's mulish parliament; if the jet plane of Yemen was taking its time achieving lift-off, if the material gap between Hadda and the rest of Sanaa, old and new, was showing no sign of narrowing that was because, in al-Sanabani's opinion, the ignorant tribesmen who accounted for the bulk of Yemen's MPs were refusing to let the government speculate to accumulate by building a duty-free port at the Bab al-Mandab for example, or a new pipeline and refinery at Mukalla, or a big duty-free port north of Hodeidah, near the Saudi border. Al-Sanabani grabbed a paper napkin and impatiently scribbled a rough map of Yemen with some pipelines and percentages for me. It was really so simple, he said. Actually, he could not see any point in Yemen having a parliament. 'What we need here right now is a dictatorship, not democracy,' he told me, 'Carrots and sticks is what it takes. We should just leave people as they are – illiterate and without electricity – they've been that way for hundreds of years, after all – and just get in the investment from outside and make a start on these big projects. That's the way to get jobs and growth –' He stopped short, belatedly aware of the damage his cynicism was doing to his cause.

American-educated, impatient with his president's costly and time-consuming dancing on snakes' heads that often looked to him like a failure of a will to rule, he was tired and out of sorts. A young friend of his, a deputy of minister of international financial relations named Jalal al-Yaqoub, might be better placed to convince me of Yemen's economic potential, he said. A few days later al-Yaqoub and I duly met, again in Hadda, in another fashionable establishment called The Coffee Trader, at an hour of the afternoon when most Yemenis were lounging at home consuming qat. The American-run café with its authentic Yemeni coffee, Wifi connection and pleasant courtyard garden was as outlandishly first world as the steak restaurant al-Sanabani had taken me to. A threesome of veiled teenage girls sat hunched and giggling over a single laptop. A few young men, dressed in jeans and T-shirts lolled in their chairs, idly scrolling up and down their screens.

In spite of a first, brave assertion that he was 'tired of whining about how bad things are', al-Yaqoub turned out to be far less persuaded of Yemen's chances of pulling off an economic miracle than al-Sanabani had hoped. After a promisingly enthusiastic start – he and Ahmad, the eldest son of the president, were about to embark on an urgent mission to the US and Europe in search of skilled and educated compatriots who could be persuaded to return home to jobs in the higher echelons of the civil service and government – he slowly succumbed to gloom. It transpired that the proposed bait for these young ex-pats – essentially, 'your country needs you' – was highly unlikely to do the trick, given the level of remuneration on offer to those they would be relying on to carry out their commands. As a US-educated deputy minister, al-Yaqoub himself was guaranteed a basic monthly salary of only $250. 'You can see now why no one with any talent wants a job in the civil service,' he grumbled.

Al-Yaqoub repeated what I had heard many times, that no matter how well-intentioned, western-educated or even well-paid government ministers were, they soon discovered there was no efficiently working structure in place to implement their directives, that any lever they tried to pull would simply come off in their hands. He explained to me that the true function of the bloated civil service was not to act as an efficient machine in the service of the government but simply as a social safety net. Employees were assured of small but secure salaries in return for doing almost nothing except voting GPC when general election time came around, and for Salih as president whenever given the chance. Naturally enough, the inadequacy of their tiny salaries had led to endemic corruption; one could not procure a sick note, a passport, a job, or permission to build, for example, without bribing a civil servant. The judiciary branch of the civil service was described by 64 per cent of people polled in 2006 as the most bribe-ridden sector of public life, with cases of judges ruling in favour of whichever party offered the largest bribe.[1] Corruption meant that discontent with Salih's regime was growing, not just in a south nostalgic for British and even Marxist law and order, or in remote and poor Saada, but everywhere.

What al-Yaqoub was saying about the dysfunctional civil service reminded me of what Abdul Qadr Bajammal, Yemen's prime minister between 2001 and 2007, had told me about really only putting in three hours work a day while in office. Other state employees I had met had similar tales to tell of chronic underemployment. A former headmaster confided to me that he had quit his job in disgust on discovering he was powerless to sack the quarter of his teaching staff who were on the payroll but had never shown their faces at the school. A tribesman acquaintance had complained to me that two of his cousins, both full-time and wealthy qat farmers, were on the army payroll but only expected to show up for training twice a year. The army, which swallowed around a sixth of Yemen's GDP, was particularly vulnerable to corruption. In 2006 it was estimated that perhaps a third of Yemen's armed forces were in fact 'ghost soldiers' like my acquaintance's cousins, for the simple reason that the size of an officer's budget depended on the number of soldiers under his command. Surplus ghost soldiers' salaries could be pocketed by the officer and extra kit sold off for personal profit. The higher echelons of the army, dominated by tribesmen, were at liberty to requisition land for military use but also to sell it on for private gain, a practice that had aroused particular anger in the south,[2] contributing hugely to the prevailing feeling that it had been 'occupied' by the north since the 1994 civil war.

Yemen's public service wage bill was swallowing 13 per cent of the country's GDP in 2000[3] but 15 per cent of it by 2005, when the World Bank stepped in to fund a biometric ID system for employees aimed at eradicating what Salih himself estimated to be a 60,000 strong plague of 'double-dippers' (employees on a number of different payrolls) and 'ghost-workers' (employees who never appeared).[4] By mid-2009, however, it was clear that little progress had been made; an EU commission had calculated that if both the army and security services were included in the purge Yemen could easily lose a grand total of 1,200,000 double-dippers and ghost-workers.[5] By one estimate, there were 45,000 employees of the PSO in Sanaa alone, some of them responsible for nothing more taxing than attending qat chews and spreading the idea that without Salih at the helm, the country would be lost.[6] It was equally clear that calling a halt to this thinly disguised dispensing of largesse by a kind and generous sheikh masquerading as a modern president would mean Salih agreeing to disband the biggest constituency with an obvious and solid stake in his remaining at the helm of a united Yemen. Without his vast army of idle and corrupt but solidly loyal civil servants, Salih's credibility as an elected president and Yemen's claim to be a democracy would look very flimsy. He would have no choice but to transform himself into a military dictator.

Judging al-Yaqoub's mood to be sombre enough already, I forbore from asking him why Yemen was buying so many MiG-29s from Russia or why the ministry of finance was not trying to replenish the state coffers by taxing Yemen's highest-earning product after oil: qat. With an estimated one in every seven Yemenis involved in the cultivation, distribution or sale of the plant, and 72 per cent of Yemeni men (33 per cent of Yemeni women) spending almost 10 per cent of their meagre incomes on it, surely it represented an obvious and immediate source of revenue, as alcohol or tobacco in any other country?[7] A former finance minister had once informed me that although in theory there was a 10 per cent tax on qat, perhaps only 20 per cent of it was ever collected. A mere 25 million dollars of annual qat tax revenue could and should have been five times that amount, but it would not have been easy, of course. There were tales of tribesmen resisting qat taxation in much the same way as their forebears had resisted the Ottomans' tax farmers. One attempt to set up an army checkpoint to levy the tax on qat-laden passing pick-ups had ended in chaos, with six soldiers taken hostage and their cars stolen.[8]

Qat is one political hot potato and diesel is another, but they are linked. Yemen currently spends $3.5 billion a year – a quarter of its budget – subsidising 2.9 billion litres of diesel, 70 per cent of which has to be imported. Thanks to these subsidies, a litre of Yemeni diesel costs roughly half what it should. Obviously, the arrangement benefits most Yemeni enterprises, but it also works dangerously to the advantage of two far less deserving groups: qat farmers and white-collar smugglers. A thirsty plant, accounting for 20 per cent of the country's water consumption every year,[9] qat would be impossible to farm without recourse to mechanical drills and pumps fuelled by subsidised diesel because only with their help is it possible to penetrate deep enough to access the sinking water table. It is fair to say that without subsidised diesel, qat-farming would not be nearly so lucrative a business, and Yemen's water supply would not be so threatened, and more arable land might be used for growing food. At least as damagingly, a steeply rising quantity of subsidised diesel is reportedly being smuggled across the Red Sea to the Horn of Africa by high-ranking civil servants who pocket up to 30 per cent of the original subsidy in the transaction.[10] Urgent demands from foreign donors like the IMF and the World Bank that these fuel subsidies must be removed before the next injection of aid can be received have only resulted in toppled prime ministers, riots and even deaths, in 1995, 1998 and again, in 2005. In September 2008, a carefully targeted and limited lifting of the fuel subsidies caused panic-buying, stockpiling and such chronic shortages that even the Sanaa public bus service was out of action.

A combination of bad luck and bad management has left Yemen dependent on foreign aid and oil for more than three quarters of its revenue, a risky position, given that neither the price of a barrel of oil nor the generosity of foreign donors can be controlled or predicted. The fact that the country's oil production is projected to diminish from its peak of 460,000 barrels a day in 2002 to only 268,000 by 2010 and that oil revenues had plunged by a catastrophic 75 per cent in the first quarter of 2009, compared to the same period in 2008, was not Salih's fault, although the business environment he had fostered certainly discouraged prospecting. Nor was the world economic recession and resulting slashing of aid budgets in the last quarter of the decade Salih's doing, but some blame him for the fact that in the spring of 2009 as much as half the money spent by the state was swallowed up by unaffordable fuel subsidies benefiting not just Yemeni qat farmers and corrupt officials but also a substantial number of East Africans, and by the wages of a gigantic surplus of civil servants.[11]

Salih's dancing on the heads of not only tribal sheikhs but civil servants and qat farmers by buying them, and his turning a blind eye to the black market in subsidised diesel could only continue while he had funds. By the end of 2009 signs that the money was starting to run low were not only visible in the form of aggravated instability but in Yemen's steady climb up the index of failing states – from twenty-fourth to twenty-first, to eighteenth position.[12] By the autumn, people were beginning to imagine how the touchpaper of collapse could be lit – when he couldn't pay the wages of the military, some said, by 2012 at the latest.

## YEMEN'S DEMOCRACY

When al-Sanabani veered wildly off his public relations message to attack Yemen's parliamentarians and declare in favour of a dictatorship, I was more surprised by his crediting parliament with any influence than by his cynicism. In the pecking order of Yemen's power centres, the House of Representatives ranked far lower than the technocrat-led government ministries, which in turn were nowhere near as powerful as the president and his kinsmen highlander tribesmen who staffed the top echelons of the military and security establishments.

Western governments had heartily applauded Salih's decision to crown the new unity of the Yemens in 1990 with the enfranchisement of every Yemeni adult, male and female, multiple political parties, a free press and the makings of a civil society. But Yemenis, at all levels of society, very soon lost faith and even interest in what even Salih soon wisely began referring to as the country's 'emerging democracy'. Coming barely a year after the Yemen's first general election, the 1994 civil war had badly complicated its birth. In second and third general elections held in 1997 and 2003, the party of the president, the General People's Conference (GPC) increased its already generous lead. Thanks in large part to the first-past-the-post-system, the 123 seats it had won in 1993 became 187 in 1997, when the south's YSP boycotted the election, and then soared again to 229 in 2003.[13]

Such results were only to be expected, it was said, while the regime controlled all the broadcast media (overwhelmingly more powerful than the press in a country with such a low rate of literacy) and while an army of civil servants directly relied on the state for payment of their wages, and while it was impossible to tell where the structures of the state or the regime ended and those of the GPC party began. For by far the larger part of its twenty-year life therefore, Yemen's parliament had been widely and routinely dismissed as window-dressing, only ever created in the first place because Salih had shrewdly calculated that a show of democracy – 'decorative democracy', as Yemenis called it – was a small price to pay for large injections of foreign aid money. The mere act of holding the 1997 elections, for example, had gained the country a package of aid equal to the size of the national debt.

But it was not as if he systematically demonstrated the parliament's powerlessness by routinely undermining its brave attempts to do its work. One serious flaw was that MPs – the majority of whom belong to the president's GPC, of course – had not been willing or able to challenge Salih's micro-management of the country via his direct control of the finance ministry and the military and security establishments he relied on to ensure his continued hold on power. Yemenis, MPs included, remained conditioned to the belief that, as in the era of the last two imams in the north or British colonial rule in the south, all power was concentrated at the very top. Instead of using parliament as a forum for calling the government and president to account, for formulating and passing laws and toeing an agreed party line, Yemeni MPs tended to treat it as they would any other civil service job, as a resource from which to extract maximum material benefit for themselves. In addition to all this, the adversarial character of western democracies held little appeal for a society that prided itself on having evolved a tribal political culture based on avoiding conflict by recourse to mediation and compromise. From the president down, Yemenis emphasised consultation, compromise and the inclusiveness of 'pluralism', rather than the confrontation and strict party allegiance that characterised western democracies. Individual reputations and family ties continued to carry more weight than political programmes. To add to these handicaps, more than a fifth of the MPs elected in Yemen's third general election, in 2003, had had no formal education, which meant they were either illiterate or barely literate,[14] a mighty obstacle to drafting and discussion of legislation and contracts.

I spoke to many who felt they were wasting their time and energies in Yemen's parliament. Tariq al-Fadhli, who had been happy to take his place in the consultative upper house after 1994, lost interest in its activities as soon as he realised he was powerless to influence the regime's conduct towards the south and had given up attending its sessions by the time I met him in 2004. A genial Hadhrami lawyer who had allowed himself to be persuaded to become a deputy speaker of the lower house was utterly disenchanted after four years in the post: 'I'm not running for parliament again because it's nothing, it means nothing,' he told me. Hamid al-Ahmar, owner of Yemen's main mobile phone network but also a powerful tribesman thanks to his late father's position as paramount sheikh of the Hashid tribes and speaker of parliament, shared his own misgivings about Yemen's malfunctioning democracy when we met at the large and fashionably glass-fronted premises of his Sabafon headquarters in early 2008. 'I'm fed up now,' he told me, 'there's no point in parliament if it continues like this – when you've got about 238 out of 301 MPs belonging to the GPC, and they're just there to do whatever he [the president] tells them to do.'

Like his father before him, Hamid al-Ahmar is a leading member of the Islah party, which struggles to unite an incoherent array of Saudi-type Salafists like Sheikh al-Zindani and moderate Muslim Brotherhood Islamists, and businessmen from the southern highlands, and conservative northern highland tribal sheikhs like the al-Ahmars under one umbrella. Deliberately created in 1990 by President Salih's most powerful supporters – Hamid's father and Brigadier-General Ali Muhsin al-Ahmar* – to attract voters away from the south's Marxist YSP, Islah had taken its time breaking free of its creators and shaping up into anything even resembling a conventional opposition party. After the 1994 war it devoted its energies to banning co-educational classes and sacking female judges in the south, and to opposing the redevelopment of Aden's port as a free trade zone on the grounds that it would attract too many foreign infidels.[15] More popularly, Islah recommended itself by sharing its name with an officially unrelated

* The paramount sheikh's family and the Brigadier-General share a name but are not directly related to each other.

charity that compensated for many of the state's shortcomings in the sphere of social welfare. But in the presidential elections of 1999, the party failed even to field its own candidate.

It was 2005 before Islah began to outgrow its original function as a shield of the northern highland tribal ruling elite and the southern highland industrialists in towns like Taiz and Ibb against the old Marxist threat from the south. In November that year the party switched allegiances to join forces with the its old enemy, the south's YSP, and three other minor parties to oppose the president's GPC in a coalition cumbrously named 'The Program of the Joint Meeting for Political and National Reform' (JMP). Ignoring Islah's original founders (Sheikh al-Ahmar, Sheikh al-Zindani and Brigadier-General Ali Muhsin al-Ahmar), who all remained supporters of President Salih, the JMP proceeded – admittedly, at the very last moment – to field a respected southerner, a former oil minister named Faisal bin Shamlan in the presidential election of 2006. Bin Shamlan went on to achieve a creditable 22 per cent of the vote. Accounting for most of the JMP, Islah is currently Yemen's fastest-growing political party.[16]

By the spring of 2009 the JMP was still being described as lacking a grass-roots base of support, as less a political party than 'a mechanism to lobby the government for greater concessions',[17] but its various component parts could agree that elections scheduled for April that year needed to be postponed for two years because there was no consensus with the GPC with regard to tinkering with the constitution. The GPC favoured keeping the first-past-the-post single-candidate system, while the JMP demanded a party list system which, it believed, would foster fairness and transparency. The JMP wanted a rule compelling voters to vote in their home electoral districts, while the GPC naturally favoured its surplus army of state workers casting their ballots en masse, in their government offices and barracks, for example. If, on the face of it, the postponement looked like a serious set-back for democracy, the decision was hailed as a victory by the JMP and tacitly approved as the lesser of two evils by western organisations such as the US's National Democratic Institute, an NGO that has been anxiously fostering democratic development in Yemen. It was felt that by refusing to go on serving as window dressing for the regime, by threatening to boycott the elections, the JMP had finally succeeded in wrong-footing Salih. At last, the JMP were all agreed that, in Hamid al-Ahmar's words, 'the country's real problem is the president'.

The following month, in May 2009, on the eve of the nineteenth anniversary of Yemen's unification, over a thousand delegates attended a two-day meeting convened by the JMP and chaired by Hamid al-Ahmar, to confront the country's multiple crises: revived secessionism in the south, the prospect of a sixth Saada war, a lively new al-Qaeda in the Arabian Peninsula, economic meltdown, electricity cuts, the rocketing price of flour, and so on. Appropriately, the mood was more sombre than celebratory: 'We should observe the event [the anniversary] with development projects rather than military parades,'[18] declared the young al-Ahmar, to enthusiastic applause. Needless to say, Salih's military parade went ahead the next day. An hour-long procession of 30,000 troops with their Russian tanks and aeroplanes, the largest ever seen in Sanaa, marched past the president who was seated on his rostrum, safely shielded by a bullet-proof glass wall, while down in Aden a demonstration of 3,000 secessionists was broken up by police, leaving three dead, thirty wounded and over a hundred under arrest. By August, Hamid was boldly telling Al-Jazeerah television that President Salih should step down and be tried for treason, for the crime of appointing too many of his relatives to high posts.

Signs of Hamid al-Ahmar's intensifying political activity came as no surprise. He had played a leading role in Islah's slow maturing process and had clearly had his sights set on power by the time I met him in the spring of 2008. A short but sturdily built man in his early forties, usually dressed as a tribesman (*thowb* or *futa*, *jambiyah* and sandals) but with the addition of a Harris tweed jacket to complement a good command of English gained at a Brighton language school, he had ushered me into a penthouse office furnished with a large desk, a display of antique *jambiyahs* and photographs of his late father. One of Sheikh Abdullah al-Ahmar's nineteen offspring, the third of his ten sons, Hamid was looking like Islah's obvious leader-in-waiting but refusing to be formally appointed. He explained that having risked loud criticism of President Salih while his beloved father still lived, he was being careful, missing his father's influence and protection.

His reluctance to act and confront had seemed to me a graphic illustration of the way Salih's snake-dancing style of rule had hampered the country's movement in a democratic direction but kept the president in power. Like so many of the larger tribal sheikhs, the al-Ahmar clan have benefited gigantically by their close association with Salih during the past three decades. Although Hamid might object to the way in which Salih was running the country, he would need to think twice before biting the hand that had been feeding him and his brothers the pick of lucrative agencies for foreign firms, for example. Nevertheless, over a lavish lunch spread for us on his boardroom table, he confided his ambition to be the next Yemeni to try his luck at ruling Yemen. 'I'm proud and willing to do the job' he told me, 'When you want to help your country, you don't count the danger.' If push (playing by the rules of modern democracy by getting elected) ever came to shove (mounting a traditional tribal armed rebellion in the manner of his Zaydi forbears) he would only, as he put it, 'need to phone about a hundred people to rally about 50,000 fighters' to his cause. Not that he was planning to take the 'shove' route to power, but he worried Salih might try and change the constitution's goal-posts by permitting himself another term as president, after his present one expired in 2013.

Hamid would not be satisfied, as his father had been, with exerting power and influence in the background, comfortable in the knowledge that he was 'not directly responsible for the hunger and suffering of the people'. His experience as a modern businessman meant that he was used to wielding direct power and taking direct responsibility, to saying what he meant and meaning what he said. My first thought was that, frustrated by the slow and disorganised pace of ordinary Yemeni life and by the endless and expensive task of balancing disparate interests, by the old need to dance on snakes' heads, he would soon lose patience and turn tyrannical. By the time we had finished tearing at a leg of lamb and scooping at a dish of honey pudding together, however, his quick intelligence and sense of humour had persuaded me otherwise and, by the time I left the premises, I believed that Yemenis could do a lot worse than elect such a likeable blend of both the traditional and the modern Yemen as their president.

Subsequently, I met a number of not just northerners but southerners too who told me they respected and trusted Hamid al-Ahmar, in spite of his family's position at the very apex of the northern highlander military-tribal ascendancy. One southerner judged him 'certainly not worse' than Salih, while another praised him as 'politically sober' and by far the best-educated member of his family. But others, northerners more closely acquainted with him, relayed tales of his thuggish business practices, of the ways in which he had abused his position to enrich himself and once badly sullied his democratic credentials by helping himself to some ballot boxes at gunpoint in Hajja, back in 1993.

In the evening of the day of that boardroom lunch, the affable and Yale University-educated Abdul Karim al-Iryani, a leading member of the GPC who had served as both foreign and prime minister, a member of the *qadhi* rather than the tribesman class, wasted no time in pouring cold water on my claim that I might have lunched with Yemen's next president. 'I very much hope not!' he declared, 'I don't doubt he's a good businessman, but if he was president he would just put members of his own tribe in power, and the Hashid are the biggest, as you know. It would be even worse than what we have now!'

## THE DANCER

An essence of that 'what we have now' had been memorably captured in a larger than life-size oil painting adorning the atrium hallway of the

GPC's central office in Sanaa. It was a portrait of President Salih, but unlike any I had seen before.

Framed portraits of Yemen's short but reasonably good-looking leader grace almost every home and public building in the country but are especially visible on the sides and roofs of public buildings in Aden, which favour an image of him head down, writing, hard at work. Others depict him in a variety of costumes: in tribal head-dress, *thowb* and *jambiyah*, in a western-style dark suit, pale blue shirt and plain tie, in military uniform, or even – by 2009 – bespectacled, tweed-jacketed and smiling in an approachably avuncular fashion. Although, as on a giant billboard on the road from Sanaa into Hodeidah, he is as gamely grinning as if he were advertising toothpaste, his expression is usually sombre, his brow knitted in visionary thought and his jaw firmly tilted resolutely forward. In this particular oil painting, however, he is dressed in a lounge suit and unsmiling but seated astride a richly caparisoned chestnut steed against a pitch black background enlivened by arcs of colourfully exploding fireworks. His shop mannequin stiffness and an outsize pair of dark glasses suggest both wilful blindness and a sinister power. I guessed the artist was obliquely criticising a leader who had deliberately blinded himself to his people's sufferings but, if I was right, the critique was too subtle to have hit its mark; the masterful satire was hanging there in pride of place where every GPC functionary who worked in the building would pass by it every day. It was hard to blame the artist for erring on the side of caution, however. Jokes at the expense of President Salih have been known to have serious consequences.

Salih's entourage had targeted Yemen's funniest satirist, Fahd al-Qarni, a young actor from Taiz, as a particularly dangerous snake. An active member of Islah, al-Qarni was hurled in jail for the third time in as many years for allegedly insulting the president and fanning the fires of southern separatism with his jokes. A cassette recording of his song 'Fed Up' first landed him behind bars during the presidential elections of 2006. In the summer of 2008, shortly before he went on trial again, a convoy of a hundred cars filled with al-Qarni's fans journeyed from

Hadhramaut to Taiz for a protest sit-in outside the courthouse, only to endure beatings by the police. The next day, treated by the prosecution to a recording of a skit featuring a clueless but reckless taxi driver with a voice identical to that of the president, the courtroom dissolved in helpless laughter, but al-Qarni was sentenced to eighteen months in jail and a large fine. Unrepentant but amnestied by the president in September, he was briefly rearrested in February 2009 for the same crime, before being released again.

Although Yemen has rejoiced in a press that is freer than that of any of her neighbours since 1990, there are subjects better left untouched by journalists who value their skins. They have learned by trial and error not to delve into four key topics: the president's family and especially the question of whether his eldest son Ahmad will succeed him; the country's sovereignty with reference to secessionism in the south and the rebellion in the north-west; religion; and the military. In 2005 the correspondent for the London-based *Al-Quds al-Arabi*'s uncovering of a corrupt trade in fighter-plane spare parts that had accounted for a number of MiG-29 crashes cost him two days' detention by air force high command and a night of interrogation, until President Salih himself ordered his release. The case of Khaled al-Khaiwani, a newspaper editor trying to report on subjects like Yemen's jails and the Saada war, was eventually taken up by Amnesty International. In 2004 al-Khaiwani spent a year in jail for insulting the president. Amnestied in 2005, he was rearrested in 2007 – snatched off a Sanaa street by masked PSO gunmen in a Toyota Land Cruiser – thrown into their security service jail and beaten up, before being amnestied again. In 2008 he was rearrested and sentenced to six years behind bars, but once again pardoned by Salih. His rearrest in January 2009 raised a storm of international protest and yet again he was pardoned, after receiving Amnesty International's Award for Journalism Under Threat. The closure of Aden's independent *al-Ayyam* newspaper in May 2009 and a physical attack on the paper's offices served as a tacit acknowledgement by Sanaa of the power of the written press to promote separatism in Yemen's second city.

Frequent arrests, amnesties and rearrests of political dissidents, whether they are journalists like al-Khaiwani, or comedians like al-Qarni, or southern secessionists like young Ahmad bin Ferid, or jihadists like the men who attacked the USS *Cole*, furnish useful proof that not only is Salih not an all-powerful dictator but he is also far from being a bloodthirsty tyrant in the mould of Saddam Hussein or Imam Ahmad, for example. Nor does the secret of his survival in power lie in a monopoly over the country's means of coercion. How could it when there are reportedly an average of three guns in circulation for every Yemeni man, woman and child and when many of the larger tribes boast their own arsenals of even heavy weaponry? And it was certainly not attributable to his having steadily improved his people's living standards, let alone to his having firmly established the rule of law.

Two Sanaani women I spoke to, both of them educated to university level, were inclined to blame his entourage rather than Salih himself – the evil counsellors, rather than the king himself – for their country's many problems. While one male civil servant swiftly diagnosed the president's problem by saying 'he still has a 1970s mentality', his female colleague, a schoolteacher, insisted that as a woman she was grateful to Salih – 'thanks to him, I can work, I can sit in Parliament, and it may be difficult but there is no law to say that I can't sit in a car with a man who is not from my family.' Back came her male colleague's reply, 'All right, he has given us some freedoms. For example, we are free to talk, but as that old man once complained to him on television "You [Salih] have taken the sticking plaster off our lips and stuffed it in your ears!" What good is being able to talk when the one with the power is not listening?'

Southerners with direct, personal knowledge of Salih tend to be far more critical of him, although all agreed that he was 'charming' and emphasised his lack of self-importance, his unrivalled 'common touch'. A wealthy resident of Hadda, a southerner and government minister, thought hard before attempting to describe him. 'When he speaks to you he gives you his full attention and you are the only person in his world. He is very, very intelligent, and he has a unique memory, and he is not a bloodthirsty person,' was how he began. 'But he is one of the best liars on this earth,' was how he ended. The verdict of a fellow southerner, a Hadhrami lawyer, was harsher still; he compared Salih to past imams who surrounded themselves with incompetent nonentities: 'He barely has a primary school education which means that he has an inferiority complex, so the last thing he wants is brilliant people around him.' An Adeni newspaper editor revealed that a far from charming Salih, an enraged and whisky-sozzled Salih, was in the habit of telephoning the paper late at night to dispute the contents of his front page, especially any coverage of unrest in the south. Abdullah Al-Asnag, the clever leader of the Adeni trade unions in the turbulent years before the British departed, who subsequently served as a minister in YAR governments under al-Iryani, al-Hamdi and al-Ghashmi as well as being adviser to Salih until 1984, confined his comment to a single sentence: 'Ignorance combined with arrogance is the end of the world.'

Most Yemenis – both admirers and critics – had no trouble acknowledging that the real key to Salih's success has been his uncannily acute understanding and encyclopaedic knowledge of Yemen's tribal society. It is his intuitive sense that he must only ever be perceived as behaving in the manner of a wise and just sheikh – mediating, balancing, reconciling, co-opting, rewarding, forgiving – that (alongside his access to the oil revenues since 1986) has preserved him from the fate of his two predecessors for so long.

No one disputes that for an uneducated tribesman with only a decent career in the army to recommend him, Salih has done astonishingly well. But there are clear signs that at the age of sixty-eight (he was born in March 1942), and with funds running short, he is flagging. As the sickness created by Yemen's chronic and interrelated and multiplying problems grows ever less curable by recourse to the sticking plasters of bribery and promises, as the complex demands of running a modern state proliferate and the money begins to run out, his hold on power is perceived to be slipping. As early as November 2005 his nervous entourage were shielding him from the shaming news that, owing to

Yemen's failure to meet various good governance criteria, Washington was withholding some $30 million of aid. Certainly, his fuse was shorter than it had been, his patience with dissent much more limited. In the spring of 2008 he shocked and disgusted ordinary Yemenis by using the occasion of a Festival of Camels and Horsemanship in the Tihaman port city of Hodeidah to tell those threatening the country's integrity, 'Our slogan is unity or death and he who does not like this, let him drink from the Red Sea and the Arabian Sea.'[19] At around the same time a government minister told me, 'Until about a year ago it looked as if he was still the strong man with all the strings in his hands. Now it's different. He issues the orders, but they're not being fulfilled. The people around him are doing what they want' – abusing their power to act with his authority.

I recalled Ahmad al-Fadhli musing along the same lines during one of our chats at his banana farm; 'the bugs in your own shirt are the ones that can really hurt you', was how he had put it.

## THE BUGS IN HIS SHIRT

The 'bugs' in President Salih's shirt are arranged in three concentric rings. First comes immediate family, his own children and his nephews who belong to the Bayt al-Affash clan of the Sanhan tribe, which itself is a member of the larger Hashid Federation. The next ring comprises other members of the Sanhan tribe belonging to the al-Qadhi clan, who include two half-brothers and his distant cousin Brigadier-General Ali Muhsin al-Ahmar. Both these Sanhan clans regard their rural heartland as the village of Bayt al-Ahmar, a half-hour drive to the east of Sanaa, where Salih was raised and has built himself a large residence. Beyond these two innermost circles are other Sanhanis and members of his predecessor al-Ghashmi's Hamdan-Sanaa tribe, which also belongs to the larger Hashid Federation of the Zaydi northern highlands.

These widening circles of people who not only hold high positions in the presidential household and offices but crucially in the military and security establishments while heading lucrative enterprises and acting as local agents for foreign corporations, are the guarantors of his security. For the time being too many people still have too vested an interest in Salih continuing in the post of president to mount a coup d'etat. As one member of the upper house of Yemen's parliament put it to me, 'If something happens to the president, they'll all suffer too, so they let him be.' However, the cost of maintaining these concentric circles, especially of his defensive ramparts in the army, security service and personal guard, is considerable; officially declared to account for 25.4 per cent of the annual budget in 2003, it is unofficially estimated by foreign observers to be nearer the 40 per cent mark.[20]

Of Salih's immediate, close family, little is generally known beyond the fact that he has three wives, ten daughters and seven sons. Among his seven sons there is his eldest son Ahmad, an affable and unpretentious person by all accounts but inclined to dissolute behaviour and lacking in charisma, who heads both the elite Special Forces and the Republican Guards and has long been viewed, though not welcomed, as Salih's heir apparent. Muhammad Duwayd, the husband of his daughter Saba, is in charge of the all-important Secretariat of the Presidential Palace. One nephew, Amar Mohammed Abdullah Salih, is deputy head of the National Security Bureau (NSB) and reputed to be a man western counter-terrorism agencies can do business with. Another nephew, named Tariq Mohammed Abdullah Salih, commands the president's close protection force and is the third most powerful officer in the army. Yet another, Yahya Mohammed Abdullah Salih, is the Staff Officer of the Central Security forces.

An attempt to get a feel for the inner circles of bugs infesting Salih's shirt by driving through the village of Bayt al-Ahmar with Walid one late afternoon in 2008 ended in failure, with Walid badly unnerved by a pair of sleek young men in plain clothes appearing from almost nowhere to politely forbid us to drive any further up the road or even to try to photograph the president's country residence, which includes a handsome domed mosque. The way one of them scribbled our car registration number on the back of his hand was what rattled Walid. Most of the top echelons of Yemen's defence establishment hail from Bayt-al Ahmar, including the Commander of the Air Force, Mohammed Salih al-Ahmar, and Brigadier-General Ali Salih al-Ahmar, the chief of staff of the general army command and, most importantly of all, the man reckoned to be the second most powerful person in the country, the commander of the north-western military sector which includes Saada and Sanaa, Brigadier-General Ali Muhsin al-Ahmar.

When Yemenis lounge at their qat chews, pondering how a future without President Salih might look, the brigadier-general's name is always mentioned, and the assumption usually made that he would be far more tolerant of Islamists of most stripes – from mildly Muslim Brotherhood to Saudi Wahhabi style, and perhaps even dyed-in-the-wool jihadists of the al-Qaeda persuasion. He had facilitated the passage of jihadists to the war in Afghanistan in the 1980s, remained close to Tariq al-Fadhli, married his sister and recruited him to the cause of unity on the side of the north in the civil war of 1994, and gone on to supervise the funnelling of Yemeni jihadists to Iraq after 2003.

As early as 2002, when the American author Robert Kaplan was in Yemen researching a book on the American military abroad, it had been clear that thanks to Brigadier-General Ali Muhsin al-Ahmar the country was quietly circumventing President George W. Bush's bellicose war cry of 'you're either with us or against us'. Instead, it was spreading its risk by being both for and against, much as the the YAR had sided with the West against Marxism during the Cold War while looking to the USSR for its armaments. Kaplan wrote: 'it was Ali Muhsen's ties to the radicals that gave the president the political protection he needed to move closer to the Americans – temporarily that is. And also to distance himself from the Americans swiftly and credibly if that, too, became necessary.'[21] It was also Brigadier-General al-Ahmar who brokered the deal that kept Yemen almost free from jihadist incidents between 2003 and 2007; if the jihadists refrained from attacking targets inside Yemen, then Yemen would neither hunt them down or extradite them to the US.

But the breakdown of the tacit agreement with the jihadists after 2007 and subsequent attacks by an Iraq-hardened generation of al-Qaeda likewise damaged his credibility among the other bugs in Salih's shirt, let alone with the general population. Some believe the brigadier-general and the president – both Sanhani tribesmen of the Hashid northern highlander tribal federation, but from different clans – long ago agreed that the former would replace the latter when the time was ripe, but that Salih has reneged on the deal by setting out, like the imams before him, to groom his son for the succession. Such people viewed all Yemen's troubles through a highly personalised prism of a two-man rivalry resembling that of Octavian and Mark Antony, or Tony Blair and Gordon Brown. For example, if Salih had used his son's Republican Guard up in Saada to humiliate Ali Muhsin's regular army, Ali Muhsin was getting his own back by encouraging his old friend and brother-in-law, Tariq al-Fadhli, to whip up trouble in the south.

By the end of 2009, no one and nothing looked strong enough to reverse Yemen's decline as a useful ally of the West or its rise as a jihadist stronghold. Thanks to southern separatism and the al-Huthi rebellion threatening the integrity of the country and Salih's apparent inability to tackle either with anything but force, events looked closer to boiling point than they had done since the civil war of 1994. Those accustomed to watching Yemen, as Kremlinologists once watched Moscow, knew that not only at qat chews in Sanaa and Aden and Mukalla and Taiz and Ibb, but among the diaspora all over the Gulf and beyond, in Britain and the United States, talks were being had, soundings being taken, new and improbable alliances being forged. While western intelligence agencies and think-tanks vaguely and gloomily forecast that a power vacuum and chaos in Yemen would open the door to a jihadist takeover and an important victory for al-Qaeda that might destabilise Saudi Arabia and so threaten the rest of the world, Yemenis able to afford the luxury of thinking about anything but their immediate daily needs felt themselves to be participating in a real and current, not an imagined and future, drama: the disintegration of their country.

# AFTERWORD

A bungled attempt at a suicide bombing aboard a Northwest Airlines flight from Amsterdam to Detroit on Christmas Day 2009 sent Yemen straight to the top of the world's news bulletins. The Yemen-based al-Qaeda in the Arabian Peninsula (AQAP) soon claimed responsibility for training the failed bomber, a young Nigerian named Omar Farook Abdulmutallab, and for supplying him with the explosives he had hidden in his underpants. Notably pious, even while a schoolboy at a British boarding school in Togo and a student of mechanical engineering at London's University College, Abdulmutallab was a loner who had broken off relations with his family in early 2009, dropping out of an MBA course in Dubai in order to make a trip to Sanaa, where he had enrolled at a language school and contacted AQAP. It soon transpired that US intelligence services had had sufficient warnings but had failed to link them; Abdulmutallab's father had even alerted the US embassy in Lagos that his radical Islamist son was missing in Yemen.

Not since al-Qaeda's attack on the USS *Cole* in Aden harbour in 2000 had Yemen claimed so much of the world's attention. But AQAP had been gaining in strength and confidence since the amalgamation of the Yemeni and Saudi al-Qaeda franchises a year earlier, and Western security agencies had been on the alert since the attack on the American embassy in Sanaa in September 2008. Already benefitting from the deteriorating economic and political conditions within Yemen, AQAP had been boosted still further by the escape of twenty-three top jihadists – one of them AQAP's present leader, Nasir al-Wahayshi – from a Sanaa jail in summer 2006, and by the enlistment of yet more enthusiastic Islamist fighters returning from the war in Iraq or fleeing US drone attacks in Afghanistan and Pakistan.

It is tempting to join up Yemen's jihadist dots and rebrand the country as the root of all al-Qaeda evil. The evidence appears to stack up: the fact that Yemen is bin Laden's 'ancestral homeland' counts for a great deal in a tribal society; Aden was the scene of a spectacular al-Qaeda attack on US interests in October 2000; many of the 9/11 hijackers and remaining Guantanamo detainees are of Yemeni origin; and last, but not least, anyone interested in Islamist terrorism, whether from an ideological or a practical point of view, can feel certain of finding in Yemen all the training and support he requires.

But it would be a mistake to write off the country as a rotten fruit on the point of falling for a Taliban-type regime or the world's first al-Qaeda state. The tangled and distinct histories of Yemen's various regions means that there are powerful forces operating against jihadist influence throughout the country. A substantial counterweight in Hadhramaut, for example, is its indigenous Sufi tradition, which has been strongly resurgent since the collapse of the Marxist state in 1990. Hadhramaut's close and profitable connections with émigré Hadhramis in Saudi Arabia and the rest of the Gulf states, and the old Hadhrami merchant diaspora in south-east Asia, also serve to work against rigorous Islamist control. In the Zaydi northern highlands the counterweight is supplied first by a small number of die-hard *sayyid* Zaydis, the followers of Abdul Malik al-Huthi, who abhor Wahhabism and Salafism of any kind and whose Shiism is detested in return, but secondly by the fact that – as history has demonstrated over and over again – the tribes of Yemen and particularly of the northern highlands care little for ideology or religion and everything for money and land. The same holds broadly true in the tribal lands around Aden, Britain's Western Aden Protectorate until 1967, where there remains a residual regard for British notions of justice and free speech as opposed to those of sharia law, and even for Marxist secularism.

If all these influences pose problems for the spread of jihadism in Yemen, they are also contributing to the strong centrifugal forces that are starting to pull the country apart, and signal the likely failure of the national project and the demise of a united Yemen. The only sentiment coming anywhere close to uniting the country today is not any powerful passion for radical Islam but a mounting resentment against President Ali Abdullah's Salih's regime, against the Sanhani northern highland tribesmen who have maintained themselves in power by helping themselves to the oil revenues that are now beginning to run out.

One of the clearest lessons of Yemeni history is that the exercise of power by the northern tribes over Yemenis of the southern highlands and coastal regions and Hadhramaut may have protected the people from foreign interference on occasion but it has never benefitted or satisfied anyone but those northern tribes, and now even some of them – the al-Huthis – are rebelling. An inevitable hiatus between the dwindling of Yemen's oil revenues and the country's new LNG revenues coming on stream means that the next five years or less may well see the fragmentation of the state. The likeliest trigger for this is economic hardship, caused by the regime's inability to pay the wages of the military and the vast numbers of civil servants who constitute the two pillars of its support. Such a break-up into two or many more fragments may not be effected without violence, for the simple reason that the northern highland regime controls the means of coercion while the remaining oil and the new LNG plant are located in the south.

As the West racks its collective brain over how best to help Yemen wage its battle against AQAP when the country's social and economic ills are already so overwhelming, it might at least resolve not to administer any aid that could be construed as propping up Salih's regime. Western governments should take particular care to avoid supplying Yemen with any weaponry that could just as easily be deployed against Yemen's southern dissidents, for example, as against AQAP. The consequences, in terms of internal suffering and worldwide anger, are easy to imagine.

It is equally worth bearing in mind that the West does not bear sole responsibility for ensuring that Yemen does not degenerate into a haven for global jihadists. In fact, there is a substantial risk that Western intervention – whether in the form of social or of military aid – will backfire by lending grist to the mills of influential Islamists like Sheikh Abdul Majid al-Zindani, who has long preached that the West is trying to re-colonise the Middle East.

We are fortunate in that, unlike Afghanistan, Pakistan and Somalia, Yemen happens to be surrounded by oil-rich Gulf states whose rulers are as hostile towards al-Qaeda and jihadism as the United States and its immediate allies, and who now realise that al-Qaeda chaos in Yemen spells al-Qaeda chaos across the entire Arabian Peninsula. These neighbouring states – each of which hosts a substantial Yemeni diaspora – are better equipped than any Western power to discover who to do business with in Yemen and how best to parley with tribesmen suspected of harbouring jihadists. Similarly, if there is a palace coup in the offing in Sanaa, it will be Yemen's neighbours who have wind of it first, and if there are useful deals to be struck and alliances to be made, the Gulf states will be more attuned to their development and significance than the West is.

Before allowing a band of inept, suicidal and deracinated jihadists to terrify us into funnelling funds, arms and expertise to a country already bristling with weaponry and on the brink of collapse, whose people moreover are fundamentally opposed to foreign interference in their extraordinarily complicated affairs, we should perhaps recall the oddly similar sentiments of three men who, at intervals over the last hundred years, pondered their experience of Yemen – north and south. The last Ottoman pasha of Sanaa, Nasser's Field Marshal al-Amer and the British diplomat Oliver Miles each admitted to feeling bewildered, wrong-footed and out-witted by the country and its people – in other words, to never having known the half of it. If the consensus of opinion is that the threat emanating from Yemen does, after all, demand action on the West's part, it would be advisable to nurture a healthy suspicion that we still do not know the half of this most beautiful and enchanting, but also opaque and unstable, corner of the Arabian Peninsula. We should also remember the weary words of a former Soviet diplomat who put his finger on the real disincentive to adventuring in Yemen: cost.

# NOTES

## INTRODUCTION

1. http://www.bloomberg.com/apps/news?pid=20601100&sid=a_aYx9Hk2V2Q &refer=germany
2. IMF Country Report, No.09/100, March 2009, p. 12.

## CHAPTER 1: UNWANTED VISITORS (1538–1918)

1. Eric Macro, *Bibliography on Yemen and Notes on Mocha*, Florida: University of Miami Press, 1966, p. 33.
2. Frederique Soudan, *Le Yemen Ottoman d'apres la chronique d'al-Mawza'i*, Cairo: Institut Français d'Archeologie Orientale, 1999, p.293.
3. Muhammad ibn Ahmad Nahrawali (trans. Clive K. Smith), *Lightning over Yemen: A History of the Ottoman Campaign (1569–71)*, London: I.B. Tauris, 2002, p. 9.
4. Ibid., p. 30.
5. Ibid., p. 16.
6. Ibid., p. 32.
7. Ibid., p. 40.
8. Ibid., p. 95.
9. Ibid., p. 89.
10. William Foster, ed., *The Hakluyt Society: The Journal of John Jourdain 1608–1617*, 2nd series, no. xvi, Cambridge, 1905, p. 105.
11. Ibid., p. 86.
12. Jean de La Roque, *A Voyage to Arabia Felix*, London: E. Symon, 1732, p. 237.
13. Bernard Haykel, *Revival and Reform in Islam:The Legacy of Muhammad al-Shawkani*, Cambridge: Cambridge University Press, 2003, p. 16.
14. Anthony Wild, *Coffee: A Dark History*, London: Fourth Estate, 2004, p. 71.
15. Soudan, op. cit., p. 59.
16. de La Roque, op. cit., p. 107.

17. Ibid., pp. 199–202.
18. M. Niebuhr (trans. Robert Heron), *Travels Through Arabia and Other Countries in the East*, vol. 2, Garnet Education, 1994, pp. 78–82.
19. Haykel, op. cit., p. 44.
20. Ibid., p. 74.
21. P.J.L. Frankl, 'Robert Finlay's description of Sanaa in 1238–1239/1823', *British Society for Middle Eastern Studies Bulletin* vol. 17–18, 1990–91, p. 23.
22. Ibid., p. 27.
23. Ibid., p. 26.
24. Gordon Waterfield, *Sultans of Aden*, London: John Murray, 1968, p. 22.
25. Richard H. Sanger, *The Arabian Peninsula*, Ithaca, NY: Cornell University Press, 1954, p. 203.
26. Ibid., p. 64.
27. Ibid., p. 71.
28. Ibid., p. 76.
29. Ibid., p. 77.
30. Ibid., p. 87.
31. R.A.B. Hamilton, *The Kingdom of Melchior: Adventures in South West Arabia*, London: John Murray, 1949, p. 74; Waterfield, op. cit., p. 82.
32. Waterfield, op. cit., p. 82.
33. Ibid., p. 121.
34. Ibid.
35. R.J. Gavin, *Aden Under British Rule 1839–1967*, London: Hurst & Co., 1975, p. 82.
36. Anonymous account of an officer of the 78th Highland Regiment – India and Aden, 1840–1853, British Library MSS EUR B277.
37. Charles Johnston, *The View from Steamer Point: Three Crucial Years in South Arabia*, London: Collins, 1964, p. 59.
38. Camp Residence in the Valley of Aden, British Library MSS10LM/2/518, Chatsworth MSS.
39. Z.H. Kour, *The History of Aden 1839–72*, London: Frank Cass, 1981, p. 101.
40. R.N. Mehra, *Aden and Yemen 1905–1919*, Delhi: Agam Pakrashan, 1988, p. 31n.
41. David Holden, *Farewell to Arabia*, London: Faber, 1966, p. 30.
42. Thomas Kuhn, 'Shaping Ottoman Rule in Yemen, 1872–1919', unpublished Ph.D. thesis, New York University, May 2005, p. 84.
43. Ibid,. p. 60.
44. John Baldry, 'Al-Yaman and the Turkish Occupation 1849–1914', *Arabica*, T.23, Fase 2, June 1976, pp. 156–96.
45. Faris al-Sanabani, a Yemeni businessman, was sent this translation by a Turkish friend, by text message.
46. S.M. Zwemer, *Arabia: The Cradle of Islam*, Edinburgh: Oliphant, Anderson & Ferrier, 1900, p. 69.
47. Aubrey Herbert, *Ben Kendim*, London: Hutchinson & Co., 1924, pp. 66–8.
48. Zwemer, op. cit., p. 68.
49. *The Times*, 4 January 1906.
50. Baldry, op. cit.
51. A.J.B. Wavell, *A Modern Pilgrim in Mecca*, London: Constable & Co., 1912, p. 257.
52. Cesar F. Farah, *The Sultan's Yemen:: 19th Century Challenge to Ottoman Rule*, London: I.B.Tauris, 2002, p. 248.
53. Paul Dresch, *A History of Modern Yemen*, Cambridge: Cambridge University Press, 2000, p. 6.
54. G. Wyman-Bury, *Arabia Infelix: or the Turks in Yemen*, Reading: Garnet Publishing, 1999 (1915), pp. 18–19.
55. Kuhn, op. cit., p. 291.

56. George Lenczowski, *The Middle East in World Affairs*, Ithaca, NY: Cornell University Press, 1952, p. 357.

## CHAPTER 2: REVOLUTIONARY ROADS (1918–1967)

1. Lucine Taminian, 'Persuading the Monarchs: Poetry and Politics in Yemen (1920–1950)' in Remy Leveau, Franck Mermier and Udo Steinbach, eds, *Le Yemen Contemporain*, Paris: Karthla, 1999, p. 213.
2. Hugh Scott, *In the High Yemen*, London: John Murray, 1942, p. 175.
3. Amin Rihani, *Arabian Peak and Desert: Travels in Al-Yaman*, London: Constable & Co. Ltd, 1930, p. 225.
4. Ibid., p. 196.
5. Wyman-Bury, op. cit., p. 39.
6. Ibid., p. 80.
7. Rihani, op. cit., p. 110.
8. Ibid., p. 93.
9. D. van der Meulen, *Faces in Shem*, London: John Murray, 1961, p. 129.
10. Sanger, op. cit., p. 268.
11. Ibid., p. 269.
12. Rhiani, op. cit., p. 117.
13. Dresch, op. cit., p. 56.
14. Ibid., pp. 56–7.
15. Chris Bradley, *The Discovery Guide to Yemen*, London: Immel Publishing Ltd, 1995, p. 267.
16. Khadija Al-Salami, *The Tears of Sheba: Tales of Survival and Intrigue in Arabia*, Chichester: John Wiley & Sons Ltd, 2003, p. 19.
17. Claudie Fayein, *A French Doctor in Yemen*, London: Robert Hale, 1957, p. 69.
18. Ibrahim al-Rashid, ed., *Yemen Under the Rule of Imam Ahmad*, Chapel Hill, NC: Documentary Publications, 1985, p. 24.
19. Ibid.
20. Ibid.
21. 'Friends & Enemies', *Time*, 14 April 1961.
22. Eric Macro, *Yemen and the Western World*, London: C. Hurst & Co., 1968, p. 118.
23. 'Friends & Enemies', *Time*, op. cit.
24. Gabe Oppenheim, 'A Collector's Eye for Artifacts – And Adventure', *Washington Post*, 20 July 2008.
25. Holden, op. cit., p. 94.
26. Dresch, op. cit., p. 84.
27. Claude Deffarge and Gordian Troeller, *Yemen '62–'69: De la Revolution Sauvage a la Treve des Guerriers*, Paris: Robert Laffont, 1969, p. 49.
28. Saeed M. Badeeb, *The Saudi-Egyptian Conflict in North Yemen, 1962–1970*, Boulder, CO: Westview Press, 1986, p. 31.
29. Scott Gibbons, *The Conspirators*, London: Howard Baker Publishers Ltd, 1967, p. 4.
30. Ibid., pp. 4–5.
31. Ham, *The Kingdom of Melchior*, p. 39; Hamilton, op. cit., p. 39.
32. Sir Tom Hickinbotham, *Aden*, London: Constable & Co., 1958, p. 104.
33. Peter Hinchcliffe, John T. Ducker and Maria Holt, *Without Glory in Arabia: The British Retreat from Aden*, London: I.B.Tauris, 2006, p. 98.
34. Mansur Abdullah (G. Wyman-Bury), *The Land of Uz*, Reading: Garnet Press, 1998 (1911), pp. 43–8.
35. Donald Foster, *Landscape with Arabs: Travels in Aden and South Arabia*, Brighton: Clifton Books, 1969, p. 90.
36. Doreen and Leila Ingrams, *Records of Yemen, 1798–1960*, Slough: Archive Editions, vol. 8, 1993, pp. 428–37.

37. Linda Boxberger, *On the Edge of Empire: Hadramawt, Emigration and the Indian Ocean 1880s–1930s*, Albany, NY: State University of New York Press, 2002, p. 43.
38. Doreen and Leila Ingrams, op. cit., vol. 10, 1993, p. 137.
39. Freya Stark, *The Coast of Incense: Autobiography 1933–1939*, London: John Murray, 1953, p. 182.
40. Hans Helfritz, *The Yemen: A Secret Journey*, London: George Allen & Unwin Ltd., 1958, p. 43.
41. Freya Stark, *The Southern Gates of Arabia*, London: John Murray, 1957 (1936), p. 194.
42. Daniel van der Meulen, *Aden to the Hadhramaut*, London: John Murray, 1947, p. 44.
43. Mohamed Alwan, *The Wind of Change*, London: Minerva Press, 1999, p. 159.
44. Johnston, op. cit., p. 152.
45. Glen Balfour-Paul, *The End of the Empire in the Middle East: Britain's Relinquishment of Power in her Last Three Arab Dependencies*, Cambridge: Cambridge University Press, 1991, p. 75.
46. Christopher Gandy, 'A Mission to Yemen: August 1962–January 1963', *British Journal of Middle Eastern Studies*, vol. 25, no. 2, 1998, pp. 247–74.
47. Gillian King, *Imperial Outpost – Aden: Its Place in British Strategic Policy*, London: Chatham House Essays/OUP, 1964, p. 48.
48. Ibid., p. 11.
49. Humphrey Trevelyan, *The Middle East in Revolution*, London: Macmillan, 1970, p. 215.
50. Ibid., p. 219.
51. Fred Halliday, *Arabia Without Sultans*, London: Saqi Books, 2002 (1974), p. 196.
52. King, op. cit., p. 4.
53. Ibid., p. 91.
54. Phillip Darby, *British Defence Policy East of Suez, 1947–1968*, London: Oxford University Press, 1973, p. 284.
55. Julian Paget, *Last Post: Aden 1964–67*, London: Faber & Faber, 1969, p. 263.
56. Karl Pieragostini, *Britain, Aden and South Arabia: Abandoning Empire*, London: Macmillan, 1991, p. 179.
57. Balfour-Paul, op. cit., p. 215.
58. Hinchcliffe et al., op. cit., pp. 58–9.
59. Ibid., p. 161.
60. Fred Halliday, *Revolution and Foreign Policy: The Case of South Yemen 1967–1987*, Cambridge: Cambridge University Press, 1990.
61. Pieragaostini, op. cit., p. 208.
62. BBC2, Scotland, 26 November 2007.
63. Halliday, *Arabia Without Sultans*, op. cit., p. 221.
64. http://www.al-bab.com/bys/articles/miles.htm
65. Paget, op. cit., p. 255.

## CHAPTER 3: TWO YEMENI REPUBLICS (1967–1990)

1. http://wwww.markcurtis.wordpress.com/2007/02/13/the-covert-war-in-yemen-1962–70/
2. Dana Adams Schmidt, *Yemen: The Unknown War*, London: The Bodley Head, 1968, pp. 211–12.
3. Ibid., p. 77.
4. Badeeb, op. cit., p. 4.
5. Muhsin Alaini, *50 Years in Shifting Sands: Personal Experience in the Building of a Modern State in Yemen*, Beirut: Editions Dar An Nahar, 2004, p. 68.
6. Ibid., p. 72.
7. BBC report from Sanaa, by Noel Clark, 24 October 1962.
8. Ali Abdel Rahman Rahmy, *The Egyptian Policy in the Arab World: Intervention in Yemen 1962–67*, Washington DC: University Press of America, 1983, p. 97.

9. David M. Witty, 'A Regular Army in Counterinsurgency Operations: Egypt in North Yemen, 1962–1967', *Journal of Military History*, vol. 65, no. 2, April 2001, pp. 401–39 (p. 425).
10. www.army.mil/prof_writing/volumes/volume2/march_2004/3_04.html
11. Abdou Mubasher, 'The Road to Naksa', *Al-Ahram Weekly*, 7–13 June 2007.
12. Ibid.
13. General Mohamed Fawzi, 'The Three-year War', *Al-Ahram Weekly*, 5–11 June 1997.
14. Anthony Nutting, *Nasser*, Boston MA: E.P.Dutton, 1972, p. 323.
15. Richard Beeston, *Looking for Trouble: The Life and Times of a Foreign Correspondent*, London: Tauris Parke Paperbacks, 2006, p. 78.
16. www.au.af.mil/au/awc/awcgate/medaspec/Ch-2electrv699.pdf
17. Al-Salami, op. cit., p. 207.
18. Yevgeny Primakov, *Russia and the Arabs*, New York: Basic Books, 2009, p. 97.
19. Halliday, *Arabia Without Sultans*, op. cit., p. 117
20. Edgar O'Ballance, *The War in Yemen*, London: Faber & Faber, 1971, p. 89.
21. Halliday, *Arabia Without Sultans*, op. cit. p. 132.
22. Ibid., p. 133.
23. Alaini, op. cit., p. 200.
24. http://www.opendemocracy.net/globalisation/global_politics/yemen_murder_arabia_felix
25. Sheila Carapico, *Civil Society in Yemen: The Political Economy of Activism in Modern Arabia*, Cambridge: Cambridge University Press, 1998, p. 6.
26. Fred Halliday, *Arabs in Exile:: Yemeni Migrants in Urban Britain*, London: I.B. Tauris, 1992, p. 15.
27. Robert W. Stookey,.*The Politics of the Yemen Arab Republic*, Boulder, CO: Westview Press, 1978, pp. 273–4.
28. Al-Salami, op. cit., p. 258.
29. Ibid., pp. 167–8.
30. Dresch, op. cit., p. 147.
31. Robert D. Burrowes, *Yemen Arab Republic: The Politics of Development 1962–1986*, Boulder, CO: Westview Press, 1987, p. 93.
32. Christopher Andrew and Vasili Mitrokhin, *The World Was Going Our Way: The KGB and the Battle for the Third World*, New York: Basic Books, 2005, p. 214.
33. Primakov, op. cit., p. 82.
34. Halliday, *Arabia Without Sultans*, op. cit., p. 250.
35. Joe Stork, 'Marxist Revolution in Arabia: A Report from the People's Democratic Republic of Yemen', *MERIP*, no.15, March 1973, p. 10.
36. Ibid., p. 230.
37. Ibid., p. 233.
38. Ibid., p. 20.
39. Ibid., p. 23.
40. Ibid., p. 13.
41. Norman Cigar, 'Islam and the State in South Yemen: The Uneasy Co-existence', *Middle Eastern Studies*, vol. 26, April 1990, pp. 185–203.
42. Ibid.
43. http://www.guardian.co.uk/world/2008/sep/28/germany.terrorism; http://www.time.com/time/magazine/article/0,9171,956703,00.html; http://www.time.com/time/magazine/article/0,9171,956703,00.html
44. Andrew and Mitrokhin, op. cit., p. 218.
45. Stookey, op. cit., p. 106.
46. Carapico, op. cit., p. 43.
47. Dresch, op. cit., p. 159.

48. Robert D. Burrowes, 'The Salih Regime and the Need for Reform', *Yemen Times*, 28–30 January 2008.
49. Stephen W. Day, 'Powersharing and Hegemony: A Case Study of the United Republic of Yemen', unpublished Ph.D. thesis, Washington Georgetown University, 2001, p. 201.
50. Halliday, *Revolution and Foreign Policy: The Case of South Yemen 1967–1987*, op. cit., p. 48.
51. Dresch, op. cit., pp. 168–9.
52. Robert D. Burrowes, 'Oil Strike and Leadership Struggle in South Yemen: 1986 and Beyond', *Middle East Journal*, vol. 43, no. 3, Summer 1989, pp. 437–54.
53. www.adenairways.com/Aden_Evacuation_1986.htm
54. Halliday, *Revolution and Foreign Policy: The Case of South Yemen 1967–1987*, op. cit., p. 42.

## CHAPTER 4: A SHOTGUN WEDDING (1990–2000)

1. Day, op. cit., p. 229.
2. Carapico, op. cit., p. 50.
3. www.yemen-nic.info/English%20site/SITE%20CONTAINTS/PRESEDENCY/PRESIDENT/Biog_pres2.htm
4. John Pilger, 'John Pilger Reveals How the Bushes Bribe the World', *New Statesman*, 19 September 2002.
5. Remy Leveau, Franck Mermier and Udo Steinbach, eds, *Le Yemen Contemporain*, Paris: Editions Karthala, 1999, p. 45.
6. Sarah Phillips, *Yemen's Democracy Experiment in Regional Perspective: Patronage and Pluralized Authoritarianism*, New York: Palgrave Macmillan, 2009, p. 63.
7. James A. Baker, *The Politics of Diplomacy: Revolution, War and Peace*, New York: G.P. Putnam's Sons, 1995, pp. 317–20.
8. Pilger, op. cit.
9. Brian Whitaker, 'National Unity and Democracy in Yemen: a marriage of inconvenience', conference paper delivered at SOAS, University of London, 25 November 1995, http://www.al-bab.com/yemen/artic/bw1.htm
10. Leveau et al., op. cit., p. 367.
11. Dresch, op. cit., p. 191.
12. 'A Real Arab Revolution', *New York Times*, 8 May 1993.
13. Day, op. cit., p. 292.
14. Phillips, op. cit., p. 177.
15. Brian Whitaker, 'North Yemen Tightens the Noose on Aden', *Middle East International*, 24 June 1994, www.al-bab.com/yemen/artic/mei4.htm
16. Simon Henderson, 'A Saudi Disaster Story: Yemen's Unity By Force', Washington Institute for Near East Policy: *Policy Watch*, no. 125, 22 July 1994.
17. 'Yemen Claims Victory in Civil War After Seizing Rebel City', *New York Times*, 8 July 1994.
18. Dresch, op. cit., p. 197.
19. Day, op. cit., p. 367.
20. Lisa Wedeen, *Peripheral Visions: Publics, Power and Performance in Yemen*, Chicago: University of Chicago Press, 2008, pp. 68–86.

## CHAPTER 5: FIRST GENERATION JIHAD

1. *Yemen Times*, 2 April 2001.
2. http://www.historycommons.org/timeline.jsp?timeline=complete_911_timeline&geopolitics_and_9/11=complete_911_timeline_yemeni_militant_collusion.
3. Burke, Jason, *Al-Qaeda: The True Story of Radical Islam*, London: Penguin, 2004 (2003), p. 140.

4. http://www.globalpolitician.com/23607-terror-yemen
5. Katherine Roth, 'War and Change in Yemen', www.icwa.org/articles/KLR-16.pdf, 19 July 1994, p. 9.
6. Lawrence Wright, *The Looming Tower: al-Qaeda's Road to 9/11*, New York: Viking-Penguin, 2006, pp. 277–8.
7. http://www.jamestown.org/programs/gta/single/?tx_ttnews%5Btt_news%5D=838&tx_ttnews%5BbackPid%5D=181&no_cache=1
8. http://news.bbc.co.uk/1/hi/uk/3752517.stm
9. Nick Owens, 'Abu Hamza Still Preaching Hate in Prison', *Daily Mirror*, 31 May 2009.
10. Brian Whitaker, 'Hostage to Fortune and Yemeni Guns', *Guardian*, 30 December 1998.
11. Andrew Higgins and Alan Cullison, 'Friend or Foe: The Story of a Traitor to al-Qaeda', *Wall Street Journal*, 20 December 2002.
12. Ibid.
13. *Al-Quds al-Arabi*, 'Bin Ladin's Former "Bodyguard" Interviewed on al-Qa'ida Strategies', 2 August 2004, www.why-war.com/news/2004/08/03/binladin.html
14. http://www.al-bab.com/Yemen/cole4.htm
15. Lally Weymouth, 'We Are Still Searching', *Newsweek*, 18 December 2000.
16. www.globalpolitician.com/printasp?=3607
17. Patrick E.Tyler, 'Threats and Responses', *New York Times*, 19 December 2002.
18. Craig Whitlock, 'Probe of the USS *Cole* Bombing Unravels', *Washington Post*, 4 May 2008.
19. Eric Watkins, 'Yemen's Innovative Approach to the War on Terror', *Terrorism Monitor*, Jamestown Foundation, vol. 3, issue 4.
20. Wright, op. cit., p. 30.

## CHAPTER 6: A TRIBAL DISORDER?

1. http://www.irinnews.org/Report.aspx?ReportId=73130#
2. *Yemen Times*, 24 March 2008, p. 2.
3. Day, op. cit., 2001, pp. 361–2.
4. Gabriele vom Bruck, *Islam, Memory and Morality in Yemen*, New York: Palgrave Macmillan, 2005, p. 9.
5. Ibid.
6. Phillips, op. cit., p. 90.
7. Patrick E. Tyler, 'Yemen an Uneasy Ally, Proves Adept at Playing off Old Rivals', *New York Times*, 19 December 2002.
8. Frank Gardner, 'Yemen Praised after al-Qaeda Action', BBC news online, 19 December 2001.
9. Nick Pelham, 'Yemeni Sheikhs Threaten Revolt over US Build-up,' *Daily Telegraph*, 16 March 2002.
10. Dale Davis, 'Red Alert', Salon.com, 13 August 2004.
11. Philip Smucker, 'The Intrigue Behind the Drone Strike', *Christian Science Monitor*, 12 November 2002,.
12. http://peacecorpsonline.org/messages/messages/467/2022573.html
13. 'Yemen's Saleh urges tribes to back State's Fight against Terrorism', Deutsche Presse Agentur, 3 February 2009.
14. Gregory D. Johnsen, 'Terrorists in Rehab', *WorldViewMagazine*, Summer 2004.
15. http://islamandinsurgencyinyemen.blogspot.com/2009/09/battle-of-marib-video.html
16. Ibid., p. 70.
17. John R.Bradley, *Saudi Arabia Exposed: Inside a Kingdom in Crisis*, New York: Palgrave Macmillan, 2005, p. 62.
18. Ibid., p. 57.
19. Ibid., p. 62.

20. Charles M. Sennett, 'Why bin Laden plot relied on Saudi hijackers', *Boston Globe*, 3 March 2002.
21. Turki al-Saheil, 'Inside al-Qaeda's Hideout', *Al-Sharq al-Awsat*, 7 May 2009.
22. 'Marib attack has no relation to al-Qaeda of bin Laden, but new one', *News Yemen*, 10 July 2007.
23. Robert F. Worth, 'Wanted by FBI but walking out of a Yemen hearing', *New York Times*, 1 March 2008.
24. http://www.longwarjournal.org/archives/2008/12/yemeni_al_qaeda_lead_2.php
25. http://www.newsweek.com/id/160694
26. Jane Novak, 'Terror Tales: Zionist Jihadis, American Pirates and Other Bedtime Tales from Yemen', *mypetjawa*, 16 January 2009.
27. Ibid.
28. Craig Whitlock, 'Bounties a Bust in Hunt for al-Qaeda', *Washington Post*, 17 May 2008.

## CHAPTER 7: KEEPING UP WITH THE SAUDIS

1. Nathan Vardi, 'The World's Billionaires: Sins of the Father', Forbes.com, 18 March 2002.
2. W.H. Ingrams, *A Report on the Social, Economic and Political Condition of the Hadhramaut*, London: HMSO, 1936, p. 54.
3. Judith Miller and Jeff Gerth, 'Honey Trade Said to Provide Funds and Cover to bin Laden', *New York Times*, 11 October 2001.
4. http://news.bbc.co.uk/1/hi/world/monitoring/media_reports/1871182.stm
5. Adam Robinson, *Bin Laden: Behind the Mask of the Terrorist*, New York: Arcade Publishing, 2002, p. 19.
6. Ingrams, op. cit., p. 111.
7. Mabel Bent and Theodore Bent, *South Arabia*, BiblioBazaar, LLC, 2008, p. 108.
8. http://yemenonline.info/news-1139.html
9. Andrew England, 'Al-Qaeda in Yemen – a threat to Saudis', *Financial Times*, 23 April 2009.
10. http://news/bbc.co.uk/1/hi/business/8130543.stm
11. Thomas Pritzkat, 'The Community of Hadhrami Migrants in Saudi Arabia and the Rationale of Investors in the Homeland', in Leveau et al., op. cit., pp. 319–418.
12. Day, op. cit., p. 413.
13. Ibid., p. 400.
14. Jaime Pueblo, 'Yemen Must Grow into GCC', *The National*, 1 June 2009.
15. Dr Christopher Boucek, Chatham House seminar, 19 January 2009.
16. 'Rebellion, Migration or Consultative Democracy? The Zaydis and their Detractors in Yemen', by Bernard Haykel, in Leveau et al., op. cit., p. 198.
17. Phillips, op. cit., p. 161.
18. 'Government Warns of Secret Extremist Schools that Attract More than 300,000 Yemenis', Associated Press, 16 April 2005.
19. www.sabanewsnet/en/news170941.htm
20. http://www.jihadwatch.org/archives/022485.php
21. Andrew McGregor, 'Yemen's Sheikh al-Zindani's New Role as a Healer', *Terrorism Monitor*, vol. 4, no. 8; Bernhard Zand, 'Are Koran Schools Hotbeds of terrorism?', *Der Spiegel*, 20 March 2007; http://www.youtube.com/watch?v=yeFr5t19aQs.
22. Evan Kohlmann, 'In Too Deep: Terrorism in Yemen', *National Review*, 17 January 2003.
23. http://treas.gov/press/releases/js1190.htm; http://hamptonroads.com/node/235681
24. Gregory D. Johnsen, 'Profile of Sheikh Abd al-Majid al-Zindani', *Terrorism Monitor*, vol. 4, no. 7.
25. Mohammed al-Qadhi, 'Yemen Accuses US of Targeting Islam', *Yemen Times*, 5–7 April 2004.

26. Gregory D. Johnsen, 'Yemen's al-Iman University: A Pipeline for Fundamentalists?', *Terrorism Monitor*, vol. 4, no. 22.
27. Nasser Arrabyee, 'Al-Qaida "not behind tourist attack" in Yemen', *Gulf News*, 10 July 2007.
28. 'Yemen Fighters Dying in Iraq', *Yemen Times*, 25–28 January 2007.
29. http://mypetjawa.mu.nu/archives/186601.php
30. Vicken Cheterian, 'Et l'Irak accouche d'une nouvelle generation de djihadiste', *Le Monde Diplomatique*, December 2008.
31. Richard A. Oppel Jr, 'Foreign Fighters in Iraq are Tied to Allies of US', *New York Times*, 22 November 2007.
32. http://armiesofliberation.com/archives/2008/07/19/yemenis-murdering-in-iraq/
33. Burke, op. cit., p. 11.
34. http://www.jihadica.com/new-issue-of-Saada-al-malahim/
35. http://www.al-tagheer.com/news.php?id=8664
36. Muhammad al-Kibsi, 'Yemen Security Breaks New Terrorist Cell', *Yemen Observer*, 17 August 2008.
37. http://www.cbsnews.com/blogs/2009/10/05/world/worldwatch/entry5364480.shtml
38. http://armiesofliberation.com/archives/2008/09/21/al-qaeda-in-yemen-timeline/
39. Gregory Johnsen and Shari Villarosa, 'Al-Qaeda in Yemen', Carnegie Endowment for International Peace Seminar, 7 July 2009.

## CHAPTER 8: AL-QAEDA, PLUS TWO INSURGENCIES

1. www.yemenonline.info/print.php?sid=803
2. Ayman Baggash al-Sayah, 'Nearly 78% of investment projects in Aden have stalled, says a recent study', *Yemen Times*, 22–24 December 2008.
3. 'Yemen: Defusing the Saada Time Bomb', *Middle East Report*, International Crisis Group, no. 86, 27 May 2009, p. 6.
4. Ibid.
5. Ibid.
6. Khaled Fattah, 'Yemen: A slogan and six wars', *Asia Times*, 9 October 2009.
7. http://www.merip.org/mero/mero040306.html
8. http://www.trendsmagazine.net/out_wordpress/wordpress/2007/05/07/the-other-insurgency/
9. www.yemenpost.net/Detail123456789.aspx?ID=3&SubID=581
10. 'Al-Qaeda calls for Islamic Rule in South Yemen', *Yemen Times*, 14–17 May 2009,
11. Abdul Hameed Bakier, 'Al-Qaeda in Yemen Supports Southern Secession', *Terrorism Monitor*, vol. 7, no. 16, 11 June 2009.
12. Tariq Alhomayed, 'No to Secession in Yemen', *Alsharq Al-Wasat*, 28 April 2009.

## CHAPTER 9: CAN THE CENTRE HOLD?

1. Yemen Corruption Assessment, USAID Yemen, September 2006, p. 12.
2. Ibid., p. 4.
3. http://www.hep.yemen.org/en/uploads/mpa_project_description.doc
4. Mohamad al-Qadhi, 'Biometric System Launched', *Yemen Times*, 12–14 September 2005.
5. Fuad Rajeh, 'EU to Government: "Spending Reforms and Layoffs" Necessary for Development', Yemenpost.net, 24 May 2009.
6. Phillips, op. cit., p. 69.
7. http://www.yobserver.com/reports/10013003.html

8. Yemenpost.net, 5 September 2009.
9. Ian Black, 'The Curse of Yemen', *Guardian*, 12 August 2008.
10. Sarah Phillips, 'Cracks in the Yemeni System', MERIP, 28 July 2005.
11. http://www.imf.org/external/pubs/ft/scr/2009/cr09100.pdf, p.13.
12. http://www.foreignpolicy.com/articles/2009/06/22/2009_failed_states_index_interactive_map_and_rankings
13. http://www.uam.es/otroscentros/TEIM/election_watch/Yemen/elections_results_Yemen.htm
14. Phillips, op. cit., p .96.
15. Ibid., p. 156.
16. Ibid., p. 162.
17. Sarah Phillips, 'Politics in a Vacuum: The Yemeni Opposition's Dilemma', in *Discerning Yemen's Political Future*, *Viewpoints*, Middle East Institute, no. 11, June 2009,, p. 11.
18. Mohammed al-Qadhi, 'Opposition groups gather to discuss Yemen's woes', *The National*, 19 May 2009.
19. Nasser Arrabyee, 'President blasts opposition parties', Gulfnews.com, 9 March 2008.
20. Phillips, op. cit., p. 70.
21. Robert Kaplan, *Imperial Grunts: On the Ground with the American Military, from Mongolia to the Philippines to Iraq and beyond*, New York: Vintage, 2006, p. 23.

# BIBLIOGRAPHY

## BOOKS

Abir, Mordechai, *Oil, Power and Politics: Conflict in Arabia, the Red Sea and the Gulf*, London: Cass, 1974

Alaini, Mohsin A., *50 Years in Shifting Sands: Personal Experience in the Building of a Modern State in Yemen*, Beirut: Editions Dar an Nahar, 2004

Allen, Mark, *The Arabs*, London: Continuum, 2006

Allen, Stewart Lee, *The Devil's Cup: Coffee, the Driving Force*, Edinburgh: Canongate, 2000

Allfree, P.S., *Hawks of Hadhramaut*, London: Robert Hale Ltd, 1967

Almadhagi, Ahmed Noman Kassin, *Yemen and the United States: A Study of Small Power and Super-State Relationship 1962–1994*, London: I.B. Tauris, 1996

Al-Rasheed, Madawi and Vitalis, Robert, eds, *Counter Narratives: History, Contemporary Society and Politics in Saudi Arabia and Yemen*, New York: Palgrave Macmillan, 2004

Al-Salami, Khadija, *The Tears of Sheba: Tales of Survival and Intrigue in Arabia*, Chichester: John Wiley & Sons, 2004 (2003)

Alwan, Mohamed, *The Wind of Change*, London: Minerva Press, 1999

Andrew, Christopher and Mitrokhin, Vasili, *The World Was Going Our Way: The KGB and the Battle for the Third World*, New York: Basic Books, 2005

Anon, Account of officer of 78th Highland regiment – India and Aden, 1840–1853, MSS Eur B277

Appadurai, Arjun, ed., *The Social Life of Things: Commodities in Cultural Perspective*, Cambridge: Cambridge University Press, 1988

Atwan, Abdel Bari, *The Secret History of al-Qa'ida*, London: Abacus, 2006

Badeeb, Saeed, *The Saudi-Egyptian Conflict over North Yemen, 1962–1970*, Boulder, CO: Westview Press, 1986

Balfour-Paul, Glen, *The End of Empire in the Middle East: Britain's Relinquishment of Power in her Last Three Arab Dependencies*, Cambridge: Cambridge University Press, 1992 (1991)

Beeston, Richard, *Looking for Trouble: The Life and Times of a Foreign Correspondent*, London: Tauris Parke Paperbacks, 2006
Belhaven, Lord (Robert Hamilton), *The Kingdom of Melchior: Adventures in South West Arabia*, London, John Murray, 1949
—— *The Uneven Road*, London: John Murray, 1955
Berg, van den, L.W.C., *Le Hadhramaut et les Colonies Arabes dans l'Archipel Indien*, Batavia, 1886
Bidwell, Robin, *The Two Yemens*, London: Longman, Westview Press, 1983
Boustead, Hugh, *The Winds of Morning*, London: Chatto & Windus, 1971
Boxberger, Linda, *On the Edge of Empire: Hadramawt, Emigration and the Indian Ocean, 1880s–1930s*, Albany, NY: State University of New York Press, 2002
Bradley, Chris, *Discovery Guide to Yemen*, London: Immel Publishing, 1995
Bradley, John R., *Saudi Arabia Exposed: Inside a Kingdom in Crisis*, New York: Palgrave Macmillan, 2005
Brent, Peter, *Far Arabia: Explorers of the Myth*, London: Quartet Books, 1979
Brouwer, C.G., *Dutch–Yemeni Encounters: Activities of the United East India Company (VOC) in South Arabian Waters since 1614*, Amsterdam: D'Flyute Rarob, 1999
—— *al Mukha: The Transoceanic Trade of a Yemeni Staple Town as Mapped by Merchants of the VOC 1614–1640*, Amsterdam: D'Flyute Rarob, 2005
Bruck, Gabriele vom, *Islam, Memory and Morality in Yemen*, New York: Palgrave Macmillan, 2005
Bujra, Abdulla S., *The Politics of Stratification: A Study of Political Change in a South Arabian Town*, Oxford: Clarendon Press, 1971
Burke, Jason, *Al-Qaeda: The True Story of Radical Islam*, London: Penguin, 2004
Burrowes, Robert D., *Yemen Arab Republic: The Politics of Development 1962–1986*, Boulder, CO: Westview Press, 1987
Carapico, Sheila, *Civil Society in Yemen: The Political Economy of Activism in Modern Arabia*, Cambridge: Cambridge University Press, 1998
—— *Arabia Incognita*, Florence: European University Institute, 2002
Caton, Steve C., *Peaks of Yemen I Summon: Poetry and Cultural Practice in a North Yemeni Tribe*, Berkeley, CA: University of California Press, 1990
—— *Yemen Chronicle: An Anthropology of War and Mediation*, New York: Hill and Wang, 2005
Churchill, Awnsham, *A Collection of Voyages and Travels*, vol. 6, London: John Walthoe, 1732
Colburn, Marta, *The Republic of Yemen: Development Challenges in the 21st Century*, London: Catholic Institute for International Relations, 2002
Crawford, Alex, *Audible Glue*, Leeds: Paragon Press, 1999
Darby, Phillip, *British Defence Policy East of Suez 1947–1968*, London: Oxford University Press, 1973
Day, Stephen W., 'Power-Sharing and Hegemony: A Case Study of the United Republic of Yemen', unpublished Ph.D. thesis, Georgetown University, Washington, 2001
Deffarge, Claude and Laffont, Robert, *Yemen '62–'69: De la Revolution Sauvage a la Treve des Guerriers*, Paris: Robert Laffont, 1969
Dresch, Paul, *Tribes, Government and History in Yemen*, Oxford: Clarendon Press, 1989
—— *A History of Modern Yemen*, Cambridge: Cambridge University Press, 2000
East India Trade, *An Essay on the East India Trade and its Importance to this Kingdom with a Comparative View of the Dutch, French and English East India Companies*, London: T. Payne, 1770

## BIBLIOGRAPHY


Farah, Caesar E., *The Sultan's Yemen: 19th Century Challenges to Ottoman Rule*, London: I.B. Tauris, 2002

Farnie, D.A., *East and West of Suez: The Suez Canal in History, 1851–1969*, Oxford: Clarendon Press, 1969

Fayein, Claudie, *A French Doctor in Yemen*, London: Robert Hale, 1957

Field, Michael, *The Merchants: The Big Business Families of Saudi Arabia and the Gulf States*, Woodstock, NY: Overlook Press, 1984

Footman, David, *Antonin Besse of Aden*, London: Macmillan, 1986

Foster, Donald, *Landscape with Arabs: Travels in Aden and South Arabia*, Brighton: Clifton Books, 1969

Foster, William, ed., *The Journal of John Jourdain, 1608-1617*, second series, no. XVI, Cambridge: Hakluyt Society, 1905

Frankl, P.J.L., 'Robert Finlay's Description of Sana'a in 1238–1239/1823', *British Society for Middle Eastern Studies Bulletin*, 1990–1, vol. 17–18, pp. 16–35

Freitag, Ulrike, *Indian Ocean Migrants and State Formation in Hadhramaut: Reforming the Homeland*, Leiden: Brill, 2003

Gandy, Christopher, 'A Mission to Yemen: August 1962–January 1963', *British Journal of Middle Eastern Studies*, 1998, vol. 25, no. 2, pp. 247–74

Gardner, Frank, *Blood and Sand*, London: Bantam Press, 2006

Gavin, R.J., *Aden under British Rule 1839–1967*, London: C. Hurst & Co., 1975

Gibbons, Scott, *The Conspirators*, London: Howard Baker Publishers Ltd, 1967

Grandpre, Louis de, *A Voyage to the Indian Ocean and to Bengal*, vol. 2, London: G. and J. Robinson, 1803

Groom, Nigel, *Sheba Revealed: A Posting to Bayhan in the Yemen*, London: London Centre of Arab Studies, 2002

Halliday, Fred, *Revolution and Foreign Policy: The Case of South Yemen 1967–1987*, Cambridge: Cambridge University Press, 1990

—— *Arabs in Exile: Yemeni Migrants in Urban Britain*, London: I.B. Tauris, 1992

—— *Arabia Without Sultans*, London: Penguin, 2002 (1974)

—— *Islam and the Myth of Confrontation: Religion and Politics in the Middle East*, London: I.B. Tauris, 2003

Hattox, Ralph S., *Coffee and Coffee Houses: The Origins of a Social Beverage in the Medieval Near East*, Seattle: University of Washington Press, 1985

Haykel, Bernard, *Revival and Reform in Islam: The Legacy of Mohammad al-Shawkani*, Cambridge: Cambridge University Press, 2003

Hickinbotham, Tom, *Aden*, London: Constable & Co. Ltd, 1958

Hinchcliffe, Peter, Ducker, John T. and Holt, Maria, *Without Glory in Arabia: The British Retreat from Aden*, London: I.B. Tauris, 2006

Heikal, Mohamed, *Sphinx & Commissar: The Rise and Fall of Soviet Influence in the Middle East*, London: Collins, 1978

Helfritz, Hans, *The Yemen: A Secret Journey*, London: George Allen & Unwin Ltd, 1958 (1956)

Holden, David, *Farewell to Arabia*, London: Faber & Faber, 1966

Hunter, Capt. F.M., *An Account of the British Settlement of Aden in Arabia*, London: Trubner & Co., 1877

—— *An Account of the Arab Tribes in the Vicinity of Aden*, Bombay Government Central Press, 1886

Ingrams, Doreen, *A Time in Arabia*, London: John Murray, 1970

Ingrams, Doreen and Leila, eds, *Near and Middle East Titles: Records of Yemen, 1798–1960*, Slough: Archive Editions, 1993

Ingrams, W.H., Issued by the Colonial Office, *Aden Protectorate: A Report on the Social, Economic and Political Condition of the Hadhramaut*, London: HMSO, 1936
—— *Arabia and the Isles*, London: John Murray, 1966
Johnston, Charles, *The View from Steamer Point: Three Crucial Years in South Arabia*, London: Collins, 1964
Jones, Clive, *Britain and the Yemen Civil War, 1962–1965*, Brighton: Academic Press, 2004
Kaplan, Robert, *Imperial Grunts*, New York: Vintage, 2006 (2005)
Karsh, Efraim, *Islamic Imperialism: A History*, New Haven, CT: Yale University Press, 2006
Kazuhiro, Arai, 'Arabs Who Traversed the Indian Ocean: The History of the Al-Attas Family in Hadramawt and Southeast Asia c.1600–1960' unpublished Ph.D. thesis, University of Michigan, 2004
Keay, John, *The Honourable Company: A History of the English East India Company*, London: Harper Collins, 1991
Kennedy, J. Gerald, *The Flower of Paradise: The Institutionalised Use of the Drug Qat in North Yemen*, Dordrecht: D. Reidel Publishing Company, 1987
Kepel, Gilles and Robert, Anthony F., *Jihad: The Trail of Political Islam*, London: I.B. Tauris, 2006
King, Gillian, *Imperial Outpost – Aden: Its Place in British Strategic Policy*, Chatham House Essays, Oxford: Oxford University Press, 1964
Knox-Mawer, June, *The Sultans Came to Tea*, London: John Murray, 1961
Kostiner, Joseph, *Yemen: The Tortuous Quest for Unity 1990–94*, London: Cassell, 1996
—— *South Yemen's Revolutionary Strategy, 1970–1985*, Boulder, CO: Westview Press, 1990
Kour, Z.H., *The History of Aden 1839–1872*, London: Frank Cass, 1881
Lackner, Helen, *PDR Yemen: Outpost of Socialist Development in Arabia*, London: Ithaca Press, 1985
La Roque, Jean de, *A Voyage to Arabia Felix*, London: E. Symon, 1732
Leigh Douglas, J., *The Free Yemeni Movement, 1935–1962*, Beirut: American University of Beirut, 1987
Lenczowski, George, *The Middle East in World Affairs*, Ithaca, NY: Cornell University Press, 1952
Leveau, Remy, Mermier, Franck and Steinbach, Udo, eds, *Le Yemen Contemporain*, Paris: Editions Karthala, 1999
Little, Tom, *South Arabia: Arena of Conflict*, London: Pall Mall Press, 1968
Luce, Margaret, *From Aden to the Gulf: Personal Diaries 1956–1966*, Salisbury: Michael Russell, 1987
Lunt, James, *The Barren Rocks of Aden*, London: Herbert Jenkins, 1966
McGregor, Andrew, *A Military History of Modern Egypt: From the Ottoman Conquest to the Ramadan War*, Westport, CT: Praeger Security International, 2006
Mackintosh-Smith, Tim, *Yemen: Travels in Dictionary Land*, London: John Murray, 1997
Macro, Eric, *Yemen and the Western World*, London: C. Hurst & Co., 1968
—— *Bibliography on Yemen and Notes on Mocha*, Florida: University of Miami, 1969
Mawby, Spencer, *British Policy in Aden and the Proectorates: Last Outpost of a Middle East Empire*, London: Routledge, 2005
Mazed, Ziad, ed., *Building Democracy in Yemen*, Stockholm: International IDEA, 2005
Mehra, R.N., *Aden and Yemen 1905–1919*, Delhi: Agam Prakashan, 1988
Meulen, D. van der, *Aden to the Hadhramaut: A Journey in South Arabia*, London: John Murray, 1947
—— *Faces in Shem*, London: John Murray, 1961

Mignan, Capt. Robert, 'A Short Camp Residence in Valley of Aden', unpublished MS, 1840, MSS Eur D616
Miller, Flagg, *The Moral Resonance of Arab Media: Audiocassette Poetry and Culture in Yemen*, Cambridge, MA: Harvard University Press, 2007
Milne, Malcolm, *No Telephone to Heaven: From Apex to Nadir – Colonial Service in Nigeria, Aden, the Cameroons and the Gold Coast, 1938–61*, Stockbridge: Meon Hill Press, 1999
Mobini-Kesheh, Natalie, *The Hadrami Awakening: Community and Identity in Netherlands East Indies, 1900–1992*, New York: Cornell University Press, 1999
Mortimer, Peter, *Cool for Qat: A Yemen Journey, Two Countries Two Times*, Edinburgh: Mainstream Publishing, 2005
*Moving Yemen Coffee Forward – Assessment of the Coffee Industry in Yemen to Sustainably Improve Incomes and Expand Trade*, USAID Yemen, December 2005
Mundy, Martha, *Domestic Government: Kinship, Community and Polity in North Yemen*, London: I.B. Tauris, 1995
Nahrawali, Muhammad ibn Ahmad (trans. Smith, Clive K.), *Lightning over Yemen: A History of the Ottoman Campaign (1569–71)*, London: I.B. Tauris, 2002
Napoleoni, Loretta, *Terror Inc.: Tracing the Money Behind Global Terrorism*, London: Penguin, 2004
Naumkin, V.V., *Red Wolves of Yemen: The Struggle for Independence*, New York: Oleander Press, 2004
Niebuhr, Carsten, *Description of Arabia, 1774*, Selections from the Records of the Bombay Government, Bombay, 1889
Niebuhr, M. (trans. Robert Heron), *Travels Through Arabia and Other Countries in the East*, vol. 2, Reading: Garnet Education, 1994
Noman, Ahmed and Almadhagi, Kassim, *Yemen and the United States: A Study of a Small Power and Superstate Relationship*, London: I.B. Tauris, 1996
O'Ballance, Edgar, *The War in Yemen*, London: Faber & Faber, 1971
Ochsenwald, William, *Religion, Society and the State in Arabia: The Hijaz under Ottoman Rule 1840–1908*, Columbus, OH: Ohio State University, 1984
Page, Stephen, *The Soviet Union and the Yemen: Influence in Asymmetrical Relationships*, New York: Praeger, 1985
Paget, Julian, *Last Post: Aden 1964–1967*, London: Faber & Faber, 1969
Peterson, J.E., *Yemen: The Search for a Modern State*, London: Croom Helm, 1982
Phillips, Sarah, *Yemen's Democracy Experiment in Regional Perspective: Patronage and Pluralized Authoritarianism*, New York: Palgrave Macmillan, 2009
Philby, H. St John, *Sheba's Daughters*, London: Methuen & Co., 1939
Pieragostini, Karl, *Britain, Aden and South Arabia: Abandoning Empire*, London: Macmillan, 1991
Playfair, Capt. R.L., *A History of Arabia Felix or Yemen*, Bombay: Education Society's Press, 1859
Primakov, Yevgeny, *Russia and the Arabs*, New York: Basic Books, 2009
*Qat Expenditures in Yemen and Djibouti: An Empirical Analysis*, MPRA, January 2007
Quin, Mary, *Kidnapped in Yemen: One Woman's Amazing Escape from Terrorist Captivity*, Edinburgh: Mainstream Publishing, 2005
Rihani, Ameen, *Arabian Peak and Desert: Travels in Al-Yaman*, London: Constable & Co. Ltd, 1930
Rotberg, Robert I., ed., *Battling Terrorism in the Horn of Africa*, Baltimore, MD: Brookings Institution Press, 2005
Ruthven, Malise, *Fundamentalism: The Search for Meaning*, Oxford: Oxford University Press, 2004
—— *A Fury for God: The Islamist Attack on America*, London: Granta Books, 2004

Sanger, Richard H., *The Arabian Peninsula*, Ithaca, NY: Cornell University Press, 1954
Schmidt, Dana Adams, *Yemen: The Unknown War*, London: The Bodley Head, 1968
Schwedler, Jillian, *Faith in Moderation: Islamist Parties in Jordan and Yemen*, Cambridge: Cambridge University Press, 2006
Scott, Hugh, *In the High Yemen*, London: John Murray, 1942
Serjeant, R.B., *The Saiyids of Hadhramaut*, London: SOAS, 1957
—— *The Portuguese off the South Arabian Coast*, Oxford: Clarendon Press, 1963
Smith, Rex, ed., *Society and Trade in South Arabia*, Aldershot: Variorum, 1996
Soudan, Frederique, *Le Yemen Ottoman d'apres le Chronique d'al-Mawza'i*, Cairo: Institut Français d'Archeologie Orientale, 1999
Stark, Freya, *The Southern Gates of Arabia*, London: John Murray, 1936
—— *Seen in the Hadhramaut*, London: John Murray, 1938
—— *The Coast of Incense*, London: John Murray, 1953
Stookey, Robert W., *The Politics of the Yemen Arab Republic*, Boulder, CO: Westview Press, 1978
—— *South Yemen: A Marxist Republic in Arabia*, Boulder, CO: Westview Press, 1982
Suwaidi, Jamal S., ed., *The Yemeni War of 1994: Causes and Consequences*, London: Saqi Books, 1995
Trevaskis, Kennedy, *Shades of Amber: A South Arabian Episode*, London: Hutchinson, 1968
Trevelyan, Humphrey, *The Middle East in Revolution*, London: Macmillan, 1970
Tuchscherer, Michel, ed., *Le Commerce du Café avant l'Ere des Plantations Coloniales*, Cairo: Institut Francais d'Archeologie Orientale, 2001
Walker, Jonathan, *Aden Insurgency: The Savage War in South Arabia 1962–1967*, Staplehurst: Spellmount, 2005
Waterfield, Gordon, *Sultans of Aden*, London: John Murray, 1968
Waugh, Evelyn, *Remote People*, London: Duckworth, 1931
Wavell, A.J.B., *A Pilgrim in Mecca*, London: Constable & Co., 1912
Wedeen, Lisa, *Peripheral Visions: Publics, Power and Performance in Yemen*, Chicago: University of Chicago Press, 2008
Weir, Shelagh, *A Tribal Order: Politics and Law in the Mountains of Yemen*, Austin, TX: University of Texas, 2007
Wenner, Manfred W., *The Yemen Arab Republic: Development and Change in an Ancient Land*, Boulder, CO: Westview Press, 1991
Wild, Anthony, *Coffee: A Dark History*, London: Fourth Estate, 2004
Wright, Lawrence, *The Looming Tower: Al-Qaeda's Road to 9/11*, London: Penguin, 2006
Wyman-Bury, G., *The Land of Uz*, Reading: Garnet Press, 1998 (1911)
—— *Arabia Infelix: Or the Turks in Yemen*, Reading: Garnet Press, 1999 (1915)
—— *Pan Islam*, London, Macmillan, 1919
Yacoob, Abdol Rauh, 'Anglo-Ottoman Rivalries in South West Arabia Prior to and During the First World War, 1906–1919', unpublished Ph.D. thesis, London University, 1995
Zabarah, Mohammed Ahmad, *Yemen: Traditionalism versus Modernity*, New York: Praeger Publishers, 1982

# INDEX

## INDEX

## INDEX